THE TROUBLE WITH FONTS

by David E. Day

alpha
books

A Division of Prentice Hall Computer Publishing
11711 North College Avenue, Carmel, Indiana 46032 USA

For Julie; the love of loves lost.

International Standard Book Number: 1-56761-030-7
Library of Congress Catalog Card Number: 92-74557

96 95 94 93   8 7 6 5 4 3 2 1

Interpretation of the printing code: the rightmost number of the first series of numbers is the year of the book's printing; the rightmost number of the second series of numbers is the number of the book's printing. For example, a printing code of 93-1 shows that the first printing of the book occurred in 1993.

Screen reproductions in this book were created by means of the program Collage Plus from Inner Media, Inc., Hollis, NH.

Printed in the United States of America

Marie Butler-Knight
Publisher

Lisa A. Bucki
Associate Publisher

Elizabeth Keaffaber
Managing Editor

Stephen R. Poland
Acquisitions Manager

Barry Childs-Helton and Audra Gable
Editorial Team

Steve Vanderbosch
Cover and Interior Illustrator

Amy Peppler-Adams
Designer

Jeanne Clark
Indexer

*Tim Cox, Mark Enochs, Tim Groeling, Phil Kitchel, Tom Loveman,
Michael J. Nolan, Carrie Roth, Mary Beth Wakefield, Barbara Webster,
Kelli Widdifield*
Production Team

*Special thanks to Ed Guilford for ensuring the technical accuracy
of this book.*

Contents

Introduction ix
Conventions Used in This Book xi
Acknowledgements xii
Trademarks xii

1 What's a Font?   **3**
Why Are Fonts Important to Me? 4
Where Do Fonts Come From? 4
The Art of Fonts 5
Font Families and Friends 7
    Use 7
    Design 8
Font Sizes 10
Font Vendors and Formats 11
How Do I Get Fonts? 12
Putting Fonts to Work 14
What Fonts to Buy 14
Printer Fonts 15
    Font Internals 17
Summary 19

2 Fonts and Printers   **21**
    Laser (and Laser-type) Printers 21
    Ink- and Paint-jet Printers 22
    Dot-matrix Printers 23
    Special Printers 25
How Printers Use Fonts 25
Printers and Pages 26
Printer Font Sources 27
Built-in Fonts 27
Font Cartridges 29
Downloaded "Soft Fonts" 29
Downloaded Scalable Fonts 30
The Infamous WYSIWYG 31
Looking Back and Looking Ahead 32

3   Fonts in Microsoft Windows   **35**
What is Windows?   *35*
How a Font Gets Onto Paper   *36*
Managing Windows Fonts   *38*
Printers Also Manage Fonts   *45*
Video Boards Handle Windows Fonts   *46*
Problems with Installing and Accessing Fonts   *47*
Selecting and Using Fonts   *49*
Displaying Fonts   *52*
Printing Fonts   *54*
Looking Back and Looking Ahead   *60*

4   Fonts in Windows Applications   **63**
Windows Font Control Features   *63*
Ami Pro   *67*
Microsoft Word for Windows   *72*
WordPerfect for Windows   *77*
Microsoft Excel   *82*
FrameMaker for Windows   *87*
Microsoft Publisher   *91*
Aldus PageMaker for Windows   *93*
Ventura Publisher   *97*
Looking Back and Looking Ahead   *99*

5   Fonts in Windows Graphics Applications   **101**
Help from CD-ROM   *104*
CSC Arts & Letters Graphics Editor   *105*
CorelDRAW!   *108*
Micrografx Designer   *112*
Microsoft PowerPoint   *115*
Harvard Graphics for Windows   *120*
Looking Back and Looking Ahead   *126*

6   Fonts in DOS Applications   **129**
Fonts That DOS Uses   *129*
WordPerfect (for DOS)   *131*
WordPerfect Font Basics   *131*
Applying Text Attributes in WordPerfect   *132*
Changing Text Size in WordPerfect   *133*
WordPerfect and Text Fitting   *135*
Font Size and Line Length   *135*
View Document Mode   *136*
WordPerfect and Printers   *137*
Using TrueType and Type 1 Fonts with WordPerfect   *138*
WordPerfect Font Problems and Solutions   *138*

Microsoft Word (for DOS)   *143*
    Setting Font Attributes in Word   *145*
Word and Printers   *146*
Word and Text Fitting   *147*
    Layout View   *148*
    Print Preview Mode   *149*
Microsoft Word Font Problems and Solutions   *150*
Quattro Pro (for DOS)   *154*
    Quattro Pro Fonts Problems and Solutions   *158*
Lotus 1-2-3 for DOS Release 3.4   *160*
    1-2-3 Graphics: the Wysiwyg Auxiliary Program   *161*
    1-2-3 Font Sets   *162*
    Lotus 1-2-3 Font Problems and Solutions   *162*
Looking Back and Looking Ahead   *170*

7   **Printers and Fonts**   **173**
Can Your Printer Print Anything?   *173*
    Step 1: Is Your Printer Plugged into a "Live" Power Receptacle and Turned On?   *174*
    Step 2: Is There Paper in the Printer, and Is It Properly Loaded?   *174*
    Step 3: Is the Printer Properly Connected to the Computer?   *175*
    Step 4: Is the Printer Properly "Configured?"   *177*
    Step 5: Is Your Computer Port Properly Configured?   *178*
    Step 6: Is There a Printer Driver Installed for Your Printer?   *180*
    Step 7: Is Your Computer Port (for the Printer) Connected to a Printer Driver?   *182*
    Step 8: Have You Selected an Available Printer from Within Your Application?   *183*
    If You Still Can't Print   *184*
Other Problems with Printers   *184*
    Working with Laser Printers   *185*
    Working with Ink- and Paintjet Printers   *193*
    Working with Dot-matrix Printers   *198*
    Looking Back and Looking Ahead   *200*

8   **Exchanging Documents**   **203**
Exchanging Documents between Different Computers Running the Same Word Processor   *204*
Printing a Document on a Different Printer   *209*
Printing the Same Document on Two Different Printers   *210*
Printing a File from Two Different Word Processors   *211*
Preparing Files for a Service Bureau   *215*
Looking Back and Looking Ahead   *222*

9	**Making a Good Font Even Better**	**225**
	Organizing Fonts	*225*
	Learning About the Fonts on Your System	*228*
	Creating Font Special Effects	*231*
	Converting Font Formats	*234*
	Creating and Editing Fonts	*235*
	Legal Aspects of Using Fonts	*240*
	My Font Is Buried in the Document	*242*
	Looking Back (and Still Looking Ahead)	*243*
A	**Font Product Suppliers**	**245**
	Manufacturer and Product List	*245*
	Product Name Cross-Reference	*259*
B	**Glossary**	**263**
	Index	**275**

Introduction

Welcome to the nasty world of fonts! If you agree (and you use an IBM-compatible personal computer) you probably need this book.

If you've ever been confused about fonts, or frustrated with how to make them work for you, I can ease your pain. I'll give you concrete descriptions of the workings of fonts. I'll also give you a wealth of solutions and answers for real-world problems you may confront (or already have).

This is not a book on typography—on how to choose the appropriate typefaces to complement your message and its esthetics. You'll find many books on that elsewhere.

Here is a brief description of this book's contents.

The first two chapters are an overview of fonts and how they work. The next six chapters describe specific areas and problems or questions and solutions. Finally, Chapter 9 explains some tools to alter fonts or create new ones; if nothing else works for you, you'll find an answer there!

A glossary defines some common terms, and an extensive list of manufacturers and products is in the appendix.

Finally, I have a special diskette offer for shareware and freeware you may find appealing.

Chapter 1 explains what a font is, how it behaves and some of the lingo of typography.

Chapter 2 describes how fonts work with printers.

Chapter 3 tells how fonts operate in the Microsoft Windows environment and discusses several font managers for Windows.

Chapter 4 gives an overview of several Windows word-processing, spreadsheet and desktop-publishing applications and describes some common problems and their solutions.

Chapter 5 continues with Windows graphics applications—design, illustration, and presentation packages—and their font solutions.

Chapter 6 explains how fonts work in DOS applications and describes specific answers for font problems.

Chapter 7 is a step-by-step troubleshooting guide for problems with printers and fonts.

Chapter 8 solves common dilemmas of exchanging documents between differing computers, word-processors, fonts, and printers.

Chapter 9 discusses several font management, editing and creation products. It also talks about the legal and ethical issues of font use.

Appendix A lists many PC applications and products for DOS and Windows—most of them described in this book. There's also a cross-reference from product name to manufacturer.

Appendix B is a glossary of common font and PC terms.

Special Disk Offer is a mail offer for a diskette loaded with shareware and freeware programs to make your life with fonts easier.

If you would like to write me about your own font interests and solutions, I'd be glad to hear from you. Either contact me at the address shown for the diskette offer or on CompuServe; my ID is 76234,3233.

Enjoy this book!

Conventions Used in This Book

To make the solutions easier to follow, *The Trouble with Fonts* uses the following conventions:

- Text that appears on your screen is printed in **bold**.

- Text that you've supposed to type is printed in **bold**.

- Commands which you should select or press are printed in **bold**.

- Selection letters which you press to pull down menus and activate menu options appear in **bold**.

You'll also find, scattered throughout the text, extra information placed in short asides called Tips, Notes, and Cautions.

These are special shortcuts and techniques that make fonts easier and faster to use.

CAUTION

These are warnings about situations in which you need to take a little extra care before proceeding.

These are simply interesting or useful tidbits.

Acknowledgements

This book comes to you through many acts of faith by the people at Alpha Books. Steve Poland gave all he had to a stranger. Lisa Bucki showed me in every chapter the value of a thoughtful and tireless editor. We were partners; I wrote this book—they gave it birth.

Another writer looms large behind me. Bob Mullen showed me what friends can be for; the gift of rejuvenation.

Trademarks

All the terms mentioned in this book that are known to be trademarks have been appropriately capitalized. Alpha Books cannot attest to the accuracy of this information. Use of a term in this book should not be regarded as affecting the validity of any trademark or service mark.

About the Author

A quarter-century ago, Dave Day was an English major who started writing about computers because he needed a job. (He's been a consultant most of the time, so he still needs a job!) He has so many interests he never knows which to pursue next, but he's never lost his fascination for computers.

Dave comes by his font knowledge from experience as a commercial phototypesetter, a technical and marketing writer, and brochure creator. He likes to be where art and science meet.

What's a Font?

For that matter, what's a typeface? These terms—*font* and *typeface*—are often used to mean the same thing, but they're not—quite.

A typeface is a specific design for a set of characters. All the letters, numbers, punctuation and other special marks look like they belong together. They have similar lines, curves and other shapes. The design usually includes italic, bold and other style variations on the basic concept.

(If you've ever read a newspaper, it probably used the most popular published typeface of all: Times Roman. Literally thousands of typefaces are available, and often they have copyrighted names to identify them.)

A font is a set of characters of one size and style derived from one typeface. For example, 12-point Times Roman bold is an example of a font. Figure 1.1 shows that font. (The 12-point part refers to the type size; more on that later.)

When in the course of human events it becomes necessary

Figure 1.1

Times Roman font.

But it's easy to get confused. Why? Because the terms *typeface* and *font* have been used in a variety of creative ways. For example, vendors will sometimes call Times Roman, Times Roman Bold and Times Roman Italic three *typefaces* when they're really three *font sets* of just one typeface. That makes the count of what they sell you seem much larger.

Even though a font used to refer to only a single type size, it's now used to mean a style (Times Roman italic, for example). That's partly because a font used in a computer can easily be changed to any size you'd like.

And in Microsoft Windows, a *font* is simply the name of a particular typeface—a much broader definition than used elsewhere. Because I'm going to emphasize Windows applications here, we'll use this definition.

When it comes to type definitions, stay loose!

Why Are Fonts Important to Me?

Let's start with a broader question: why are *typefaces* important to you? It's because type is a special kind of art form. It's art used to add complex nuances of meaning to the written word. Think of how much poorer our written language would be if we didn't have **bold** words for emphasis, or *italic* words to signal unusual situations.

Think of the overall emotional impact of type designs you've seen: for example, the flowing, pen-like script of a wedding invitation with its gentle, even fanciful style. Or the strong assertiveness of a newspaper headline demanding your attention. Typefaces contribute to meaning and understanding.

Fonts are important because that's what you select using your trusty computer application: a typeface of a particular design, style and size.

Where Do Fonts Come From?

A typeface design consists of a set of images, one for each character. Somebody has to create these drawings, and that used to be done by a designer on paper. To yield better quality, these master drawings were often very large, perhaps a foot high or more.

Next the designs were electronically scanned and converted into a special master format, then stored in a computer as a set of numbers. These days, a designer does all the design work on a computer screen, and the computer creates the electronic masters without scanning.

From the master formats, a font vendor can create typefaces in any format needed for different computer systems and printers.

Bold, italic and other styles are all created separately. A complete typeface can easily contain over 1000 separate master drawings.

The Art of Fonts

A font is a special blend of art and science.

The trick to art is to make the entire typeface faithful and consistent with the visual effect the designer intends. Every character has to look right when combined in any order with other characters on a line, and also has to look good in every size.

Good typeface designs can easily take thousands of hours of careful, even tedious work.

Science adds methods of automatically adjusting a typeface for the best results when it's used. There are two words used for this process: *hinting* and *kerning*. Together, they're sort of an automatic pilot for fonts.

Hinting refers to rules built into the typeface design to adjust the type characters for the size being used. That's because a small character shouldn't be simply a large character that's been shrunk down. The proportion of line shapes needs to be subtly adjusted; hinting does this automatically. It's a little too subtle to show here, but hinting is an important feature—chiefly for small type sizes.

If all the characters on a line are spaced the same distance apart, some of them will appear too far apart. Kerning is an automatic feature that spots certain pairs of characters in a line and reduces the space between them. Sometimes spacing for the entire line is adjusted; this is called *track kerning* or simply, *tracking*.

In some computer applications, you can even adjust kerning manually to get just the right look. That can make an important visual improvement, especially for headlines. Figure 1.2 shows the difference.

Figure 1.2

Characters before and after kerning.

You Win

You Win

Sometimes, italic and bold characters aren't in the font design at all, but are created by the computer on the spot. To make italic characters, the program simply tilts the letters. (That's called making them *oblique*.) To make bold characters, it simply adds thickness to the lines. The results aren't nearly as good as you'd get with designed characters, but they are often good enough for casual work. Figure 1.3 shows the difference in quality for italic characters.

Figure 1.3

Real italic and made-up italic characters.

When in the course of

real

When in the course of

made up

Font Families and Friends

Typefaces are described in several general categories that often overlap. The two basic categories are *use* and *design*.

Use

A face that's meant for the main text or body of a document is called a *text face*. If it's meant for headlines and titles, it's called *display type*. A *decorative face* is a fancy design used for a special effect. (It may be used for either text or display.)

Symbol fonts contain symbols used for mathematics or musical notation. Or, they can be special characters used for emphasis, such as arrows and bullets. Some symbol fonts contain little pictures, or icons.

Figure 1.4 shows some samples of these font types.

Text *font*

DISPLAY FONT

Decorative font

Figure 1.4

Text, display, decorative and symbol fonts.

Symbol font:

AαBβXχΔδEεΦφΓγ

Icon fonts:

Design

The basic distinction between type designs is called the *serif.* That's the little curve or ball ornament at the end or edge of each character. Type that has these elements is called *serif* type; if it doesn't have them, it's called *sans serif* (literally, without serif). Figure 1.5 shows the difference between these two.

Serif typeface
Sans-serif typeface

Typically, serif type designs are used as text faces, and sans serif is used for display type and for captions. But that's only a general guideline.

Another variant on type design is *style.* A *font family* usually consists of four faces (four variations of the same font): regular (sometimes called "roman"), italic, bold and bold-italic. Figure 1.6 shows a serif family and Figure 1.7 shows a sans-serif family.

Regular (roman) face
Bold face
Italic face
Bold-italic face

Regular face

Bold face

Italic face

Bold-italic face

Figure 1.7

Basic font family in a sans-serif design.

Sometimes there are variations to the thickness or weight of characters. Characters that are "bolder than bold" can be called demi-bold, extra-bold, heavy, or black. Characters that are less bold than the regular face are called light or thin. Figure 1.8 shows some of these variants on the basic theme.

Light weight (condensed)

Regular weight

Bold weight

Extra-bold weight

Black weight

Figure 1.8

Font family variants.

One last design element describes the difference between the width and height of a character. If the characters are high and narrow (compared to regular ones), the font is called *condensed* (or sometimes a *narrow* font). If it is low and broad, it's an *expanded* font. Condensed fonts help you squeeze more text on a single line—helpful for overloaded tables. Examples of these are in Figure 1.9.

Condensed and expanded fonts.

Regular font
Condensed font

Font Sizes

Type is measured in a unit called a *point*, which is equal to about 1/72 of an inch. The abbreviation is pt. This means that a 72-point (72pt) character should be an inch high. Body text usually uses type that measures 10pt or 12pt. Headlines (display type) are often 18pt to 48pt, but can be much larger of course.

Unfortunately, the point size of a font isn't the same as its size on the printed page. Type is usually a little smaller—10 to 20 percent smaller than you'd expect. And some faces—notoriously script—are even smaller. Compare some of the sizes of type in Figure 1.10; all of them are 18pt fonts.

A description for the *width* of type depends on whether it's *proportional-spaced* or *fixed-space*. Fixed-space (or "monospace") characters are all exactly the same width. That's what most typewriters have traditionally used. Monospace type is useful for tables where all the numbers have to line up. But it isn't very appealing to read in body text.

Each proportional-spaced character has its own distinct width. A "W" character is much wider than an "I." The effect is to make the spaces between characters much more uniform than in monospace type. That makes for easier reading and a nicer-looking page.

Text face

HEADLINE FACE

Brush face

Light script face

Medium script face

Brush script face

Figure 1.10

Type sizes for various styles.

Figure 1.11 shows examples of both monospace and proportional-spaced fonts.

```
Monospace 1234--0
```

Figure 1.11

Monospace and proportional-spaced fonts.

```
You Win
```

Proportional 1234--0

You Win

Font Vendors and Formats

Literally dozens of vendors sell fonts in a variety of formats. But by far the most popular format is *TrueType*.

TrueType is the new font format that's directly handled by Microsoft Windows 3.1. It was orignally developed by Apple computer and is licensed by Microsoft. If you buy a font in

TrueType format, all you need do is install it in Windows, using the built-in utility. Windows will create all the screen and printer fonts you need automatically. (Much more on this in Chapter 3.)

Some basic TrueType fonts are included with Windows. Microsoft sells some more, and many vendors also now offer type in this format.

The second most popular format is from Adobe Systems; it's called *PostScript Type 1* or sometimes *Postscript* or simply, *Type 1*. Before TrueType, it was the reigning standard for the highest quality type. Adobe offers hundreds of excellent typefaces in this format, and literally thousands are available elsewhere.

Runner-up font formats include Bitstream's *Speedo* and Agfa's *Intellifont* (also used by Hewlett-Packard). Hundreds of fine fonts are also available in these formats.

Be wary of *converted* fonts. Because TrueType is such a runaway success, it created a large interest in the format before many fonts were available for it. Vendors have sometimes resorted to using programs to convert fonts from another format to TrueType, with very mixed results. A converted font is rarely as good as one generated directly from the original type masters.

If you're going to use Type 1, Intellifont or Speedo fonts with your application, you'll need a font manager. That's software that uses the electronic pattern supplied on the font diskettes to create screen and printer fonts.

Some vendors sell fonts that include more than one format in the same package (TrueType and Type 1, for example). That way, you can use them on different systems or with different font managers.

How Do I Get Fonts?

You usually buy computer fonts by buying them as products packaged just like computer programs. They come in a box with floppy diskettes, and usually a short booklet explaining how to install and use them.

Fonts are sold through retail computer stores and mail-order catalogs. Only a couple of years ago, the price was typically $75 to $300 each. But now, with the mass market created by Microsoft Windows, you can buy some decent fonts for under $5 each—and some for less than a buck!

Just like commercial computer programs, fonts are copyrighted, and it's illegal to make copies to use on other computers or pass out to your friends.

A novel way to distribute fonts is on *CD-ROM* disks. A CD-ROM looks just like an audio CD disk that you could play on your stereo system. Instead of music, it contains computer programs or data. You need a special CD-ROM drive installed on your computer to access them.

A single CD-ROM can contain many hundreds of fonts. You get to use a few of them right away, as part of the original purchase price. If you want others, you phone a special number and give them your credit card info. They give you a special code that unlocks the fonts you choose. That way, you have immediate access to any font on the disk—for a price!

Many fonts are available these days as *shareware*; you can download them from computer bulletin boards or get copies for free on floppy diskettes. These fonts are often for special or unusual purposes, and vary widely in quality and usefulness.

With shareware, you get to try all the fonts you have any interest in, and you only need to pay for the ones you decide to continue using.

Another way to buy fonts for your printer is in *font cartridges*. These little boxes contain memory holding several fonts at once, and plug directly into a socket on your printer.

The advantage of font cartridges is speed—they're directly available where they're needed and don't have to be created by the computer and sent to the printer. The disadvantage is price and the limited variety of fonts available. Although the cartridge serves the printer's need for font information, you may still have to load a diskette into the computer to provide fonts for display on the video monitor.

Putting Fonts to Work

This should be the easy part. You buy a font, and you want to use it. But wait! A font is just an electronic pattern that represents characters. Something has to convert that pattern into formats your computer display and printer can use. Enter the *font manager.*

A font manager is built into Microsoft Windows. If you're going to use Type 1 fonts, you need the Adobe Type Manager. For Speedo fonts, you need Bitstream Facelift (which handles Type 1 fonts as well). If you want a single font manager that handles these types and several others, try Zenographic's Superprint. First you install one of these font managers and then use one of their utilities to install the fonts you've bought.

Often an application program such as a word processor, desktop publisher or graphics program will contain or include a font manager. Or, one may be included as part of a font package.

What Fonts to Buy

Just like the galaxy, billions and billions of fonts are out there (or so it seems). You need to make same choices, for several reasons. First is compatibility, next is design and finally, storage limitations.

Not all fonts work with all systems. Buy fonts that are compatible with your PC. If you're working with a DOS application, there may be serious restrictions on fonts you can use. In

Windows, it depends on which font manager you're using; you can always use TrueType in version 3.0 and later because its font manager is built-in.

> **TIP**
>
> *Document design is much like making music; it demands variety within unity. Fonts add variety and interest, but they also unify the document—make it seem as one piece. For that reason, the rule-of-thumb is never to use more than four typefaces in one document. Otherwise, it may become as disconcerting as a font sample sheet!*

> **TIP**
>
> *The typefaces you use should complement each other, except in the rare case when you want a reader to be jarred or startled. Often, you can use a sans serif headline face combined with serif text for a clear distinction.*

For most users, ten or twenty well-chosen fonts are more than adequate for nearly all uses. That will cost you from $5 to $500 or more depending on the vendor.

When you buy a font, you have to store it on the hard disk for use. The more fonts, the more space; especially if you must also create and store faces for display. You'll need to balance your desire for font choices with your available disk space—and with your budget.

Printer Fonts

These are the fonts that are managed directly by your printer. They include *internal* (built-in) fonts, *soft* fonts and font cartridges.

Many printers have at least a few fonts built in. These internal fonts are provided in a limited number of sizes and styles.

NOTE

If you're installing a font cartridge on your printer, you simply plug it in. Then, you make the program that sends characters to the printer (called the driver) aware that these new fonts are available. More on this later.

TIP

A font cartridge in effect adds to the internal font list of a printer. It also has the advantage that these fonts don't need to be stored on your hard disk.

Soft fonts are sent to the printer's memory by a loader program. You select the style and size you want, and the loader puts the pattern for that specific font into the printer. A soft font remains available until it is deleted (erased from the printer memory) or until you turn the printer off.

One printer type is in a category all by itself: the Adobe PostScript-compatible. This printer contains dozens of fonts; your font manager can also download your Type 1 fonts to it. The printer itself can scale all of these fonts to any size you need and can also rotate them to any angle and create some other special effects.

In other words, the PostScript-compatible printer is a set of scalable fonts, a font manager *and* a printer.

Font Internals

Why explain the internal workings of a font? Because it helps you understand some of the interesting problems you can run into, and also some of the solutions.

Most fonts are one of two kinds: *bitmapped* and *outline*. The difference is in the way they store the shapes of the characters. A bitmapped font stores the shapes as patterns of dots (see Figure 1.12). An outline font stores characters as a sets of lines, curves and points, along with the directions for making them into any size (see Figure 1.13).

Figure 1.12

Bitmapped font.

Figure 1.13

Outline font.

Because a bitmapped font stores every character as a pattern of dots, you need a font for every character size you are going to use. That can be an enormous disk storage problem!

If you use a large font and the right size bitmap isn't available, the font manager may have to expand a smaller one. Figure 1.14 shows what happens.

With outline fonts, creating characters of any size is no problem at all. Your font manager simply uses the directions to manufacture any size you need—that is, it *scales* them (see Figure 1.15). That's why these are called *scalable outline fonts*.

Figure 1.14

An expanded bitmapped font—"jaggie."

Figure 1.15

An outline font expanded to any size.

All the font formats I've mentioned—TrueType, Type 1, Intellifont, and Speedo—are scalable outline types. That means they handle the creation of fonts in the printer very well. They do have some differences in the way they handle screen fonts, and I'll discuss that later.

Fonts contained in printer cartridges or downloaded to the printer as soft fonts are bitmapped. That creates some limitations in how you can use them. For example, you don't have much control over size selection, and they can't be scaled.

Fonts provided internal to the printer are often bitmapped too. The major exception is the PostScript-compatible printer I discussed earlier.

Summary

In this chapter I've given you a very broad view of what type-faces and fonts are and some of the terms used to categorize and describe them. I've introduced the popular font formats and how to put them to use. And I've hinted at some of the problems that might crop up (but frankly, not the solutions—yet). But that's coming!

Next: some specifics—fonts and printers. From now on, I'll be describing problems and their solutions a lot more.

chapter

2

Fonts and Printers

Why a chapter on printers in a book about fonts? Because putting your carefully crafted characters on paper is what makes them useful. It releases your work of art to the world. (The only other way is to take pictures of your computer screen—expensive and tedious.)

Now I'm going to fill you in about each popular printer type, and what the trade-offs are in each case.

Laser (and Laser-type) Printers

The most popular printer for quality computer graphics work is the laser printer. They used to cost $3,000 or more, but now you can find one at under $600. They deserve their reputation for sharp, clean printing.

By far the most popular manufacturer of laser printers is Hewlett-Packard. They make models in several price ranges and speeds. Many other vendors vie for this aggressive market, including Lexmark, Canon, NEC, Panasonic, and Sharp.

(Just to be technically accurate, not all "laser printers" are laser printers at all. Instead of a laser light beam, some of them use a row of tiny lamps and a special liquid-crystal light shutter to control the creation of the dots. They still do a good job.)

So when should you consider buying a laser printer? When you want quality. All of them will create 300 dots per inch of paper. (That's 300 times 300 in every square inch, or 90,000 dots!) And some of them will do 600, 1,000 or even 1,200 dots per inch. Unless you go to a printer, this is the highest quality font output you can get. Higher-quality laser printers are now commonly used for commercial typesetting.

Laser printers will do characters and graphics of any size. Many of them have built-in fonts that can be sized and rotated

90 degrees. PostScript-type printers usually have at least 35 fonts built in; these can be any size and any angle of rotation. (I'll explain them shortly.)

Buy one for speed and economy: four to eight pages a minute is common; it costs you two to five cents to print a standard page.

When shouldn't you buy a laser printer? When you can't afford it (obviously), but also when you must have color images. If you want to buy a color laser printer, you can get one for $4,000 and up, and they're very expensive to operate. But hang in there: prices are dropping quickly.

If you must have multi-part forms, you can't use a laser printer; you need a printer that stamps an image through the carbon paper mechanically.

The laser's the one to buy, if you're buying all-around quality and versatility.

Ink- and Paint-jet Printers

These printers do just what their name implies: they squirt ink (or paint) at a page. It sounds simple, but imagine the quality a squirt gun has to have to put 90,000 dots on a single square inch of paper!

The squirt gun consists of a little reservoir of ink and a tiny nozzle that slides back and forth in front of a piece of paper. Every place your page needs a dot, an incredibly tiny droplet of ink is thrown at the paper. You can imagine that all this takes some time, because of the huge number of dots on a page. But it's whisper-quiet!

Because any ink has a tendency to spread out and soak in, the ink-jet image varies with the paper. If you use fancy (and expensive) coated paper, you get a really sharp image; if you use ordinary copy paper, it tends to be a little mushy.

Here again, Hewlett-Packard is the most popular brand, although there are a few other vendors, including Canon and

DataProducts. H-P's inexpensive and versatile *DeskJet* printer is a price-performance leader.

Why buy an ink-jet printer? When you need *almost* laser-quality output at a lower price. You can buy an ink-jet for $400 or less. It also has an advantage when you need almost complete quiet—all you hear is a gentle whirr!

The best reason to buy one is color! You can get a color printer for under $700. If you use special paper, the colors are striking, and you can even print on transparency film for overhead projections.

Why not buy one? When you want print-quality text or graphics, it's just not as sharp as a laser printer. You could use one for a business letter, but it's not quite as convincing as you might want. When you're concerned about speed and cost per copy, an ink-jet or paint-jet printer might not be the best choice. Special paper and ink cartridges are a little pricey, and color output especially is slow, but these aren't killer issues.

Dot-matrix Printers

Simple translation: *dot-matrix* means "patterns of dots." This kind of printer uses a series of miniature hammers to put rows of dots on paper. It has a little box (called a *head*) loaded with thin wires (called *pins*) that it slides along the sheet of paper.

When the printer needs to form characters, it puts dots on the paper by pushing out a pattern of pins. The pins strike a ribbon, the ink gets put on paper, as shown in Figure 2.1.

A head contains eight to 24 pins, so it can make lots of dots at the same time. When it finishes as many lines of dots as it can on one row, the head returns to do more rows until it covers the whole page.

Why would you want to buy a dot-matrix printer? Three reasons: low price, a desire for color, or to make "carbon" copies.

Figure 2.1

A dot-matrix printer uses pins to create an image on paper.

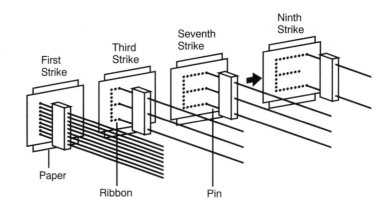

Dot-matrix printers are the low-cost leaders in the game; you can buy one from about $100 to about $500, depending on how many pins the head has, how fast it prints, and the size and kinds of paper it will accept.

Some models have multi-color ribbons so they can make fair-quality color images. The colors can be a little murky, and are not very accurate, but they're good enough for posters, newsletters and other casual work.

Because those little pins push dots into the paper, you can use multi-part forms for printing invoices and receipts.

Why not buy this printer? Don't forget those pins—they're really miniature hammers—and hammers make noise. It's not as bad as a typewriter—more like a low staccato hum—but it can be annoying close-up.

Because there's a limit to how close the dots can be on a page, there's a limit to quality, too. Some of the more expensive models do a pretty good job of putting characters on paper, but they're just not as crisp as a laser printer. Don't forget—there's a ribbon to replace, and the intensity of the printing goes down as the ink gets used up.

These printers are the last of an old technology. Unless you're looking for casual-quality printing or are on a strict budget, you'd do better to stretch a little to get a laser or ink-jet printer.

Special Printers

Some printers are so rare that you'll probably never see one (although you often see the results from one—you're seeing it now). For example, if you want to publish the very best text quality, go to your local commercial printer. They probably have a device that takes your diskette and creates very high-quality images. It acts like a PostScript printer, but it prints on photographic film, ready for publication.

Another print specialty is slides or overhead transparencies for presentations. If you need these, you can get them from companies that use expensive gadgets that put images directly on color film. You supply the original material as a file on a diskette.

Finally, one printer that you might need if you're an architect or designer is called a *plotter*. This machine prints graphics or text by moving pens in automated arms across the paper. Some of them draw in many colors, and may accept very large sheets of paper. Not for desktop publishing!

How Printers Use Fonts

Today's printers (except for daisy wheel printers) don't really put characters on paper at all. They actually draw pictures. The pictures *can* be characters—or they can be any other shape you want. That's why they're called *graphics* printers.

These printers work a lot like two common household items: your television and your newspaper. Take a good close look at the picture on your TV. (Don't stare too long—remember what your mother warned you about.) Notice how it's made up of horizontal lines of little dots.

Look closely at a newspaper photograph (you may want to use a magnifying glass). You'll see the same thing—line after line of little dots.

A printer gets a picture (an image) of what it needs to print, then breaks it down into many very thin lines of dots. It puts little dots of ink or other black stuff on paper in just the right places (see Figure 2.2).

Figure 2.2

Most printers create an image on paper by breaking it up into small dots.

Why go to all this trouble to break apart a perfectly good picture? Because that gives the printer the ability to make any shape you need. You can have characters of any size or drawings of any kind, anywhere you want them on the paper.

The technique of making an image out of little dots is called *rasterizing*, and each line is called a *raster*. It's the same term your TV repairman would use to talk about your video picture.

You need to know about rasterizing to make sense out of the way printers use fonts and the way applications make them available. It also helps when we're discussing font problems and their solutions.

Printers and Pages

There's a big difference between the way laser printers get ready to print and the way ink-jet and dot-matrix printers do. Ink-jet and dot-matrix printers have little assemblies ("heads") that shuttle back and forth across the page to print a line at a time. That means the computer has to make up the bitmap for all the characters on one line and send it to the printer and wait until it's done.

But the laser printer prints a full page at one quick pass. That means the computer must send the information for the *entire* page before the printer can start. It also means the printer must have the ability to store or remember all the dots on the page at once. If your printer doesn't have enough memory, you can't print a full page of text or graphics.

Printer Font Sources

Now it's time to talk about where printers get their fonts. Another way of saying this is: where do they get their graphic images of characters to print?

The term for the graphic image of a character (and for an entire page) is a *bitmap*. That's because each character is made up of a set of dots or "bits" arranged in a pattern, or "map." When the printer gets a whole page ready for printing, the bitmaps may include an assortment of characters and other graphics—drawings or pictures.

Remember from Chapter 1 that a bitmap is formed in a process called *rasterizing*. That occurs in your computer, which uses a font manager and printer driver to send the bitmaps to your printer. Or, character bitmaps may be built into your printer. I'll discuss that more fully below.

One detail about character bitmaps you may need to consider is their *orientation* on the page. If the characters are printed on a vertical (tall) page, that's called *portrait* orientation; if they're on a horizontal (wide) page, it's *landscape* orientation. That small distinction can be important with fonts.

That's because soft fonts in your computer are really prebuilt bitmaps. Because a landscape page is tilted on its side (rotated 90 degrees) from a portrait page, it needs an entirely different set of bitmaps—also titled over.

Built-in Fonts

I'm going to talk more specifically about how the major printers we've already discussed—laser, ink-jet and dot-matrix—handle fonts.

Most printers are built with some fonts permanently stored in them. Laser printers tend to have the most, perhaps 20 to 80 fonts. Ink-jet and dot-matrix printers usually have between a dozen and 20 fonts.

These internal (or "resident") fonts are stored as ready-to-use bitmaps, or dot patterns. These patterns are stored in the printer using read-only memory components, or *ROMs*. ROM storage is permanent, even when the power is turned off.

Because the printer stores characters as read-to-use bitmaps, that means they are available only in specific, commonly-used sizes—usually 8, 10 and 12 points. You can sometimes get away with using a little larger size, but the bits get spread out and the character looks odd. Also, separate fonts are required for portrait and landscape orientation because their bitmaps are rotated 90 degrees from each other.

Recent laser-type printers include not only bitmaps, but also *scalable outline fonts*. The beauty of these scalable fonts is that you can see them in almost any conceivable size and they'll look the same. That's because each character is stored as a *definition of its shape* rather than as a bitmap. From them, the printer creates bitmapped characters as needed for your document.

(If you want a refresher about the difference between bitmapped and scalable fonts, look back at Chapter 1.)

Although internal fonts have obvious limitations, their big advantage is speed. Internal fonts print faster than any other kind.

Remember that when printer manufacturers count fonts, the regular, italic, bold and bold-italic styles count as four!

One type of laser printer offers unique versatility: the *PostScript-type*. First made by Apple and developed with Adobe, this type is available from several vendors. It also contains built-in fonts (usually 35 or more), all stored as *scalable outline fonts*. That gives you many quality font choices.

Another advantage to the PostScript-type printer is that it brings many page-layout and graphic functions under computer command, including rotating fonts to any angle. (That means every font is available in both portrait and landscape orientation—and everything in between.)

The disadvantage is speed. The PostScript-type printer has to create its own bitmap for each character on the page. That takes a smarter printer, as well as time and lots of memory, to create and store the complete image for the page.

Font Cartridges

One way of extending the number of fonts in your printer is to use a *font cartridge*, which contains a permanent bitmap of a set of fonts. A wide selection of fonts is available in these cartridges, and one kind even lets you load more fonts into it after you buy it.

Many printers have one or more special sockets or slots to accept font cartridges. When you plug them in, they become (in effect) internal fonts.

One other cartridge that's available for some laser printers contains not just fonts, but a computer program. When you plug it in, it converts your printer to a PostScript-type, including a basic set of scalable fonts. Because this cartridge relies on lots of storage, you may also have to add memory to your printer.

Downloaded "Soft Fonts"

If you want a font that isn't built into your printer (or isn't available in the size you want), you can download one. This kind of font is called a "soft font," because it's not permanently built-in.

A *soft font* is a set of bitmaps—one for every character (in every size) you plan to use, in portrait and landscape orientation. It's usually created in advance, ready for downloading to the printer. If you use many fonts, a soft font is a large storage burden on your hard drive.

Your computer application sends whatever soft fonts you need for the current pages to the printer. It sends a bitmap of only the requested sizes. Any fonts downloaded to the printer are stored in its memory, and are lost or "forgotten" when you shut off the power.

There's a limit to the number of fonts you can download at one time, because they all occupy some of the printer's internal memory. That means you may need to add more memory to use soft fonts at all. Soft fonts are often provided in either portrait or landscape orientation; consider which ones you'll need for the pages you're printing.

Downloaded Scalable Fonts

PostScript-type printers also accept downloaded fonts. (Strangely enough, they're called "PostScript fonts," or more accurately, "Adobe PostScript fonts.") But such fonts are downloaded from the computer as scalable outlines, just like the internal fonts for these printers. That means you can request any character point sizes you like without overtaxing the printer's memory with bitmaps.

(With the help of a font manager, other printers can use Type 1 fonts used in your document and sends them to the printer as bitmaps. Every character on the page is an individual bitmap. That takes much longer to download than does one set of outlines for the entire font. But the quality is the same as if they were internal scalable fonts.)

The latest H-P printer—the LaserJet 4— contains not only bitmapped and scalable fonts but also a rasterizer for TrueType fonts. (*TrueType* is a new font format developed by Microsoft and Apple and built into Microsoft Windows; more about TrueType in Chapter Three.) Your computer can download

TrueType outlines to this printer in the same way it can download Type 1 fonts to a Postscript-type printer.

Printers that aren't lasers can take advantage of scalable fonts (either PostScript, TrueType or a number of others). But the printer itself doesn't handle them directly. Instead, your computer has a program called a *driver* that converts the scalable fonts into bitmaps, and then downloads them into the printer.

The Infamous WYSIWYG

WYSIWYG is the widely-renowned desktop publishing acronym for "What You See Is What You Get." That means simply that your computer monitor display of your text is supposed to look just like the printed page. It's often been more of a hope or a mantra than a reality.

I've left this part for last because it's a coordination game between your computer and your printer. In other words, your computer application has to know what to expect from the printer in every situation. Then it has to create a replica of the expected page on your monitor. Some trick!

The way a computer application knows about a specific printer is through a driver, and sometimes through a *font manager* program. The driver and font manager contain information about available fonts and also has access to fonts specially designed to be presented on the monitor, called *screen fonts*. These are bitmaps designed to look good on your display.

The driver needs specific information about the fonts, including the shape and size of each character and the width of each character on a line. These attributes are called the font's *metrics*.

When you set up your computer for printers, you must specify the exact model printer you'll be using, and any enhancements made to it. That selects the appropriate driver.

Your printer driver contains a complete list of the printer's original internal fonts and standard font cartridges. If it's a Windows printer driver, it may also contain the associated screen fonts. Or, you may be able to install the screen fonts when you install the driver. If the screen fonts aren't available, Windows will substitute a similar style it already has.

If you add a font cartridge to your printer, you'll need to notify the printer driver. For Windows, if you're using a non-standard cartridge, you may have to install new screen fonts and font spacing information (*"metrics"*). That info is often provided on diskettes with the cartridge.

Soft fonts and scalable fonts employ a font manager to create screen fonts. When you print your document, the manager then creates the bitmaps needed, and downloads them to your printer.

For PostScript-type printers, a font manager creates screen fonts too. Because the printer does the work of creating bitmaps, the manager needs to download only the size and position for characters used in your document.

If you're using TrueType fonts, the Windows font manager creates bitmaps for both the printer and screen fonts automatically as needed. (For the H-P LaserJet 4, it downloads the actual character outlines instead of bitmaps.)

Looking Back and Looking Ahead

There's a lot to be said about printers—maybe too much. It's a "feature war," with manufacturers trying to outdo each other in competing for a brisk business. In this chapter, I've given you the background info to help you understand the various types of printers, and perhaps to select one that's right for you. I've explained how printers use fonts, and the advantages, disadvantages, problems and solutions for each type of printer.

Next, we'll look at the premier personal computer environment for fonts: Microsoft Windows.

Fonts in Microsoft Windows

If you care about fonts, you probably are already using Microsoft Windows, Version 3.1. It's the most exciting software development in the PC world today.

I'm going to explain a little about Windows and the way it operates, and a lot about how to make fonts work the way they should.

What is Windows?

Windows is called a graphical user interface ("GUI" for short). Windows is like a super operating system; that's why it's also called an *environment*. It does what DOS does, and much more—and it does it in a visually appealing way. Windows is Microsoft's answer to the Apple Macintosh and its graphical way of operating.

When you use most DOS programs, you're stuck with a single (fairly ugly) font—like an old-time typewriter. Characters are all the same width and style, as shown in Figure 3.1

With Windows, when you type some characters into your word processor or other application, you actually see them on the display as they will be printed. You can mix character styles and sizes easily. You experience the visual impact of all the qualities of the text, as shown in Figure 3.2.

Figure 3.1

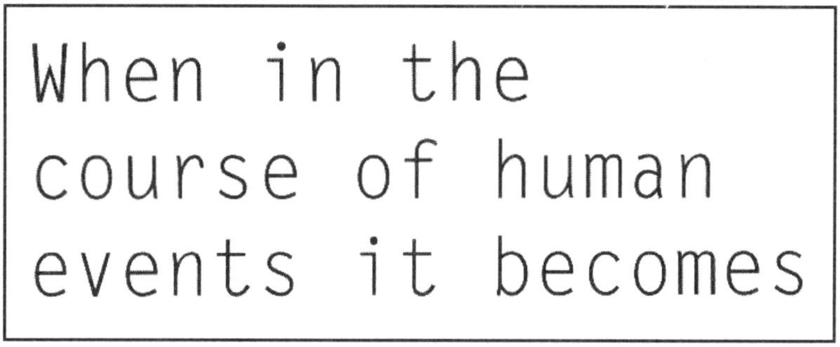

The plain font offered by most DOS programs.

When in the course of human events it becomes

Figure 3.2

Complete font control using Windows.

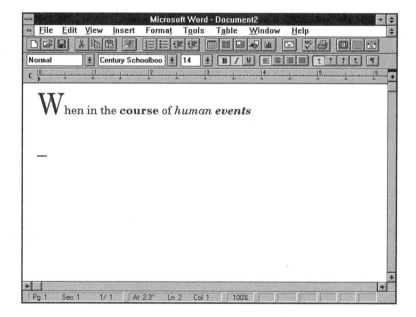

None of this comes for free, of course. Windows needs more of everything than DOS: a faster computer, more memory, more disk storage space—the works. But Windows gives you what everybody wants more of—control! And it's a lot more fun to use. Let's see how this all works.

How a Font Gets Onto Paper

Every time you type a character, the Windows font system goes into action. From its stored font file, it finds the style and type of character you chose. It then creates an image of the character in the size you selected, and sends it to the display system. You see something very close to what you'll get on paper when the document is printed. Figure 3.3 illustrates this process.

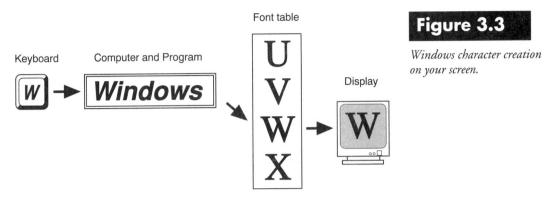

Font table

Keyboard   Computer and Program

Display

Figure 3.3

Windows character creation on your screen.

Windows repeats this graphic creation process for every character you type—it's called *rendering* the font. That includes the rasterizing I've already discussed and also adding hinting and handling kerning and other spacing. It's a lot of extra computing; that's why you'll probably want a faster computer and a better display than the one you'd need for a DOS word processor. Figure 3.4 shows a font created on-screen in Windows.

Figure 3.4

Windows screen character.

When you print your document, Windows creates a completely different set of graphics characters. That's because they have many more dots in them. Printer characters for a laser printer are about four times more detailed than those you see on a typical video display. (See Figure 3.5.)

Figure 3.5

Windows printer character.

Windows also comes with two other kinds of fonts: *raster* and *vector*. These raster fonts are used to improve the screen display for Windows itself, and the vector fonts are often used for plotters.

No matter where a font comes from, it ends up either on paper or on your display as a pattern of little dots. The pattern is called a *raster*. The more dots per character, the better the quality.

(If you want to recall more about font types, turn back to Chapter 1. That's where I talk about the difference between raster, vector, and scalable fonts.)

Managing Windows Fonts

A font manager is the function that creates characters for your screen or printer from your fonts—it renders the fonts. Whenever you use a font, the manager creates the required bitmaps automatically, and saves them in a temporary storage area called a cache.

The big font news in Windows Version 3.1 is *TrueType*. It's a new type of scalable font new to Windows. With its built-in font manager, TrueType assures that your screen display closely resembles the printed page. You get some TrueType fonts with Windows and you can buy more at great prices from many different vendors.

TrueType was developed by Apple Computer as a segment of its TrueImage document handling technology; it is part of the Macintosh System 7 operating system. Microsoft licensed its use and integrated it into Windows 3.1

Because TrueType is built-in, it automatically starts when you run Windows. You access TrueType functions using the Windows Control Panel; you usually find its icon in the Main program group. Figure 3.6 shows the Control Panel box with its applet selection icons for Windows for Workgroups 3.1. (The only addition over regular Windows 3.1 is the Network icon. The Tablet icon is a special one I've added.)

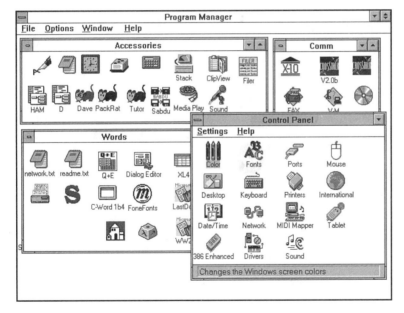

Figure 3.6

Shows the Control Panel box with its applet selection icons for Windows for Workgroups 3.1.

Only the Fonts and Printers applets directly affect fonts and their application. Figure 3.7 shows the box you get when you double-click on the Fonts icon. The scrolling list at top shows all installed TrueType fonts. Because I've selected the font called *Arial* (a clone of Helvetica), a sample of a few of the actual characters appears in the bottom box. One feature that's missing is a display of a font before it's installed.

Other controls let you add, remove or control use of TrueType fonts; I'll discuss them in the problem/solution section later in this chapter. I'll also visit the Printers applet later!

Figure 3.7

Shows the box you get when you double-click on the Fonts icon.

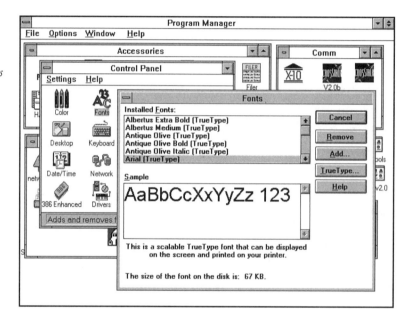

Windows handles only TrueType fonts by itself. If you plan to use Adobe PostScript fonts, Bitstream Speedo fonts or Agfa Intellifonts, you'll need to install their font managers into Windows. These managers create both screen and printer fonts as you use them, automatically.

Adobe Type Manager (ATM) is probably the most often-seen installable font manager, and is often included (bundled) with word processing applications. Bitstream's FaceLift handles not only Bitstream's proprietary Speedo font format, but also Type 1. It also gives you some special font effects. Agfa and

Hewlett-Packard support their Intellifont font format, and provides a matching manager. And Zenographics' Superprint is a versatile font manager that handles fonts from several different vendors, including Type 1, Speedo, Intellifont and others

Figure 3.8 shows the Control Panel for the latest version of ATM. As with TrueType, you can add and remove fonts. (There's no font sample viewer.)

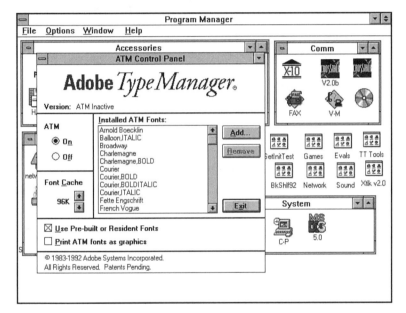

Figure 3.8

Shows the Control Panel for the latest version of ATM.

To install fonts, you click on the **A**dd button and a box like the one in Figure 3.9 appears. You can choose any directory for the fonts you want to install; they're usually provided on a diskette (for drive A or B). At the bottom of the box you can choose any destination or target directory for the installed fonts (or actually two directories). That's because each Type 1 font consists of two files (with PFB and PFM extensions).

Figure 3.9

Directory of fonts to install.

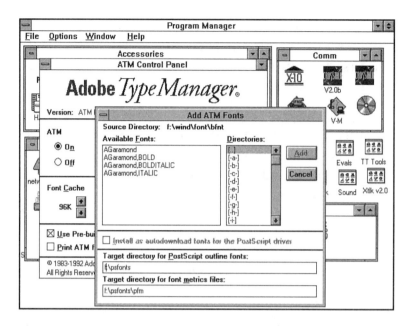

Figure 3.10 shows FaceLift, Bitstream's font manager for both Speedo and Type 1 fonts. It's shown here in "Advanced" mode, with all its feature buttons displayed. FaceLift gives you some extended features: font special effects such as shadows, fills and outlines, font groups and access to alternate character sets.

Figure 3.10

Shows FaceLift, Bitstream's font manager from both Speedo and Type 1 fonts.

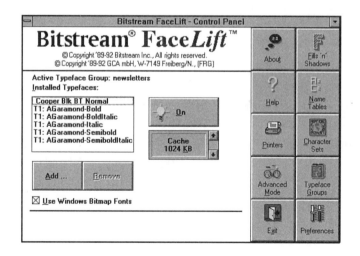

It's always fun to play with special effects, and Figure 3.11 shows what you see when you click on FaceLift's "Fills 'n Shadows" button. Here, I've created a shadow font using Cooper Black as my base. I chose a solid character face and a shadow consisting of diagonal lines, for a 3-D effect. The shadows are rotated at 315 degrees (45 degrees to the left).

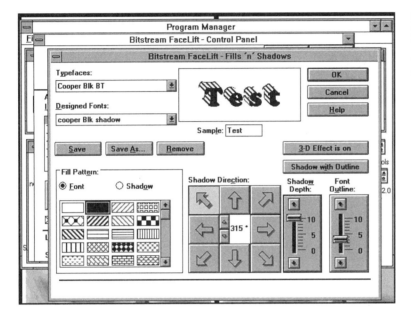

Figure 3.11

FaceLift's "Fills 'n Shadows" button.

One font product that's difficult to categorize is SuperPrint from Zenographics. That's because it's all over the place: it's a font manager for several formats, a print manager (or "spooler") *and* a set of high-quality printer drivers that often improve on the one supplied with Windows.

Figure 3.12 shows the control panel for the font manager, called SuperText. Separate windows show how some of the font formats handled: Type 1, FaceLift, Intellifont and Nimbus Q (rarely seen). At the bottom left is a box with the controls for fonts "on the fly," meaning that SuperPrint will make screen fonts for your applications as you type in the characters. That saves much disk space if you use a wide variety of fonts.

43

Figure 3.12

SuperText.

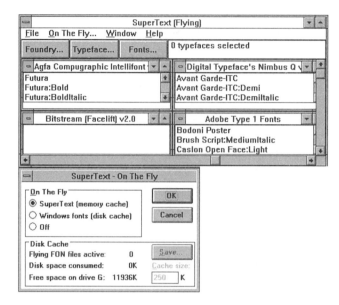

If you often use a few specific fonts, you can create and store matching screen fonts, as shown in Figure 3.13. Although screen fonts use disk space, they are instantly available to an application. You can choose to build fonts in various point sizes, character sets and screen resolutions. When you're done, you can view your results in a window as shown at bottom right.

Although not shown here, SuperText will let you revise some internal information used by Windows to categorize fonts, and also to change their names as they appear in applications. That can help you manage fonts better. SuperQueue (also not shown), handles multiple documents for release to printers. Like the Print Manager in Windows, it lets you continue working without waiting for the document to finish printing.

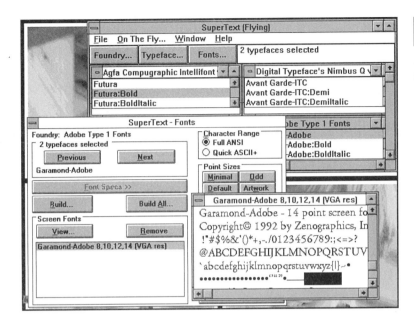

Figure 3.13

You can create and store matching screen fonts.

Printers Also Manage Fonts

As I described in Chapter 2, some printers create their own bitmaps for characters instead of having a Windows font manager do it. These printers have fonts either built-in, on a plug-in cartridge, or sent to them by your PC as "soft fonts."

Laser-type printers such as the H-P LaserJet family often have built-in scalable fonts and a rasterizer to create characters for printing. For example, the new LaserJet 4 contains both TrueType and Intellifont scalable fonts and rasterizers for each.

Microsoft has recently introduced an add-on product for some of H-P's LaserJets, called the "Windows Printing System," or WPS for short. It's a plug-in cartridge (like a font cartridge) and a program set that together give a LaserJet model II, IIp or III the ability to rasterize TrueType fonts. WPS adds some other Windows features, including a voice that announces when document printing starts and finishes. (Good for shock value at least!) More on WPS in Chapter 7.

Some printers are smart enough to not only create characters, but also contribute to composing the entire page of text. These are *PostScript-type printers.* For these, Windows sends strings of commands telling the printer what characters to use, lines, shading and simple shapes and where they are to be placed on the page. The printer completes the work—creating the page image and putting it on paper.

Video Boards Handle Windows Fonts

One interesting product I'll mention only in passing is a new kind of video board that not only generates Windows graphic images but also the fonts themselves. ATI Technology's Ultra Graphics Pro creates both TrueType and Type 1 screen fonts using what they call "CRYSTAL fonts."

CRYSTAL Fonts are created using screen dots ("pixels") of various shades of gray, filling in character shapes and resulting in screen resolution approaching that of a laser printer page. These fonts are only created for high-resolution displays (1024 by 768 pixels and higher). That means you'll probably want to use at least a 15-inch monitor for best results using Windows.

Windows displays change often as you enter text or graphics or switch between applications. If you're using Windows with lots of graphics and fonts, you'll want to buy a video board that contains a "graphics accelerator." That speeds up the process of creating pixels on your screen. Otherwise, you may have annoying delays as you work with fonts and documents.

Problems with Installing and Accessing Fonts

Here are some questions people often have about installing fonts and some solutions for common needs and problems.

PROBLEM: I have some fonts from Adobe, but Windows won't let me install them (doesn't even recognize them).

SOLUTION: Windows only handles TrueType fonts directly, but not the Type 1 fonts from Adobe. If you want to use fonts from another vendor, install their font manager. In this case, it's ATM—the Adobe Type Manager.

PROBLEM: I have some new TrueType fonts, but I can't find a way to install them.

SOLUTION #1: TrueType only works with Microsoft Windows Version 3.1 and above—not with older versions. Install your fonts by choosing the **Fonts** icon in the **Control Panel** and then selecting the **Add** button.

SOLUTION #2: If Windows still won't install your font, it may be one converted from another format into TrueType. Some of the early attempts to convert font formats resulted in corrupted files that yield errors.

PROBLEM: When I try to use one of my TrueType fonts, my computer "locks up" (won't respond).

SOLUTION: TrueType fonts are like little self-contained programs that create fonts. A corrupted font can lock up your computer when you use it. Exit and restart Windows, then remove the font that caused the problem. You can do this by double-clicking on the **Control Panel** icon, selecting the **Font** icon, then selecting the offending font and clicking on the **R**emove button.

At this point, you can try re-installing the font to see if the problem was caused by a load error. But be careful about using older shareware or converted TrueType fonts; some are corrupted.

PROBLEM: When I try to use TrueType fonts, my computer gives me fault errors or acts erratically.

SOLUTION #1: If you're using a display that has a special *driver* (program that runs your display system), it may be out of date and not compatible with TrueType. Either get an updated one from the manufacturer, or use one of the drivers that come with Windows 3.1.

Install the new driver using the Windows **S**etup application. It's usually in the Main Windows group. One of the pull-down menu items is **O**ptions. From that menu select **C**hange System Settings and select your **D**isplay from the list. (The option to install an Other display is at the very bottom of the list.)

When you select any listed display, you'll be asked to load a Windows installation diskette. If you select an Other display, you'll be asked to load a diskette from the display's manufacturer (an *OEM*).

SOLUTION #2: You may have too little RAM memory in your computer for TrueType; you need at least 2MB. If you're using Windows in 386 enhanced mode, I recommend you have at least 4MB. (I use 8MB—a safe amount for almost any single-user system.)

While you're waiting for your new RAM, don't use TrueType. You can turn off TrueType fonts by starting the **Control Panel** (double-click on its icon in the **Main** group). Double-click the **Fonts** icon, click on the TrueType command button, and clear the **E**nable TrueType Fonts check box.

PROBLEM: I have a font that isn't TrueType, and I've converted it to TrueType using a font converter program. But it doesn't work right.

SOLUTION: Some early font conversion programs didn't convert to TrueType properly. Get the latest version and try again. But don't expect perfect quality printing results from a converted font. (Some poorly-designed fonts can actually be improved by the conversion process!)

Selecting and Using Fonts

Once you have some fonts installed, here are some unexpected things that may occur—and what to do about them.

PROBLEM: I just installed some new fonts, but they don't appear in my application's font dialog box.

SOLUTION: Not all applications are notified by Windows when you add fonts. Go to the **Printer Setup** menu in your application, and select your printer again. Click on **OK**. If the new fonts still don't appear, restart Windows and start your application again.

Be sure you're not using an application intended for Windows Version 3.0 or earlier. These programs weren't designed to use TrueType fonts; they didn't exit in Windows before Version 3.1.

PROBLEM: I know I have some TrueType fonts installed in Windows, but none of them appear in any font dialog box.

SOLUTION #1: Your TrueType fonts may have been disabled. Open the **Control Panel** and double-click on the **Fonts** icon. Click on the **TrueType** button. Select the **Enable** TrueType Fonts check box.

SOLUTION #2: You may have selected a printer that can't use TrueType fonts, or one with an outdated driver that doesn't support TrueType. Use a different printer, or install a new driver. (See the answer in the "Printing Fonts" section below.)

PROBLEM: I have both TrueType and other types of fonts, but only the TrueType fonts appear in the font dialog box.

SOLUTION: You may have chosen to show only TrueType fonts. Use the **Control Panel Fonts** icon and click on the TrueType button. Unselect **S**how only TrueType fonts in Applications.

PROBLEM: I know my fonts have all kinds of special characters for foreign languages and other uses, and I want to use them. Where are they?

SOLUTION: Windows includes a special application called *Character Map* to show you special characters and allow you to insert them in any document. Select **Character Map** (which is usually in the **Accessories** group), and choose any available font. As many as 224 characters in the font are shown in a table. **S**elect one or more characters, and click on **C**opy; they will be copied to the Clipboard, ready to paste into your application. You can then close the Character Map.

If you're using a lot of special characters in your document, you might want to keep the Character Map open on part of your screen (see Figure 3.14). That way, you can select a character instantly when you need it.

Figure 3.14

Windows Character Map application.

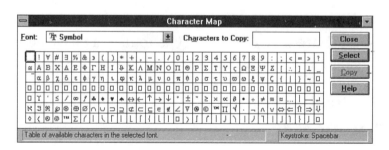

Some applications also allow you to enter a special character as a numeric code. (The Character Map shows the code in a window at its lower right. For example, the code for the copyright symbol © is **alt+0169** in most fonts.)

Once you know the code, you can simply enter it on the keyboard while you're in the application. In this example, hold the **Alt** key down and enter the numbers **0169** on the numeric keypad. Don't try to use the numbers along the top row of the keyboard—they won't work.

Microsoft Word for Windows also includes a function similar to the Character Map. It allows you to view only the special symbol fonts (not all available fonts like the Character Map). To use it, select **I**nsert **S**ymbol, and then select a single special character using the keyboard or the mouse.

PROBLEM: I loaded an old document into a Windows text application, and a font I don't even have appeared in the font dialog box. What's going to happen?

SOLUTION: Windows doesn't change font references automatically in documents. Instead, it substitutes a screen font that looks something like the original font. If you print the document, Windows will attempt to select an available font that's as close to the original as possible. Sometimes that's not very close.

Select the entire document, and choose a font that you *do* have. The original font name will disappear. If your word processor uses style sheets, you can change the font references in them instead.

(There is a feature in Windows that allows you to choose which fonts are substituted for the ones that aren't available. It's a little outside the scope of this book. But it's in your Windows reference manual, and relates to the [FontSubstitutes] section of the WIN.INI file.)

PROBLEM: I've selected a new font, and when I type, all I get is weird characters.

SOLUTION: A font is really a set of little "pictures"—not always pictures of alphabetic characters. You've selected a special font that has Greek characters, math (or other) symbols, arrows, bullets, or even icons.

Many characters in the font can be typed in using the regular alphabetic and numeric keyboard keys. Look in the information that came with your font. You should find a table that shows which key is associated with each special symbol.

To view the entire special font and select characters to insert in your document, use the Character Map application included in Windows (refer back to Figure 3.14).

Displaying Fonts

Now that you have some fonts installed and working, they may not look the way you expected. Here's what to do.

PROBLEM: Characters on my display have jagged edges.

SOLUTION: This happens when Windows doesn't have a screen font to match the desired size, and has to create one from a smaller size bitmap. If you use a TrueType font (or another font with its own manager), the screen fonts are created automatically.

Switch to a scalable font which has an installed and active manager. (If you've forgotten what a scalable font is, take another look at Chapter 1.)

If you're using a soft font, use its associated font installer program to build a screen font of the size you're now using.

TIP

Sometimes it just makes sense to ignore the "jaggies" on your screen fonts—especially when it's a font you don't use often. Every time you have your font installer build a new screen font, it uses some hard disk space. That might be more important to you than the temporary inconvenience. Remember, the font should still print correctly, regardless of how it looks.

PROBLEM: My TrueType fonts won't display properly.

SOLUTION: Either you have very little RAM memory, or you're using a display driver that's outdated. See the "Installing Fonts" section above.

PROBLEM: Every time I type a character, the whole line of text flickers.

SOLUTION: You're using a font for which you don't have a pre-built screen font. Use your font installer program to build a screen font of the size you're now using.

This flicker problem often occurs when you've selected a different screen display (or "zoom" factor) other than 100% in an application. That makes all the screen fonts different from their standard (pre-built) sizes.

TrueType and ATM make screen fonts of any size you need, automatically. You could simply switch to a TrueType or Adobe font.

PROBLEM: The text I type goes outside of the document margins.

SOLUTION: You have a screen font that doesn't have the proper character widths, and your application makes an error trying to determine how many characters to put on a line. Switch to TrueType or another scalable font, which will create an accurate screen font automatically.

Some text applications (including Word for Windows) don't display screen text properly in all cases—especially with combinations like bold italic type. You could simply ignore the disparity after you've verified that the printing is correct.

PROBLEM: I entered some special characters into my text, but now they've disappeared (or changed).

SOLUTION: You've changed fonts in that section of text, from its original symbol font to another font that doesn't have those symbols. Highlight the special characters and reselect the symbol font.

PROBLEM: I switched printers, and now the font I was using doesn't show up in the fonts dialog box.

SOLUTION: When you select a printer, Windows shows only the fonts it can print currently. The font you were using may be built into the printer, or available in an installed printer font cartridge. The new printer doesn't have the same fonts. You can either return to the original printer, or select another font this printer can use.

Your printer driver may not support TrueType fonts; an updated one may be available from Microsoft or from the printer manufacturer. See the answer in the "Printing Fonts" section that follows.

Printing Fonts

Your fonts appear on your display the way you want them, but somehow they don't appear on the printed page that way. What to do?

PROBLEM: I can't print anything!

SOLUTION: (This is an abbreviated list that is repeated in greater detail in Chapter 7.)

1. Make sure your printer is working using DOS; ignore Windows for the moment. Start your computer in DOS (don't run Windows). Find out which port your printer is on (COM1, COM2, LPT1, LPT2, LPT3). Try printing a directory using one of the following DOS commands (type the command at the DOS prompt, then press Enter):

   dir > com1   (or **com2**, **com3**, or **com4**)

   or

   dir > lpt1   (or **lpt2** or **lpt3**)

(Be sure to type the right triangular bracket (>)—usually located on the keyboard above the period key. That tells DOS to send the directory to the printer instead of your screen.)

If this doesn't print the directory, make sure the printer is plugged in, turned on, properly connected to the computer port, on-line, and has paper. Then try this DOS print test again.

2. If your printer works under DOS, Run Windows. Go to the **Control Panel** and check the following settings.

   - If your printer uses a COM port, select the **Ports** icon and make sure the port is set for the right speed. (Most printers can be set for different speeds; check your printer manual for the settings, and verify the speed. It will usually be 1200, 2400, 4800 or 9600.)

   If you make a speed change, you'll need to reboot your computer to make it effective.

   - Select the Printers icon from the Control Panel, and check to see if a driver for your printer is installed.

     If it isn't, install one. Click on the Add button, select your printer from the list, then click on the Install button and follow the on-screen directions. (If your printer isn't shown on the list, you'll need to select Install Unlisted or Updated Printer from the list; you'll also need a printer driver diskette from the printer manufacturer.)

   - Click on the **C**onnect button and make sure the printer is connected *in Windows* to the same PC serial or parallel port to which it's connected by cable.

3. Go to your application. Select P**r**int Setup from the **F**ile menu, and make sure the printer you want to use is

selected for this application. If you've missed anything, the **F**ile **P**rint menu item will be grayed out, indicating the printer still isn't available.

PROBLEM: I try to print, but the computer locks up.

SOLUTION: Your computer needs space on the hard disk to store printer font information temporarily. For printers like the HP PaintJet, the printer driver stores the bitmap for the entire page. If it runs out of space, it may lock up.

Be sure there is enough hard disk space for the Windows TEMP directory, which is usually on drive C [**C:\TEMP**]. You may need between 1 and 3MB disk space.

PROBLEM: My printed text is garbled.

SOLUTION #1: Are you using a font manager, such as ATM? These programs need to use at least 1 to 2MB of temporary space on your hard disk for temporary storage while they're creating printer files. Make sure you have well over that amount of space free on your disk.

Even when the disk space is available, the font manager has to be able to access it. Check the font manager documents to be sure that its disk access is properly set up. (For example, you may need a DOS **TEMP** statement in your **AUTOEXEC.BAT** file.)

SOLUTION #2: Are you using a *print sharing device* (an electronic box used to connect two or more printers to one computer)? If so, you may have to change a Windows setting. Select **Printers** from the **Control Panel**, choose your printer, and click on the **C**onnect box. Clear the box labelled **F**ast Printing Direct to Port.

PROBLEM #1: Fonts that I print don't match those on my display.

PROBLEM #2: The number of characters on displayed lines don't match those on lines as printed; thus I have different line breaks.

SOLUTION: You're using an installable font on your printer that doesn't have a matching screen font. To compensate, Windows has substituted another font for use on the screen; your application is using that to determine character width.

You can either use the font installer supplied with your fonts to create a screen font, or switch to a scalable font such as TrueType (or Adobe Type 1 fonts, using ATM).

PROBLEM #1: I'm using a new printer, and now my TrueType fonts don't appear in any font dialog box.

PROBLEM #2: Text using TrueType fonts won't print.

SOLUTION: Many older printer drivers can't use TrueType fonts. Contact the printer vendor for a new driver, or use one of the new Windows drivers.

If you have access to the CompuServe Information Service, you'll find the latest drivers on the Microsoft Library forum. Type **GO MSL**.

To install a new driver, select the **Printers** icon in the **Control Panel**. Click on the **A**dd button. On the printer list, choose Install Unlisted or Updated Printer. You'll be prompted to insert the diskette with the new driver.

PROBLEM: I print one document, but I have to wait until the first one is finished printing before I can print another.

SOLUTION: Enable the Windows Print Manager. Select the **Printers** icon in the **Control Panel**, and check the box called **U**se Print Manager. Now the Print Manager will accept all print requests from your applications, and print them in the order received. You won't have to wait.

(But you'll still have to wait while your application sends the documents to the Print Manager; the net result may not be very much time saved.)

PROBLEM #1: Only part of the page will print—the rest is blank.

PROBLEM #2: I get an **Error 21** message on my LaserJet.

SOLUTION: You don't have enough memory in your LaserJet or other page printer. If you're printing a full page of high-quality graphics, you need at least 1.5MB of RAM in the printer itself.

Either install more memory in the printer, or reduce the quality of the output from 300 dpi (dots per inch) to 75 or 150 dpi. (That reduces the need for memory because the printer doesn't have to store as many dots.) To change quality, select the **Printers** icon in the **Control Panel**. Select the printer you're using, and click on the **S**etup button. Change the **G**raphics resolution, and click on all the **OK** buttons.

Some applications and printers allow you to select *draft quality* output, which also lowers the resolution and may allow you to print the entire page.

If you're not using TrueType fonts, try switching. Because TrueType files sent to the printer are somewhat smaller than other formats, you might get by with the printer memory you already have.

PROBLEM: My documents are printed on the wrong printer.

SOLUTION: Select Print Setup on your application's menu. Select the printer you want. If the printer hasn't been installed before, you may also have to click on **C**onnect and **S**etup buttons and make those selections. Click on **OK** when you're done.

To make this printer the one your application will use automatically in the future, go to the Windows Program Manager.

Click on the Control Panel icon, then the Printers icon. Find and select your printer in the Installed Printers list box. Finally, click on Set As Default Printer before leaving the Control Panel.

PROBLEM: My HP DeskJet printer doesn't print TrueType fonts.

SOLUTION: The driver from Hewlett-Packard that was shipped with Windows doesn't support TrueType. Get the new Hewlett-Packard driver and install it. (Or you can get one from Microsoft that will work almost as well.) Either driver is available from the manufacturer, and is also available on the CompuServe Information Service. See the appendix for manufacturers and their telephone order numbers.

To install the new driver, select the **Printers** icon in the **Control Panel**. Click on the **A**dd button. On the printer list, choose **Install Unlisted** or **Updated Printer**. You'll be prompted to insert the diskette with the new driver.

PROBLEM: I reset my LaserJet printer in the middle of the job, and now the only font it prints is Courier.

SOLUTION: Fonts used by your page printer were loaded into its memory at the beginning of printing. Those fonts were erased from the printer's memory; the printer is substituting another font that it has built-in.

Abort the print job from Windows if it's still running. (Go to the **Print Manager** if you have it enabled.) Reset the printer to clear everything from its memory, and do the print command again. If that doesn't work, you may have to close and then reopen the application.

PROBLEM: I've installed a new font cartridge on my printer, but the new fonts don't appear in the font dialog box.

SOLUTION: You need to make the printer driver aware that the cartridge exists. Select the **Control Panel**, choose

Printers, and select the one with the cartridge. Click on **S**etup and select the font cartridge you've installed. Click on all the **OK** boxes and exit the Control Panel.

Some font cartridges are not shown on the printer driver list. They are shipped with a diskette that provides the printer driver the font information it needs. In that case, while you are still in Printers Setup, click on **Fonts**, choose the **A**dd Fonts button, and install the files from the diskette.

When you're done, click on the E**x**it, OK and Close buttons to leave the Control Panel.

Looking Back and Looking Ahead

What I've done in this chapter is give you a concept of how Windows creates and uses fonts. We've also spent a lot of time resolving common problems you might encounter.

Next, we're going to turn to the more popular Windows applications that employ fonts. You'll probably find your favorite word processor, spreadsheet, desktop publishing, or graphics program there.

So read on in Chapter 4 for more info and solutions!

chapter 4

STEVE
VANDERBOSCH

Fonts in Windows Applications

Microsoft Windows applications exert a large amount of control over fonts and how you can use them. Although Windows includes the TrueType font manager and makes the fonts accessible, the application controls which fonts and styles are available to you and how they appear.

Because an application directs its own display, it also influences the quality of the text presentation. Some applications give you a more faithful approximation of the printed page than others. What you see is not *always* what you get!

In this chapter, I'll discuss some of the more popular Windows applications, their special font features, and some problems and solutions.

But first, a general look at the Windows font features that affect all text applications. (By *applications*, I mean the programs you buy that are meant to run under Windows—such as word processors, desktop publishing packages, or graphics and drawing programs.)

Windows Font Control Features

All applications can take advantage of the general font-control features that Microsoft Windows 3.1 provides. Many of these apply specifically to TrueType fonts.

The Windows Control Panel, shown in Figure 4.1, contains font controls that let you install, remove, enable, disable, and preview TrueType fonts. It's a fairly simple feature—for example, the Control Panel doesn't let you preview (look at a sample of) a complete font, but only a few selected characters (usually **AaBbCcXxYyZz123**).

Figure 4.1

Windows Control Panel.

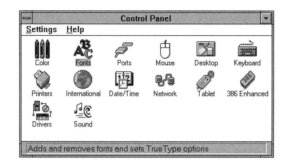

Figure 4.2 shows the Font dialog box, with its font controls and its preview screen. The Font system maintains the list of all available TrueType and a few internal fonts.

Figure 4.2

Windows Font control dialog box.

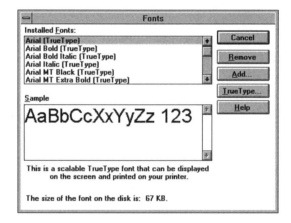

When you install a TrueType font, Windows ordinarily copies it to the WINDOWS\SYSTEM subdirectory, where it has a file extension of TTF. (For example, Arial—a version of Helvetica—has the file name ARIAL.TTF.) At the same time, the Font system creates a second small file with the same name, but with the extension FOT (for example, ARIAL.FOT). That file describes the font and its location so Windows can list and access it quickly.

Windows maintains a list of all available TrueType fonts, and also of some bitmapped internal fonts. When you select a font in your application, the application asks Windows for that list, and displays it for you.

When the font you've selected needs to be displayed or printed, Windows creates the appropriate bitmapped fonts. (This is called *rasterizing.*) The TrueType font files store the shapes of the characters (their *outlines*) and information about character spacing, kerning, and hinting (called *metrics*).

One confusing aspect of Windows fonts is that some font files contain only one style, while other files may have several. For example, Arial is in a single font file which contains four styles (regular, bold, italic, and bold-italic) within it. Other fonts may have other styles; they may have only the regular style, or a light or extra-bold, or other variations. You can't tell by looking at the font file directory what styles are in each file.

> ### TIP
>
> *Remember: the Windows Character Map application will give you a look at all the characters in all available font files. But it only shows the base—regular—font in a file and not any style variations. This is likely to be improved in future releases.*

Windows 3.1 can provide more font information to your applications than the older Windows 3.0 could. The newer Windows can provide a list of all the font types and all the styles within a font family—no matter where they're found in the various font files. For this arrangement to work, all the font files of each family must have the same internal family name. Font files from different vendors often don't have the same family names.

The *Adobe Type Manager* (or *ATM*) is an application that runs in Windows to allow you to use PostScript Type 1 fonts. You also use ATM to install your Type 1 fonts, which are then available to all Windows applications. You must first install, load, and enable ATM before running text applications. You can buy ATM as a product by itself, and it is often included with Windows fonts and text applications.

An application that uses Windows fonts will have a menu item that allows you to choose one by name. This list shows all your TrueType fonts, and also any Type 1 fonts available via ATM. In the menu item, you also choose the font attributes you want—regular, italic, bold, bold-italic, underline, small caps, color, and others.

Many applications let you change the size of the text display on your monitor. To see the entire page on the screen, for example, you might choose a display size of 60 percent. This would make 12-point type appear at a size of about 7.2 points (60 percent of 12-point).

Some applications have difficulty displaying such fractional point sizes. You may see some screen flicker as you enter characters on a line. Other applications may simply substitute the nearest whole-size font on the screen (in this case, 7-point). If that happens, the lines may not display with the appropriate length or number of characters, but they will print correctly.

The Windows TrueType system gives you more than just font styles. You can select variations like small capitals, underlining, and tightness of character spacing.

TrueType has the capacity to add even better control over type generation. You will see better kerning and other special effects added in future applications. As type vendors become more familiar with TrueType, you can expect to see better-looking type faces generally.

Now for some discussion on how real-life Windows text applications handle fonts.

Ami Pro

Here's a very popular word processor for Windows. *Ami Pro* was developed by Samna Corp. of Atlanta, and Lotus Development Corporation bought the company. Version 3 was released in mid-1992, and takes advantage of new Windows 3.1 features such as OLE (Object Linking and Embedding) and drag-and-drop. (It can run under Windows 3.0 as well.) Figure 4.3 shows the main Ami Pro screen.

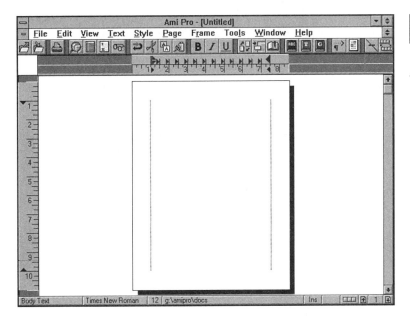

Figure 4.3

The main screen in Ami Pro 3.0.

Ami Pro does a good job of displaying an accurate screen representation of what will be printed. Other word processors sometimes run text lines which contain bold or italic characters past the edge of the screen "page." That can be somewhat unnerving.

Like other Windows applications, Ami Pro uses the built-in TrueType font handler. To allow you to use Type 1 fonts, the Adobe Type Manager (ATM) Version 2.0 is included.

When you use the **Text** menu to format your words, Ami Pro shows you a fonts list that includes both TrueType and Type 1 fonts. For each font, you choose the styles and attributes you want, as shown in Figure 4.4. Font files are not combined to show all the styles in a font family, although that feature is sure to be included in the next major revision.

Figure 4.4

Ami Pro font selection dialog box.

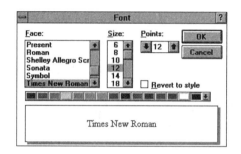

You can select attributes for any character or block of characters, but there's no provision for saving character formats. If you select small capitals ("small caps"), and they don't exist in the font you're using, Ami Pro will generate them for you on the spot.

NOTE

If you're going to use Ami Pro's extensive scientific features and math equation editor, you'll need to have a symbol font available. The one that's included with Windows will do the trick; just make sure you don't delete or disable it.

Although there's no provision for manual kerning of letter pairs, you can adjust the overall spacing of characters on a line. You choose between tight, normal and loose spacing.

Here are a few problems you might encounter with Ami Pro—and some solutions.

PROBLEM: I tried to print a row of characters in reverse—white on black instead of black on white—on my laser printer, and it doesn't print.

SOLUTION: Make two changes. First:

1. With Ami Pro not running, start the Windows **Notepad** application by double-clicking its icon in the **Accessories** program group.

2. Choose **File O**pen to open the file in your \WINDOWS directory called AMIPRO.INI.

3. In the section with a heading of **[AmiPro]** you'll find a line that reads: **HPLJClipping=0**. Change the 0 to a **1**.

4. Choose **File S**ave to save the file.

   Then:

1. Start the Windows **Control Panel** from the **Main** program group, and double-click on the **Printers** icon.

2. Select the printer you're using, choose **Setup**, and then **O**ptions.

3. Check the box that says Print TrueType as **Graphics**, then click on **OK**. (Not all laser printers have this option available. If your laser printer is set to a low resolution (75 or 150 dots per inch instead of 300), you won't be able to check this option.)

4. Click on the **OK** button, and then the **Close** button to exit.

PROBLEM: I am using some large TrueType characters in a headline, and I expected them to be kerned. But there are big gaps between letters like "W" and "i". What can I do?

SOLUTION: Switch to a similar font in the Type 1 format. Ami Pro doesn't kern TrueType fonts at present, but it does kern Type 1's.

PROBLEM: I'm trying to edit some bold justified text, and the characters are displayed overlapping each other; I can't read them.

SOLUTION: There's a problem with an early Ami Pro file called AMIFONT.DLL that makes justified or right-aligned text with attributes display incorrectly. You can get a corrected one called AMIFNT.EXE from Lotus by calling their technical support line (or you can download it from CompuServe). Here's how to install the file you need.

▼ **NOTE**

CompuServe is an on-line information service you can sub-scribe to if you have a modem. It features forums about a variety of software products; there users discuss problems they have encountered, and the solutions. You can also download (transfer) many handy files to your system to help you use applications more effectively.

1. Insert the diskette with the AMIFNT.EXE file into a floppy drive (drive A or drive B).

2. Copy AMIFNT.EXE to an empty directory on your hard disk. At the DOS prompt, type **COPY AMIFNT.EXE**, a space, then the directory's letter, a backslash, and the subdirectory's name. For example, you might type **COPY AMIFNT.EXE C:\TEMP**. (If the diskette is in drive B, simply change the "A:" to "B:" in the line.) When you're done typing the line, press **Enter**.

3. Change to the directory where you copied the AMIFNT file (see step 1). For example, if you've used the C:\TEMP directory, type **CD C:TEMP** and press **Enter**. While in that directory, type **AMIFNT** to run this self-unpacking file. This will produce the AMIFNT.DLL file you need.

4. Copy AMIFNT.DLL to the Ami Pro program directory (where the older AMIFNT.DLL will be) by typing **COPY AMIFNT.DLL C:\AMIPRO**. Now you can start Windows and run Ami Pro. (You may first want to delete both the files now in the temporary directory you were using.)

PROBLEM: I want to use ATM (Type 1) fonts with my newly-installed Ami Pro, but all the style sheets I got specify TrueType fonts. What do I do?

SOLUTION: On the Ami Pro installation diskettes are some style sheets specifying ATM fonts. Because they're in a special compressed format to save space, you need to decompress them before use. Get the decompression utility called DECOMP from Lotus Development Corporation's technical support or download it from CompuServe (where it's called DECMPS.EXE).

While still in DOS, copy the file DECMPS.EXE to a convenient directory on your hard disk (see the previous Solution for examples of how to copy files). While in that directory, type **DECMPS** to run this self-unpacking file. This will produce two files: DECOMP.EXE and COMPRESS.DLL.

Next, find the directory where your Ami Pro style sheets are stored (usually \AMIPRO\STYLES) and rename, delete, or move the TrueType-based style sheets (all the ones that Ami Pro automatically installs).

You can now run Windows for the next steps.

1. Place the Ami Pro program diskette—3 1/2-inch Disk 1 or 5 1/4-inch Disk 2—in a floppy drive.

2. From the Windows Program Manager, select **F**ile **R**un and enter **DECOMP.EXE** (preceded by its directory path) in the **C**ommand Line: text box. (For example, if you placed the program in the Ami Pro program directory, you'd type **C:\AMIPRO\DECOMP**.) Then click on the **OK** button.

3. When DECOMP runs, double-click on the letter of the floppy drive you put the Ami Pro diskette in. In the list box, double-click on the name **STY30MST.CMZ.**

4. From the **Files** list box in the next dialog box, select **ALL,** then **ADD**.

5. In the **Destination Path** box, type the full path to the Ami Pro styles directory (usually **C:\AMIPRO\STYLES**).

6. Finally, choose **Decompress** to start the action.

7. When the action stops, and you see **Decompress more files?**, click on **YES** and insert the next program diskette into the floppy drive.

8. Again, double-click on the letter for the floppy drive you're using. In the list box, double-click on the name **STY30.CMZ.**

9. Again, select **ALL** and then **ADD**, and enter the styles directory.

10. Choose **Decompress** again to start.

11. Finally, in response to the line **Decompress more files?**, choose **NO**. When you next start Ami Pro, you'll have your new style sheets referencing Type 1 fonts.

Microsoft Word for Windows

Without doubt the most popular word processor for Windows, Word for Windows (or WinWord, as it's often called) sets the standard others are compared against. It's currently in version 2.0c, reflecting three minor maintenance revisions. (Registered users can get them at no charge from Microsoft Customer Service.) Figure 4.5 shows you the main WinWord screen.

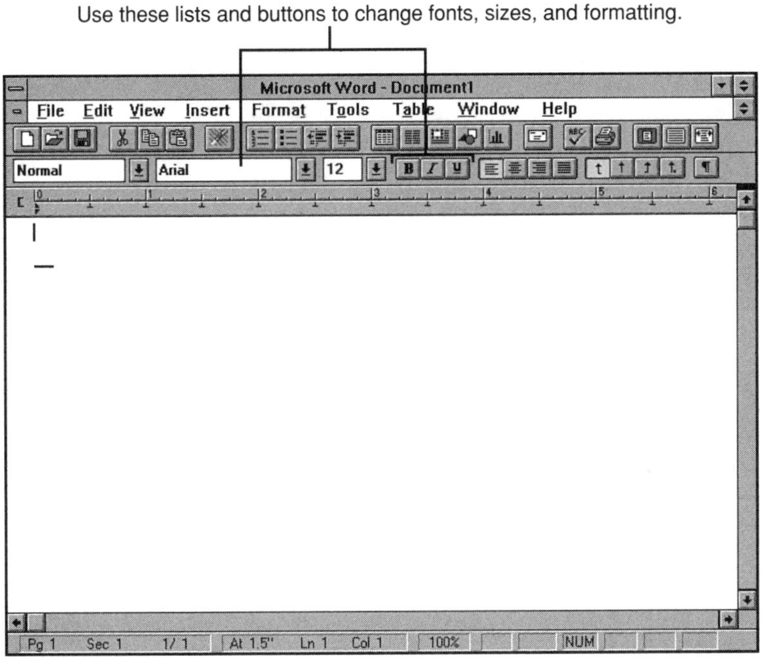

Use these lists and buttons to change fonts, sizes, and formatting.

Figure 4.5

Word for Windows 2.0.

WinWord allows you to choose a font from a list which includes all available fonts. That includes TrueType of course, and also Type 1 fonts *if* you are running Adobe Type Manager. (ATM is not included with WinWord.) You can use the WinWord Toolbar to change the font, its size, and its bold, italic and underline style attributes.

For more complete font control, select the Forma**t** **C**haracter menu item. There you'll find the font list and styles, as well as color and line spacing controls (shown in Figure 4.6).

To view and insert special characters, WinWord has its own font display tool, selected on the menu **I**nsert **S**ymbol. It appears in a window, and looks and acts much like the Windows Character Map application. But the Symbol tool only shows specially designated icon and symbol fonts and a font called "Normal Text." That means the currently selected text font, which usually has a regular character set.

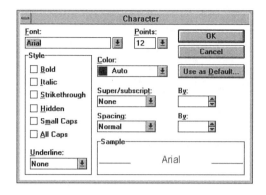

Figure 4.6

Word for Windows Format Character dialog box.

WinWord has an entire application just for headline creation, linked to the word processor—it's called WordArt. You enter this application by choosing the **I**nsert **O**bject command and choosing **MS WordArt** from the **O**bject Type list. WordArt starts automatically, giving you nineteen display fonts and a variety of special text effects to use. You see it in Figure 4.7.

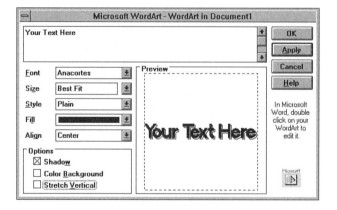

Figure 4.7

Microsoft WordArt.

When you've composed a text string in WordArt, the text is placed in your document as an object—a graphic in an enclosed box. Except to change size, you can't edit an object while it is displayed on the WinWord screen. If you want to modify the headline you created, double-click in the object box. WordArt reappears automatically, with the current text displayed inside it.

TIP

*If you want to view your fonts and lines on-screen the way they'll be printed, be sure to choose Tools Options View, and check the **Line Breaks and Fonts as Printed** box. Otherwise your display may not look much like the printed document. If you select a font that's not available for your printer, WinWord will substitute an existing font that best matches it.*

Here are a few WinWord problems and solutions.

PROBLEM: I've just inserted a picture or object into my WinWord document, but I can see only a tiny piece of it. Now what?

SOLUTION: Select Format Paragraph from the menu bar, set Line Spacing to **Auto**, then click on **OK**. That allows WinWord to use as much "line" spacing as it needs to display the graphic.

PROBLEM: I'm trying to print reverse (white on black) text on my laser printer, but it doesn't work. How do I fix this?

SOLUTION: There are two procedures to follow. First:

1. Start the Windows **Notepad** application by double-clicking its icon in the **Accessories** program group.

2. Choose File Open, and open the **WIN.INI** file in the **\WINDOWS** program directory.

3. Find the section headed with [**Microsoft Word 2.0**]. In that section, add this line: **SlowShading=Yes**.

4. Choose File Save, then exit Notepad.

Second:

1. Open the Windows **Control Panel** from the **Main** program group, and double-click on the **Printers** icon.

2. Select the printer you're using; choose **S**etup, then **O**ptions.

3. Check the box that says Print TrueType as **G**raphics, then click on **OK**. (This helps if your printer is close to running out of memory for your printed pages. Not all laser printers have this option available.)

4. Click on **OK**, then **Close** to exit.

PROBLEM: My TrueType fonts don't appear on the font list when I select an HP-compatible laser printer. But when I look for them in the Windows Write accessory, they're OK. How do I get to use them?

SOLUTION: Some older versions of WinWord were shipped with printer drivers, which were installed in the WinWord program directory. Those drivers weren't TrueType-compatible.

Delete the files named HPPCL.DRV and HPPCL5A.DRV from your WinWord program directory (*not* from your \WINDOWS\SYSTEM directory). Now start WinWord and re-select the printer. You should now see all your TrueType fonts listed in WinWord.

PROBLEM: I'm using the Equation Editor, but the special math characters are the wrong size or shape. I want the right ones.

SOLUTION: You may have some old math fonts with the same name as new ones which do match. In the **\WINDOWS\SYSTEM** directory, look for files named **MTEXTRA** and **FENCES**. If there are two copies of them—one with the .FON and the other with an .FOT extension—delete the ones with the **.FON** extension.

PROBLEM: I'm using 12-point TrueType Courier—the one that comes with Windows 3.1. My display shows some characters extending outside the margins. What does this mean?

SOLUTION: Not much. There's a small problem with this Courier display on-screen. It shouldn't affect printing, and you should ignore it until it gets fixed in a maintenance release of WinWord.

PROBLEM: Whenever I change my mind after selecting **File Print** and **Cancel**, my ruler changes from inches to centimeters scale. Then I have to change it back. Can I prevent this?

SOLUTION: No. This was a problem with the original release of WinWord, and may have been fixed in a maintenance release. Get the latest release from Microsoft Customer Service; it's usually free of charge.

To change the ruler scale, choose **T**ools **O**ptions, select the **General** icon, and choose the **M**easurement Units you prefer.

WordPerfect for Windows

WordPerfect for DOS is likely the world's most popular word processor. WordPerfect for Windows (also from WordPerfect Corporation) is its Windows cousin and is shown in Figure 4.8. The current version is 5.2; a completely revised edition is expected late in 1993.

One of the special appeals of WordPerfect for DOS (at least to version 5.2) has been its ability to run on simple PCs with only basic amounts of memory (640K). But, like every other Windows word processor, WordPerfect for Windows needs lots of hard disk space and a reasonable amount of memory (RAM)—4M is an adequate amount for most users. (WordPerfect Corporation also recommends that you use a 386 or higher level PC.)

WordPerfect for Windows maintains quite a lot of compatibility with its DOS counterpart: it shares the same document and dictionary file format. There's also an alternate keyboard layout you can select if you want to use command keystrokes that match the DOS version of WordPerfect.

Figure 4.8

WordPerfect for Windows 5.2.

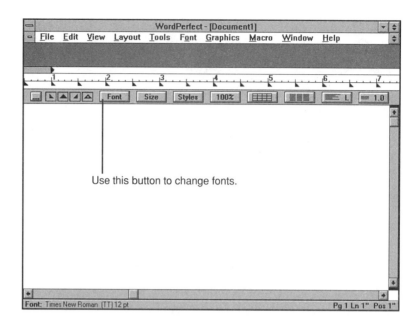

WordPerfect defines a font in the "classical" way, as a set of characters of one typeface design, and of a specific size. For example, 12-point Helvetica is a font. This is a more narrow definition than Microsoft uses, because it specifies a single size. Figure 4.9 shows the main font list.

Figure 4.9

WordPerfect for Windows Font dialog box.

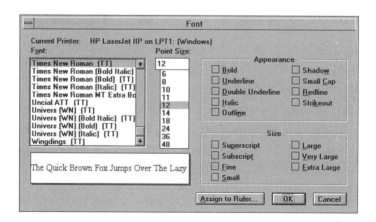

WordPerfect offers even more extensive control over type management. A Typesetting window, shown in Figure 4.10, lets you set word and letter spacing, and either manual or automatic kerning.

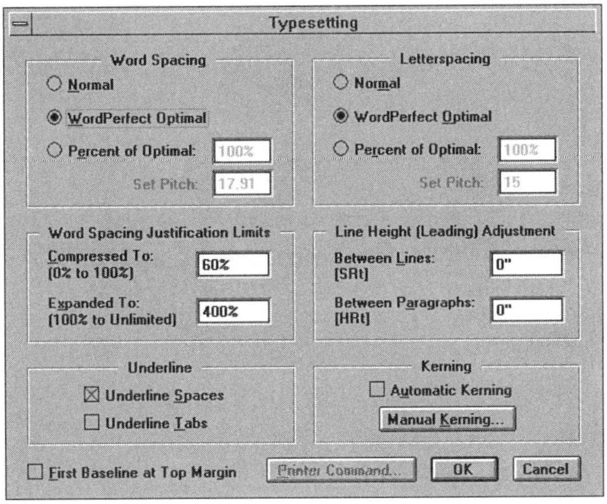

Figure 4.10

WordPerfect Typesetting options dialog box.

From the main font list, you can select as many as 21 fonts to be available for quick access on the Ruler bar at the top of the display window (shown previously in Figure 4.8).

WordPerfect for DOS provides drivers for more than 1,000 printers, including many printers not supported by Windows. These drivers support built-in, cartridge, and downloadable soft fonts—but not scalable fonts. You can select either a Windows printer driver or a WordPerfect one.

WordPerfect for Windows uses the same printer drivers that WordPerfect for DOS uses. This gives you access to printer types and options not usually found in Windows. For example, your print job can pause automatically to let you change a daisywheel to provide another font. You can also include special command codes in your document to control a printer's operation. The drivers are even customizable for special printer needs. (These are not features for beginners!)

Here are a few problems you might encounter in WordPerfect, and some answers.

PROBLEM: I'm using a WordPerfect printer driver, and my graphics aren't printing.

SOLUTION: You're using an old printer driver file. Get a new printer driver from WordPerfect. (This problem has been fixed in later releases.) WordPerfect Customer Service will mail the drivers to you on diskette if you give them a call. If you have a modem, you can also download them from the W-P bulletin board or from CompuServe.

To install a W-P printer driver in Version 5.2, place its diskette in a floppy drive. Then double-click on the W-P Install icon in your WordPerfect program group. The install program will then run. Choose **Install New Printer Drivers** and select the drive the diskette is in. Now you can choose the proper driver from the displayed list. The install program will place the new driver in the C:\WPC directory, over-writing the old version.

If you're using W-P Version 5.1, first exit to DOS. Then run the install program in your W-P program directory (usually C:\WP51). At the DOS prompt, type C:\WP51\INSTALL. The rest of the procedure is as above for version 5.2.

In any case, *don't* simply copy a driver from the supplied diskette; it is in compressed format and will not work.

To enable the new printer driver, you must add the printer. Exit the install program and return to your WordPerfect word-processor. From the command menu, select **F**ile **S**elect Printer, then **D**elete; then choose the printer name that you've updated. Next, select Add and follow the prompts to over-write the old printer setups. (When you do this, you'll lose all the setups for forms for this printer. You'll need to recreate them manually for the new printer driver.)

PROBLEM: Some of my lines are underlined, and I see breaks in the underlines between characters.

SOLUTION #1: Try changing the Letterspacing option in the Typesetting dialog box from WordPerfect **O**ptimal to Nor**m**al. (The Nor**m**al setting uses the character spacing data from the font file, and the **O**ptimal spacing is a WordPerfect special effect.) You access this box from the command menu using **L**ayout Typesetti**n**g.

SOLUTION #2: If you're using an old version of the Windows driver for your printer, install the latest one. You can often get them directly from the printer manufacturer (see your printer manual), or download them from CompuServe.

You could also try switching to a WordPerfect printer driver if there's one for your printer. See the solution above about selecting a printer driver.

To install a Windows printer driver, open the Windows Control Panel and double-click on the **Printers** icon. First click on the **R**emove button, then find the printer name in the list and click on **Yes**. That deletes the old driver.

Next, click on **Add**, choose **Install Unlisted** or **Updated Printer** (first line in the list of printers) and click on Install. Place the diskette with the new printer driver in a floppy drive and select the drive. This loads the new printer driver.

You may want to check the printer setup while you're in the Control Panel Printers box. Just click on **S**etup.

PROBLEM: I'm putting symbol characters in my document. I see the symbols on the screen, but they print in the regular font—not as symbols. That's not what I expected.

SOLUTION: Instead of selecting the symbol font directly, try using the WordPerfect F**o**nt **E**xtended Character menu item to select your special characters.

PROBLEM: I've selected a portion of my text to add a bold attribute, and the text prints as a completely different font (such as condensed). How do I get the proper effect?

SOLUTION: WordPerfect is confused about the font name, and about whether to change to a completely different font or find the attribute in the current font.

Select (highlight) the text and choose the menu item Font Font. . . to open the Font dialog box. If a bold version of the face you're using is listed separately in the font list, change all your bold characters to that face (instead of applying the bold attribute for the regular face).

PROBLEM: I made a few small changes to my printer setup, such as changing the orientation from portrait to landscape. Now WordPerfect is doing something with my hard disk and won't let me continue working. What did I do wrong?

SOLUTION: Nothing. Whenever you make a change to a printer setup, WordPerfect updates its internal file that holds all the font information for the printer. That could take anywhere from a few seconds to several minutes, depending on the number of fonts you have. Just be patient. WordPerfect is bound to be working on a better way to update printer information files selectively.

Microsoft Excel

Excel is the Microsoft spreadsheet application that's won wide acclaim. In its latest version (4.0), it's packed with useful features. (Microsoft has recently made available a minor maintenance release you can get at no charge.) Figure 4.11 shows Excel with a blank spreadsheet, ready to be filled out.

Although you might not expect a spreadsheet to emphasize font control, Excel does. In fact, it's the first Windows application to display the "new-style" list of fonts within the families I described earlier.

Tools for changing font size, bold, and italics

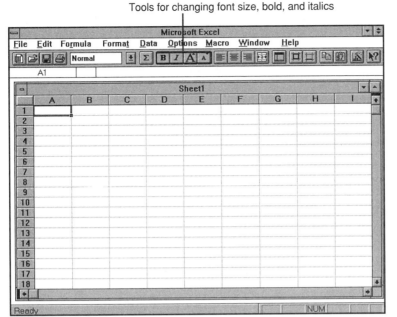

Figure 4.11

Microsoft Excel 4.0.

To choose a font, select Forma**t F**ont from the menu bar. Excel displays the window shown in Figure 4.12, with three scrolling list boxes: **F**ont, Font St**y**le, and **S**ize.

Use these lists to select and format fonts.

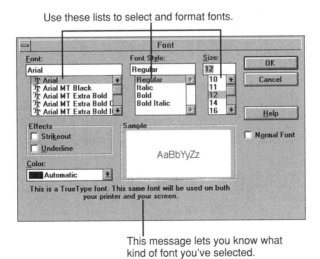

Figure 4.12

Excel Font selection dialog box.

This message lets you know what kind of font you've selected.

The **F**ont box might better be called the "Font Family," because there should be one entry in that list for each font file in the family. (There may be one or several files in a family.) The Font Style box shows you styles contained in all the font files in the family. You can also select font size, effects, and color.

A message line at the bottom of the Font menu's dialog box tells you whether you've selected a TrueType, printer, or screen font. If you've selected a font style that's not in the font family, it tells you that style is being "imitated"; Excel will select the closest font, or create the bold or italic effect.

If you select (click on) the Normal Font check box, Excel displays the current default font —MS Sans Serif at first, which is an available Windows screen font. (This is a screen font *only*, and an available sans-serif font will be substituted for printing.) You can easily change the default font by changing the normal style. (Go to the Format **S**tyle menu, choose the **Normal** style, select **D**efine, and then select the font and other attributes you want.)

You can have as many as 256 different font styles on a single spreadsheet. That's at least 250 more than you will (very likely) need. You can apply font formats to individual spreadsheet cells, or to groups of them. Remember that your font choices affect only the currently selected cells. If you want to change formatting for the entire spreadsheet, be sure to select all cells first.

You can also select fonts for Excel charts wherever text or numbers are used. Each item in a chart is an *object*; for example, a horizontal or vertical scale is a single item. You simply click on the chart object you want to modify; small square boxes appear on each end of the selected object. Then select the Forma**t F**ont command and choose the font you want.

From the Excel Toolbox (previously shown in Figure 4.10), you can select bold and italic attributes, and also increase or decrease the font size by increments. (Excel doesn't let you select a font name from the main screen; here it differs from most word processing applications.)

Here are some problems you might find using Excel—and their remedies.

PROBLEM: Some of my Excel dialog boxes (and the labels on my Windows icons) are very hard to read.

SOLUTION: Excel substitutes a small font for some dialog boxes (intended for print preview) if it can't find the proper screen font. What you need is the HELVE.FON or a similar font for your video adapter.

You can use the Windows Setup applet (see Chapter 3, "Problems with Installing and Accessing Fonts") to reinstall the driver for your video adapter (with its associated screen fonts), using the Windows Setup applet. Or you can try to simply reinstall the missing font using the Control Panel/ Fonts applet. The details of how to do that are in your *Windows User's Guide*.

PROBLEM: I want to format some characters in a text line as bold for emphasis. But Excel wants to format all the characters the same. Is there a way to do this?

SOLUTION: Yes and no. Excel is all-or-nothing about attributes for all text in a single cell. If you can split your text line into separate cells, you can format each cell separately.

PROBLEM: I'm using a font that prints well, but I'm having trouble reading it on the display. How can I improve its readability?

SOLUTION: Because MS Sans Serif was specially "tuned" to look good on-screen, it may be more readable than the font you want to use for printing. In that case, stay with MS Sans Serif as your default font while you create your spreadsheet, then change to your favorite font just before you print.

PROBLEM: I've just installed PowerPoint for Windows, and now my Excel screen shows huge characters in some dialog boxes. What do I do?

SOLUTION: PowerPoint (or some other application) may have modified some settings in your WIN.INI file, so that the screen font is the wrong one for your video adapter. (The screen font in this case is probably the HELV sans-serif font.)

Either reinstall the driver for your video adapter board (using the procedure in Chapter 3), or reinstall the associated screen fonts.

To reinstall the screen fonts, you probably will have to go through the driver installation procedure again. Refer to the user's guide for your video adapter board to find out what's needed.

You install Windows video drivers by double-clicking on the Windows Setup icon (usually found in the Main group). Then choose **O**ptions **C**hange System Settings Display and select your display from the list. Put the driver diskette in a floppy drive, select the drive in the setup program, and click on **OK**. The driver and related screen fonts are installed.

PROBLEM: I've selected portrait orientation for my printer using the Windows Control Panel Printers applet, but when I print my Excel document, it's in landscape orientation (or vice versa). Help!

SOLUTION: This is actually a feature—not a problem. Excel's **F**ile Page Se**t**up menu item controls page orientation for the current document. It ignores whatever default orientation you've chosen when you set up the printer in Windows.

This means you can select a different orientation for each Excel document—a distinct advantage. Just be sure to select the orientation you need (with the **F**ile Page Se**t**up command) before you print.

PROBLEM: I have set some of my spreadsheet row heights very narrow. When I print it on my laser printer, some of the characters in one row print on top of those in the row above.

SOLUTION: Obviously, if you increase your row height, this won't occur. But if you must use narrow (compressed) rows, try using a Windows vector font—Modern or Roman—for the affected text.

PROBLEM: I've set some spreadsheet columns to be print titles, and I'm scaling the document to fit into the page. When I print, the titles appear okay, but I see duplicate columns or columns from earlier pages.

SOLUTION: This is a bug for sure. Either don't reduce or enlarge your page (use 100%), or don't use columns as print titles. This was fixed in the 4.0a maintenance release. If you have Version 4.0, it's available at no charge from Microsoft Customer Service.

PROBLEM: I get an "Error 21" message on my H-P LaserJet.

SOLUTION: See Chapter 3, "Printing Fonts."

FrameMaker for Windows

One of the more exciting new releases of 1992, FrameMaker for Windows blends a competent word processor with extended features used in desktop publishing. Shown in Figure 4.13, FrameMaker is also available on several other computer platforms.

True to its name, FrameMaker provides frames you can use to contain text or graphics and freely place them on the page. Regular text on the page can flow through or around these frames.

Chapter 4

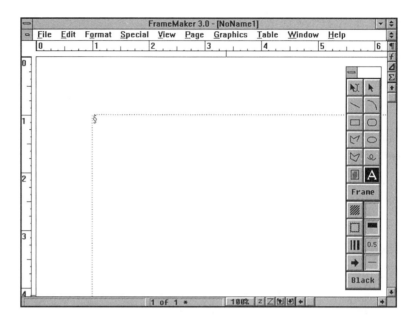

Figure 4.13

*FrameMaker for
Windows 3.0.*

FrameMaker allows you to have multiple documents open
at one time. If you do, you'll probably need a large, high-
resolution display to view the documents and access the many
formatting features.

To allow you use of Type 1 fonts, FrameMaker includes a
copy of Adobe Type Manager. FrameMaker has all the expected word-processing controls over fonts; it lets you select
the font family, style, size and color. But some of its menu
options are unusual for Windows applications. Instead of
regular/bold/italic/bold-italic, FrameMaker gives you separate
selections for angle, weight, and variation. This is because
other versions of FrameMaker run on computers that don't
define font characteristics in the same way as Windows.

An *angle* is the "tilt" of the character—regular, italic, or
oblique. A *weight* is regular or bold, and might also include
extra-bold, black, or light. A *variation* is a style variant in the
family—regular, narrow, condensed, or expanded.

You can also disable *pair kerning*—the feature that reduces excessive spacing between certain pairs of characters. You'd want to do that if you were using a monospaced font like Courier.

To adjust spacing between characters, FrameMaker provides *spread*—a percentage variation from normal spacing. A negative spread makes the characters tighter; a positive spread makes them looser. This feature gives you more precise control than the usual tight/normal/loose selections other applications have.

In what FrameMaker calls *advanced properties*, you can set minimum and maximum spacing between words.

FrameMaker provides true *character formats* that let you save sets of font attributes by name, and apply them to selected text anywhere in your document. Figure 4.14 shows the character format dialog box that pops up when you choose the Format Character menu item. All the font attributes are shown as well.

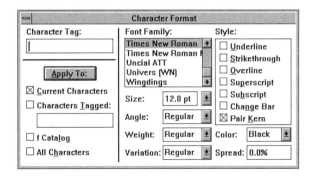

Figure 4.14

FrameMaker character and font formats.

If you'd like a list of all fonts used in a document, FrameMaker can generate one for you. The list shows every font family, size, and weight combination. It can be a very helpful check to see whether your document is consistent, and whether all the fonts you need are available.

FrameMaker has a unique feature to create font *aliases*. You can create a table that associates various fonts with font families and variations. No matter what the font name, you can make it appear as a particular variation, angle, and weight of a selected family.

Another table lets you specify a font you want to substitute for one that's specified in a document but isn't available to you. This might happen if you open a document created elsewhere, or select another printer. (It's beyond the scope of this book to describe how to set up these features; you'll find that information in the "Customizing FrameMaker" appendix of your *Using FrameMaker* manual.)

Here are a few issues for you to consider.

PROBLEM: When I start FrameMaker, I get an error message that says I don't have the right fonts, and asks me if I want to continue. What's the problem?

SOLUTION: FrameMaker expects to have available the four fonts that are provided with Adobe Type Manager (ATM): Courier, Helvetica, Times Roman and Symbol. If it doesn't find them (because you haven't loaded ATM with these fonts—or because you don't have ATM turned on), it's an error.

But there's no real harm done; if you continue, FrameMaker will find TrueType fonts that match closely. If you'd rather not see the error, reinstall just ATM (and be sure to also install these four fonts). Refer to the discussion of ATM in Chapter 3, and be sure to turn it on, as described below.

PROBLEM: I'm using an ATM Type 1 font, and it doesn't display properly. Can I fix it?

SOLUTION: Yes. Go to ATM and delete, then reinstall the font. That will correct any errors that might have crept into the font file or into WIN.INI. Refer to the figures in Chapter 3 and the ATM's user's guide.

PROBLEM: I can't access my ATM Type 1 fonts.

SOLUTION #1: You might simply have ATM turned off. Start ATM (either double-click on the **ATM** Control Panel icon where it appears, or run ATMCNTRL.EXE— which appears in the \WINDOWS directory—by using the **F**ile **R**un command). Then click on the ATM O**n** button. Exit ATM and click on the button that's offered to restart Windows in order to make the change effective.

SOLUTION #2: A few users have had problems with Type 1 fonts if they installed FrameMaker *before* they installed ATM. If you're one of those lucky ones, you should reinstall ATM, *then* reinstall FrameMaker.

PROBLEM: I'm trying to rotate type, but the results are not what I expect. Characters are out of place.

SOLUTION: Are you using a font manager and fonts other than those for Type 1 and TrueType? If so, you may have problems with alignment after rotation. Switch to ATM or TrueType-based fonts.

Microsoft Publisher

Considered one of the best low-cost desktop-publishing solutions, Microsoft Publisher uses frames to contain all text and graphics.

You can begin creating a document using a template that defines the page layout, or you can start with a blank page, as shown in Figure 4.15.

Once you've placed a frame on your page, you can simply type text into it. But it's probably easier to import text from a word processor, especially if you want to use extended tools such as a thesaurus and grammar checker. These aren't in Publisher.

Figure 4.15

Microsoft Publisher 1.0.

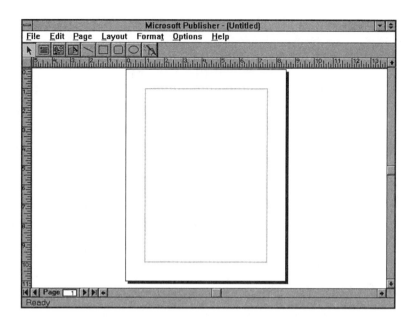

You choose fonts and attributes with the Forma**t C**haracter command, which displays the dialog box shown in Figure 4.16. Most of these selections—font, size, bold/italic/underline—are available directly on Publisher's Toolbox as well (but you have to have text selected or highlighted for the formatting tools to appear).

Figure 4.16

Publisher Format Character dialog box.

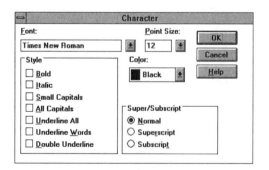

You can use any fonts available via Windows, including Type 1 fonts if you have Adobe Type Manager; ATM is not supplied.

Publisher's emphasis is on page layout, and it omits some of the font controls found even in Word for Windows. It has no strikethrough or hidden text, and no control over overall character spacing or the degree of superscripting or subscripting. But Publisher does have manual kerning (to reduce spacing between selected characters), which is also available in Word for Windows.

For fancy headlines, you can use WordArt to create special color, outline, and rotation effects. This is the same application also included with Microsoft Word for Windows and shown in Figure 4.7. You do all the headline creation and editing in WordArt, which includes nineteen typefaces.

Aldus PageMaker for Windows

PageMaker has for years been the premier Windows application for page layout, especially for short, design-intensive documents such as brochures. While users with lesser needs have migrated to low-cost desktop-publishing tools, PageMaker has been the tool of professionals. Version 4.0 has been around for awhile.

One welcome feature of the new version is the ability to open several documents at once; Version 4.0 can only handle one.

PageMaker begins with an open screen that is meant to resemble a "paste-board" that a layout artist might use to make up a page. It's shown in Figure 4.17, with a blank layout for a simple one-page single-column document.

PageMaker can use any fonts available in Windows—including Type 1, if you use Adobe Type Manager (provided). The reference manual includes a good discussion of the advantages of using a font manager.

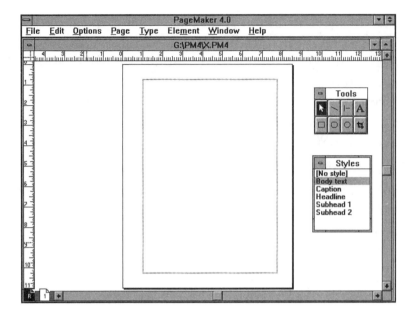

Figure 4.17

Aldus PageMaker 4.0.

PageMaker provides the complex font controls that advanced users need. It provides both automatic and manual pair kerning, and also lets you set the range for character spacing on a line. You can tightly control word and line spacing. You can specify spacing in inches, millimeters, picas, and even ciceros (a seldom-used typesetting unit).

On top of all this, PageMaker also provides five levels of *track kerning*. This feature adjusts the spacing of words and characters on a line mathematically, from very loose to very tight. Track kerning is proportional to the font size in use, and to the design. It lets you "fine-tune" a page to yield a "heavier"- or "lighter"-looking page (and perhaps pack in a few extra characters when needed).

If for any reason PageMaker can't get the spacing right, it highlights the offending line so you can correct it.

PageMaker has probably the most comprehensive font specification tools available in a Windows document application. Figure 4.18 shows the dialog box displayed from the menu command **T**ype **T**ype specs. You select the font, style, size, and color. You can also select the width of each character, from five to 250 percent of normal. If you select the **O**ptions button, you can specify individually the size of small caps, and the size and position of subscript or superscript characters.

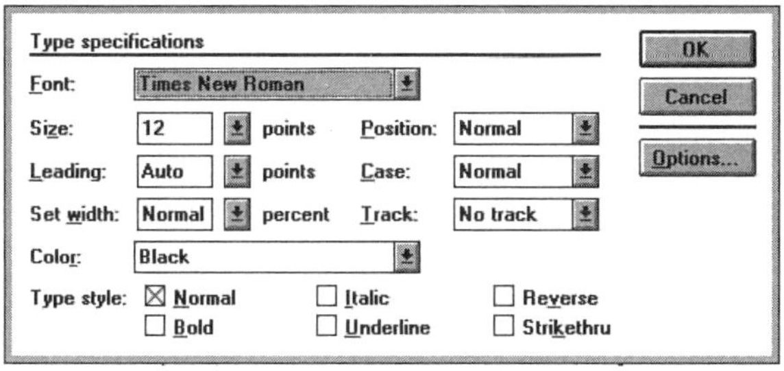

Figure 4.18

PageMaker Type specification dialog box.

Line spacing is called *leading*—a typesetter's term—pronounced "ledding." It is derived from the original practice of using actual metal strips—lead of various thicknesses—to space out lines of metal type. Leading can be set to any size, or to automatic, which allows PageMaker to calculate the spacing for you.

You can make adjustments to individual font and spacing settings directly from the **T**ype menu, shown in Figure 4.19. You can select the font, size, style, character and word spacing, and the amount of track kerning.

To enter special characters that aren't on the regular keyboard, you use a combination of control and shifted key characters. That gives you access to such special typesetting characters as the *em*, *en*, and *thin* spaces and dashes. You can also use the Windows Character Map application to copy characters to the Clipboard, where PageMaker can retrieve them.

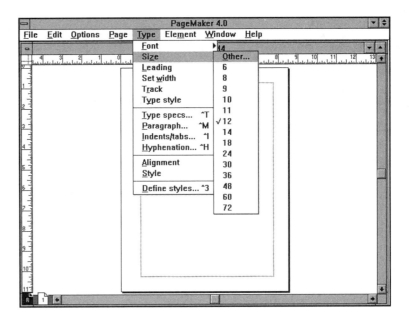

Figure 4.19

PageMaker Type menu.

Here are a few PageMaker problem situations.

PROBLEM: I have "zoomed in" on a portion of my page layout to see how some headlines fit. But all I see are thin-line "stick" characters instead of the fonts I could see in the normal view. How do I check the fit?

SOLUTION: PageMaker switches automatically to a vector font above a size (in pixels) that you specify. That greatly speeds up the page image generation. To view actual fonts for headline placement, either increase the **Vector Above** setting, or use a lower magnification zoom.

From the command menu, select **E**dit Preferences and click on the **Other** button. This displays the Screen font options dialog box. Select the **V**ector text above box and enter a new value. A 24-pixel setting is the default; a larger number will let you see fonts more accurately, but will be slower.

PROBLEM: I have "zoomed-out" on my page layout. Now I see my headlines in the right font, but the body text is just a bunch of unreadable bars.

SOLUTION: This is just the other extreme of the problem above. PageMaker "greeks" any displayed characters that are below a size (in pixels) that you choose. The "greek" characters are simply placeholder bars that help you check the text position, but not read it.

Either change the setting for "greeking" to a lower value, or use a higher magnification for display. From the command menu, select **E**dit Preferences Greek **t**ext below and change the number in the box. A higher number will cause larger-sized type to be "greeked" and will also display the layout faster. The default is 9 pixels (or picture dots).

PROBLEM: I select the drop-down font list from the menu, but it only shows about 25 fonts or so, and it doesn't let me scroll to see the rest of my fonts.

SOLUTION: Select the font list using the key combination **Ctrl+T**. You'll get a drop-down list that lets you scroll through all available fonts.

Ventura Publisher

This product has been vying with Aldus PageMaker for years to capture the interest of desktop publishers. Ventura Publisher, or V-P, has found special favor with book publishers and others with long documents to produce.

V-P was not originally designed for Windows, but for another graphical environment called GEM. The latest V-P, version 4.1, has a fresh Windows face, but also allows you to choose the old GEM look if you prefer it.

The new V-P lets you use a mouse more freely for menu selections, and has a customizable toolbox at the top of the screen. It's now much more like other Windows desktop publishing applications.

V-P has extensive controls to prepare a document for commercial printing. Version 4.0 had four separate add-on programs (at extra cost) to handle scanning, color separation, color effects, and database management. You now get the scanning and separation features included.

Desktop publishers expect good control over both graphics and type. V-P gives you control over type size (from 2 to 254 points), as well as letter kerning and line tracking. It allows text rotation in 90-degree increments.

V-P can use a math co-processor for its color separation and graphics calculations. If you have a co-processor in your computer (included in the 486DX type), you'll see a performance improvement.

Here are a few difficulties you might run into using Ventura Publisher.

PROBLEM: I have a lot of fonts on my system. When I installed V-P, it didn't finish loading for a long time. Is something broken?

SOLUTION: No. V-P creates a font table that identifies each of your fonts by a special code. It has to "build" the table and create the unique code for each font. (The table is different from the one V-P 4.0 used.) This can take several minutes when you install version 4.1.

PROBLEM: I was used to the font ID's that V-P 4.0 gave me for all my fonts. Now that I've installed version 4.1, they've all changed. I'm confused!

SOLUTION: Version 4.0 had a list of all fonts it expected. It only "knew" about a certain number of fonts, and any new ones were a problem. Version 4.1 creates a unique code for every font (called a *hashed code*). While it's different from 4.0, at least you can install new fonts easily, from any vendor, and have them uniquely identified. In the long run (probably) there will be less confusion.

PROBLEM: I know I have some special characters in my font, but V-P won't let me print them. How do I get access to them?

SOLUTION: V-P preceded Windows in the marketplace, and uses a slightly different internal character set. (It uses the ASCII, not ANSI, character set.) The next version will likely switch to the Windows set.

V-P may let you enter certain characters by code instead of from the keyboard. Refer to the user's manual for the codes and techniques to do that.

PROBLEM: V-P lets me work on documents created on a Macintosh. But I'm getting incorrect letter spacing on some of my fonts. Why does this happen?

SOLUTION: Earlier versions of V-P and the Macintosh version use different base units for font widths. You can't share the *font metrics tables* (the *VFMs*) between these platforms.

(This is beyond the scope of our discussion, but refer to the V-P documents for the whole story.)

Looking Back and Looking Ahead

This chapter began with a look at some of the font control features in Windows, which affect all applications. Then I reviewed the font features, problems, and solutions for a number of the most popular Windows text applications. (These are word-processors, presentation managers, or desktop-publishing products.)

Next, I'll focus on Windows applications whose main purpose is to create graphics—drawings, illustrations, and sometimes photos. Not only do you use fonts to add text to graphics, but you can also use some of them to create new character shapes. It's a fascinating subject—just ahead!

chapter

5

Fonts in Windows Graphics Applications

We've just looked at a slew of word processing and desktop publishing applications for Windows. They access and apply fonts in a fairly consistent way. That's because they use the built-in Windows TrueType font manager.

But the graphics applications I'm going to discuss here are far more varied and elaborate. Although they may let you use TrueType or Type 1 fonts, they also provide their own special fonts. These applications can make characters into graphic *objects*—images to be changed in any way you like.

A familiar example of a graphic object is the headline you create using Microsoft WordArt (provided with Word for Windows). Here, the entire headline is a single object that you can size or crop in Word. To change text characters, you double-click on the object to open WordArt again.

Graphics applications take this object concept another step. You can select individual characters, change their outlines and add numerous special effects. A graphic object can be a character, a block of text or a mix of characters and art. You can place a graphic into most any Windows text document.

A special function in Windows called OLE (for Object Linking and Embedding) makes graphics easier to work with. When you design a graphic and then insert it into a document, that's *embedding*. It can represent a link to another application.

If you want to make changes, you must return to the application you used to create the graphic. With OLE, that's simple: you double-click on the object, and your graphics editor opens automatically, with the object ready to modify. WordArt works just that way.

I chose Arts & Letters to create my examples. (I could have used any of the applications I'll describe in this chapter.)

Here's our example: I want to create a special headline that reads, "Text Here" and I want the right portion of the "T" to hang over the "e". Why? Because I want to make a "word picture," perhaps to imply the "T" is a lamp shedding illumination on the "e". (Later I might want to draw in some "rays" to complete the effect.)

First, I enter the characters in a text dialog box, shown in Figure 5.1. I've entered four rows of text. I've selected a font from the ones Arts & Letters provides. Nothing tricky so far.

Figure 5.1

Arts & Letters Enter/Edit Text dialog box.

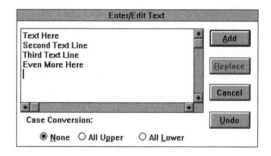

Next, I place the text block on the screen page, and drag it to any size I want. (This could yield expanded or condensed characters.) I can also choose the thickness of the lines, and the "fill" (or interior) of the characters. You see the result in Figure 5.2; all these operations affect the entire block of text.

Now I choose an unwitting victim, the letter "T". It's shown in Figure 5.3 as an outline—a group of connected lines and curves—with little boxes called *handles* or *nodes*. I can drag any of these boxes with my mouse pointer, pulling the outline with it. I created the bizarre overhang on the "T" by dragging out the handles on the serif.

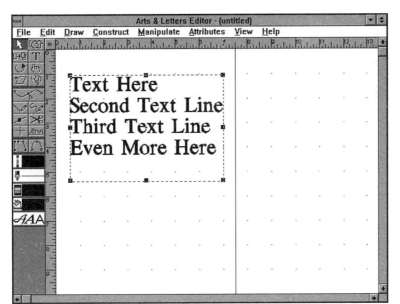

Figure 5.2

Arts & Letters text block applied to page.

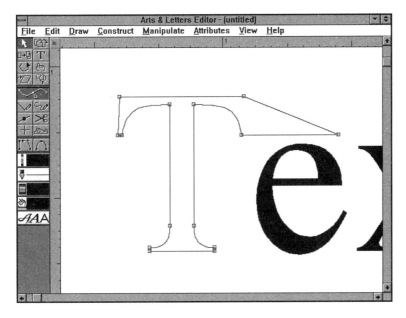

Figure 5.3

Arts & Letters text outline editing.

When I'm through editing, I'll return the "T" to its regular filled (solid) display, the handles disappear and the effect is complete. I could also change size and color, perspective, and rotation—many more special effects than I can show you here.

*Before I could edit an individual character I first had Arts &
Letters convert the line of text to freeform—that is, break it
up into individual graphic elements. I also selected options
to show the character in outline form, and to display the
handles.*

The graphics objects are much like the scalable outline fonts
I described in Chapter 1. That's what makes it possible to
stretch them to any size you choose.

Now that you have the concept, let's look at some actual
graphics design packages. We'll focus on the tools they give
you for working with fonts and characters.

Help from CD-ROM

But first, a background note on the value of CD-ROM.
Graphics programs are very large. They are nuisances to install
because they typically occupy ten to twenty floppy diskettes.
Combined with their generous clip-art libraries, they can soak
up well over 10 megabytes (million bytes or characters) of
your hard disk space.

CD-ROM solves this problem. This new storage device
looks just like an audio CD disk player, but instead of music,
it stores over 600 megabytes of data. (That's over 500 floppy
diskettes' worth!) Expect to see virtually all graphic applications available sooner or later on CD-ROM.

Let's use CorelDRAW! as an example of the benefits of CD-
ROM. The edition on floppy disks has some TrueType fonts,
and about 3,000 items of clip art. The "bonus" CD-ROM
(included) contains over 250 fonts (duplicated in Type 1 and
TrueType formats), and over 15,000 clip-art items. If you
want to access everything the floppy edition has, you'll use

over 20 megabytes of hard disk space—and you still won't have most of the clip art.

If you were to install everything on the CD-ROM, you'd consume well over 50 megabytes of hard disk! But if you install just the program files, that's about 11 megabytes—and you can still access the extra fonts and clip-art from the CD-ROM when you need them. And if you run the applications from the CD-ROM, you'll use a measly 1 megabyte of your hard disk!

You might want to know, however, that running applications directly from CD-ROM has a down side. It's at least three times slower than your hard disk and you'll have annoying delays. It's better to install just the entire application on your hard disk, and use the CD-ROM for the very large, seldom-used clip-art libraries.

To use a CD-ROM you need a computer drive to "play" the disks on. It serves the same purpose as a hard disk drive, except you can only read information from it, and cannot record. (A special drive is available that does record, but it's very expensive and not widely used.)

For fonts, the main value of CD-ROM storage is choice and availability. For example, with CorelDRAW!, you get many more fonts on the CD-ROM version than you do on diskette. Entire libraries of fonts with hundreds of selections are now commonly available on CD-ROM.

CSC Arts & Letters Graphics Editor

I've already given away some of the secrets of Computer Support Corporation's Arts & Letters in Figures 5.1 to 5.3. This is version 3.12 of a multi-purpose drawing and charting application that includes several thousand pre-drawn images, or *clip art*.

The opening screen of Arts & Letters is shown in Figure 5.4. Expect to see a fully-upgraded version of Arts & Letters to be released on CD-ROM in 1993.

Figure 5.4

Arts & Letters opening display.

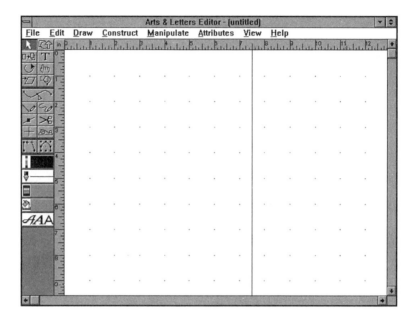

You can enter or import as many as 5,000 characters into a text block (shown back in Figure 5.2). The entire entry is a graphics object. You can easily select position and size for the entire block.

You can use any typeface available in Windows, including Type 1 fonts provided via Adobe Type Manager (which is not provided). Only the more than eighty typefaces included with Arts & Letters can be edited in freeform, as I showed you in Figure 5.3.

Not only can you drag text to set size and shape, but you can choose type and spacing from an attributes dialog box. You can select character and line spacing (as well as kerning) just the way you would with a word processor.

Arts & Letters goes far beyond a word processor to allow you to fit text into (or around) any line or graphic shape you like. You also have fills, blends, textures, wraps, slants, and perspective controls.

Here are a few items that might confuse you. I'll try to shed some light on them.

PROBLEM: I want to create a special character effect just like you did, but I can't figure out how. How do I do it?

SOLUTION:

1. Open the **Enter/Edit Text** dialog box, using the **D**raw **T**ext command.

2. Enter any text you like, up to 5,000 characters. Click on **Add**.

3. Place the text outline box on the page, and drag it to the size you want—leave the text selected.

4. Select **D**raw **C**ut to Freeform from the menu bar (the command will have a check mark on it).

5. Click on a character to edit.

6. Select **D**raw **E**dit Freeform from the menu bar (the handle boxes will appear), and edit the outline (you may want to zoom in on the unsuspecting character).

7. Deselect **D**raw **E**dit Freeform when you're done with the character. (You can repeat steps 5 through 7 for each character.)

Once you've converted your text to freeform, each character becomes a separate object. You might want to regroup them so they don't wander off from each other. Select the characters to be together, then select Manipulate Group from the menu bar.

PROBLEM: I've done all the steps above, but the text I've chosen refuses to be converted to freeform. Why?

SOLUTION: Although any font you have in Windows can be placed on the page as an object, only the Arts & Letters special fonts can be converted to freeform.

Select the Attributes Type option from the menu bar, and the Type Attributes dialog box appears. You have two general choices for fonts: the ones that come with Arts & Letters, or your printer-based fonts (or sometimes screen fonts—which are bitmaps); choose the Arts & Letters fonts. Choose the closest match from the scrolling list. You can view a short sample if you wish.

When you click on the **OK** button, the selected text will change to the new one. Now you can edit it as freeform.

PROBLEM: I converted my text to freeform, edited the shapes, and grouped the text together. Now I want to edit the text (add or delete characters) using the Enter/Edit Text box, but Arts & Letters won't let me. Why?

SOLUTION: Converted text is now one or more graphics objects, and is no longer a string of characters. You must edit text strings *before* you edit them as graphics. If you're really stuck, you can select individual characters and delete them. You can also enter some words or characters as text, convert them, and then manually insert them in a line with other previously converted text. Don't try this if you're in a hurry!

CorelDRAW!

This product from Corel Systems in Ottawa, Canada, is in a highly-acclaimed Version 3.0B, which even includes a CD-ROM as an alternate storage form. If you can take advantage of the CD-ROM, you'll use much less of your hard disk storage and will have direct access to over 250 fonts and well over 10,000 clip-art graphics.

You can use either TrueType or Type 1 fonts in your graphics. On the CD-ROM, Corel includes all fonts in both formats; on the floppy diskettes, only TrueType is provided.

CorelDRAW! is extremely capable of handling text. You can import or enter a block of text as long as 4,000 characters. For text to which you want to add special effects (Corel calls this *artistic text*), you can enter as many as 250 characters at a time.

For all characters, you can choose standard attributes (from the dialog box shown in Figure 5.5). Before you can work with text, you need to place some characters on the page. First, click on the character icon (the large letter "A" shown at the bar at left). Then click on the page where you want to begin the text line. Now you can display the Text dialog box from the command menu using Text Character.

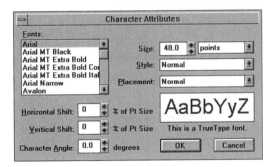

Figure 5.5

CorelDRAW! text attributes dialog box.

You also enter the text and character spacing you need in a similar dialog box, shown in Figure 5.6. Here, I've activated the *Text Roll-Up*—a movable dialog box with text controls—shown to the right of the screen. I did that from the command menu, using Text Text Roll-Up. Then I clicked on the Text icon at left, clicked on the page, and typed in "Hello." I selected the text by holding the left mouse button down and dragging it across the text. (Text is now displayed in the darkened "highlight" form you see.)

Finally, I clicked on the Text Roll-Up button, Character Kerning to display the dialog box shown in the figure. This dialog box shows line spacing (leading) selections in both horizontal and vertical directions. You select them as a *percentage* of point size, rather than as point size (as in other applications). I prefer this approach because spacing stays proportional even if you change character size.

To change spacing for the selected (highlighted) characters, fill out the box, click on **OK**, and then click on the **Text Roll-Up Apply** button.

The angle selection lets you "oblique" (change the vertical angles) of characters. A negative angle tilts characters right (as in italics); a positive angle tilts them left.

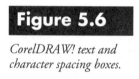

Figure 5.6

CorelDRAW! text and character spacing boxes.

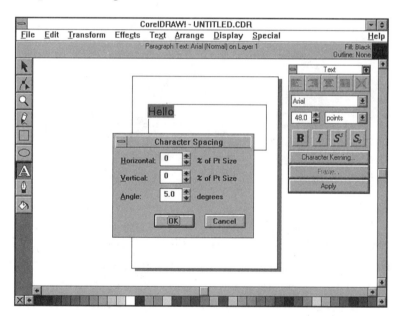

For any "artistic text," you can select rotations, shading, color, and fill effects. Corel includes a large variety of fill patterns you can apply and modify in several ways. There's even a special editor that lets you create a bitmap of any graphic design you want to use to fill a character.

Using CorelDRAW!, you can actually create custom characters—or a complete font—in either Type 1 or TrueType format. A source for a character shape can be hand-sketched, scanned, traced, or even extracted from an existing font. Corel suggests an intriguing use for this feature: creating a custom font from samples of your own handwriting. (There's only one catch: to enter character widths, you must import a width file from an existing font. Check the User's manual for more info.)

To edit character outlines, you must first enter characters as "artistic text." (This means to enter text directly on the page without first placing it in a box or frame.) Next, you convert them to freeforms: with the text selected, choose the Arrange Convert to Curves command from the menu. To edit the shape of a single character, choose the command **Arrange Break Apart**.

The freeform shapes can now be edited by dragging the handles with the mouse. When you're done with a collection of character graphics, you may want to join them as a unit, using the commands **Arrange Group** and **Arrange Combine**. (See the CorelDRAW! user's manual for more on these commands.)

Here are a few problems you might have with CorelDRAW!, and some possible solutions.

PROBLEM: I'm using some Type 1 fonts, and also some TrueType ones. When I use the Type 1 fonts, they appear on my display much slower than the TrueTypes. What can I do to improve this?

SOLUTION: This revision of CorelDRAW! is highly optimized for TrueType fonts. It's probably no slower than earlier revisions for Type 1 fonts, but the disparity is frustrating. Expect another revision to come along and increase speeds for Type 1 fonts too.

PROBLEM: I created a custom font, using the directions given in the user manual. But when I try to use the font, I see some (or none) of the characters on my display, and nothing prints. Can I fix it?

SOLUTION: Possibly. If you created a font with characters numbered above 128 (the second half of the character set), CorelDRAW! corrupts the entire file. You'll have to restrict yourself to creating characters only to number 127 until Corel fixes this one.

PROBLEM: I've been getting various error codes that appear sporadically. It doesn't seem to have any specific cause. Is there a way to clear this up?

SOLUTION: Try deleting your configuration file; it's **CDCONFIG.SYS**, found in the directory **\CORELDRW\DRAW**. You'll lose all your preference options, but that's a small price to pay if it fixes those bugs!

When CorelDRAW! finds its configuration file missing the next time you start it, it will create a new one with default settings. You should then choose your preferences; Corel-DRAW! will save them automatically when you exit and use them thereafter.

Micrografx Designer

Designer is a venerable, well-respected graphics application from Micrografx that is best-equipped for technical drawing. The current version, 3.1 Plus OLE, is a re-release to add object linking and embedding (OLE) services, some fonts, and a number of new features. It also improves display quality and speed in several areas.

Designer has an austere, businesslike appearance compared to other graphics applications. Its on-line help is informative, but looks downright Spartan. For a snappy, colorful screen, look at Windows Draw, a less expensive and simpler package that Micrografx calls "fun, fast and friendly."

Many of Designer's new features are for handling text. In Version 3.0, you could adjust line spacing (leading); now you can also adjust letter spacing (kerning). You can also place text on a curve or on an outline of a graphic shape.

With Designer, you also get both Adobe TypeAlign and Adobe Type Manager (ATM) Version 2.0. ATM gives you access to Type 1 fonts, and TypeAlign lets you create special type effects with them, such as rotating, stretching, twisting, and other type tortures. To inform you of your legal obligations, there's Adobe's 35-page license agreement in nine languages.

TIP

TypeAlign is an independent program; when you've used it to create special effects, you export the resulting graphic image to Designer to complete your drawing. The quickest method is to use the Windows Clipboard; the recommended format is encapsulated PostScript (EPS).

In this latest version, Designer includes 180 fonts compatible with ATM, 35 Bitstream Speedo format fonts, and six fonts from a type foundry named URW in a proprietary format called Nimbus-Q. You can use any of these scalable outline font formats and also any TrueType fonts you may have for text entry.

For quick entry of a block of characters, Designer provides a "text editor" in a scrolling window above the graphics area. Although characters you type there are unformatted, the font, size, and style appear when you place the block in the graphics drawing area.

You can import as many as 64,000 characters at a time into the text editor or the drawing area. You can move selected blocks of characters freely between the editor and the drawing area.

Designer gives you full control over fonts, styles, and color; Figure 5.7 shows the dialog box that appears when you select the menu bar command Text Font. At the top left of the screen is the selected word "Hello" in 24-pt Arial bold.

Figure 5.7

Designer font selection dialog box.

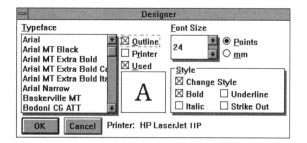

You can select—separately—the proportion of spacing between characters, words, and lines (leading), as shown in Figure 5.8. Here, I've selected a modest kern of five percent. If you look closely, you can see that this "Hello" is more tightly spaced than the one in Figure 5.7.

Using other Designer features, you can mix any font size and styles in any paragraph. You can also use the mouse to drag text segments to change size, rotate, or tilt.

If you want to edit the shapes of characters in outline fonts, you must change them to graphic objects; Micrografx calls this process "convert to curves." You select that feature using a convenient outline letter "T" in the on-screen toolbox. You can then use the mouse to drag control points of the freeform character outlines to any shape you choose. (Once converted, characters can no longer be edited as text.)

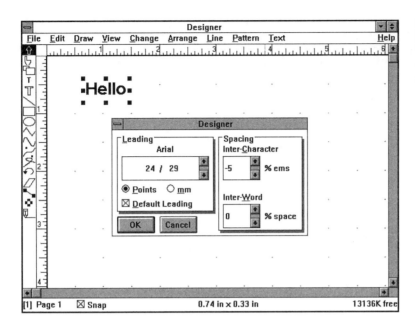

Figure 5.8

Designer Text Spacing dialog box.

Microsoft PowerPoint

PowerPoint is a *presentation application*, meant to create and display a sequence of images. It lets you put together a "slide show" of words and graphics. While its focus is different from that of the other applications I've discussed, PowerPoint is—at heart—a combined graphics and text tool.

Shipped with PowerPoint are 22 TrueType-format fonts, selected for good appearance on presentations. You can use these fonts in other applications for headlines. While still in PowerPoint, you can also use any other fonts you may have available in Windows. (To use Type 1 fonts, however, you'll need Adobe Type Manager, which is not supplied.)

PowerPoint first appears on-screen ready for business, with an outline for a presentation slide ready to begin filling out, as Figure 5.9 shows.

Figure 5.9

PowerPoint main display.

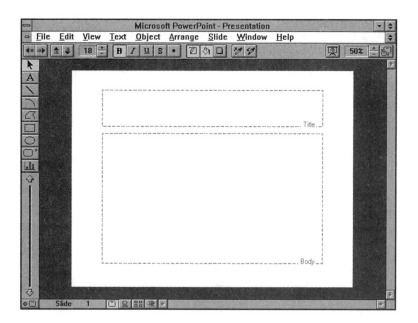

To describe only text features (which is to ignore a lot of features): PowerPoint is a word processor of about the capabilities of Microsoft Write (included with Windows), with powerful outlining features added. You can display a ruler above your text as a guide to page makeup. There's an included spelling checker (but no thesaurus). You can create and apply templates that define the default text font, size, color, and special effects.

Text controls for font size, style, and color are like those in a word processor. Figure 5.10 shows the drop-down menu list that appears when you select the Text menu. Size and style controls are also provided on the PowerPoint Toolbar; so is a "bullet" button that automatically places a bullet at the beginning of each line as you enter it. (You can choose any character in any font as a bullet.)

When you select the command Text Font, a page appears listing all your available fonts. This is different from the usual scrolling list box. Since the selected font doesn't appear on the Toolbar, this is the only way to verify what font is in use.

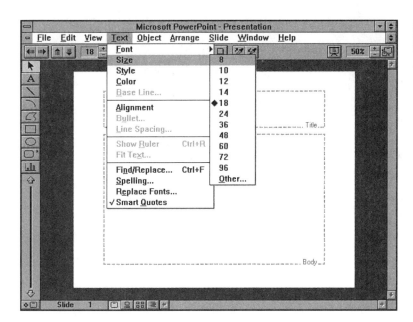

Figure 5.10

PowerPoint Text menu.

A handy aid for text lists is *proportional sizing*. When you select two or more lines of differing size, and change size using the Toolbar, the text increases or decreases while the lines maintain their relative sizes.

One unusual feature is a "global" font replacement table, shown in Figure 5.11. (This dialog box appears when you select from the command menu, Text Replace Fonts.) You can select fonts to substitute for the ones in your presentation—wherever you've used them. That saves you a time-consuming search through all your slides.

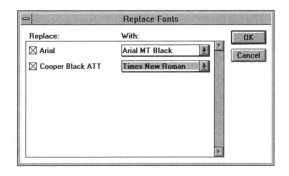

Figure 5.11

PowerPoint Replace Fonts dialog box.

PowerPoint does not allow you to convert text to freeform graphics objects. If you want a modified character shape, create it using one of the full graphics applications I've discussed above. Then you can copy it from the Windows Clipboard, insert it into your slide as a "picture," or embed it as an "object."

PowerPoint supports Microsoft's powerful Object Linking and Embedding (OLE) technology, which lets you create documents in one application and insert them into the application with which you're currently working. One familiar embedded object might be a headline created in Microsoft WordArt, as shown in Figure 5.12. (This application is included with Word for Windows.)

Figure 5.12

PowerPoint with WordArt.

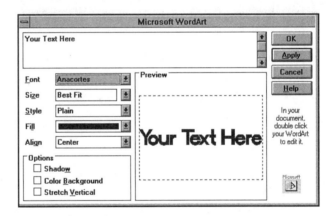

Here are some items to help you with using PowerPoint.

PROBLEM: I want to change the text size using the Text command on the menu bar. But whenever I slide the mouse pointer down the list, I slide past the Font command, and a big list of my fonts appears. How do I select another command without this distraction?

SOLUTION: Simply click once on the Text command on the menu bar. That drops down the menu. Now move the mouse pointer to the command item you want and click on it. You'll get only the item you select.

PROBLEM: My slide has text of several different sizes. But I think they're all too small for my presentation and I want to make them larger. Can I "blow up" all the type without selecting each size and adjusting it individually?

SOLUTION: Sure. First select all the type, using the Edit Select all command. Then, on the Toolbar at the top of the screen, click on the + or the – buttons next to the Type Size box (refer back to Figure 5.9) to enlarge or reduce the type. All type will enlarge or reduce proportionally.

PROBLEM: Somewhere in my presentation, I have a slide with some key words on it. But I can't find it—it's buried in the pile somewhere. Can I find that slide without looking through the whole presentation?

SOLUTION: You can, and quickly. Use the Text Find/Replace command. You can either search or search-and-replace a word or phrase. (In most word processors, this command is under the Edit group, but here it's a Text command.)

PROBLEM: PowerPoint gives me text control, but I want to edit some characters as graphic elements, as you described at the beginning of this chapter. How do I put them in my presentation?

SOLUTION: Do your graphics editing in a full graphics package. Let's say you created some character "art" in CorelDRAW!. First you save the work in a file, as usual.

You have the choice of inserting the art as a picture or as an "object." A picture must be in one of the standard bitmap formats, such as TIFF or BMP, that PowerPoint can accept. An object is created by an application (such as CorelDRAW!) that supports OLE (Object Linking and Embedding).

To insert a picture, use the Edit Insert Picture command and choose the file where you've stored the picture. Then place and size the picture where you want it on the slide.

To insert an object, use the Edit Insert Object command. In this case, choose **CorelDRAW! Graphic**. That opens CorelDRAW! and you can select and edit the art. When you exit CorelDRAW!, the art is placed on your PowerPoint slide.

Whenever you want to edit the art, just double-click the mouse with the pointer on it; CorelDRAW! will again open automatically, and you can make any changes.

Harvard Graphics for Windows

Harvard Graphics for DOS has been a very successful and easy-to-use presentation application. Building on that popularity, Software Publishing Company has recently introduced Harvard Graphics for Windows. It's now in its first issue, with a few maintenance releases.

Harvard Graphics for Windows is an application that lets you develop a "slide show" of text and graphics for presentation. While not as full-featured as PowerPoint, it is easy to understand and use. You can even use it to play some Windows multimedia sound and animation to accompany your slide show!

As you could expect, the Windows version of Harvard Graphics can import and export to the DOS version, to share presentation material you developed using either one.

Its main screen, shown in Figure 5.13, provides a template for the a slide and a toolbar along the left side. You choose from three views: Slide Editor (shown), Slide Outliner and Slide Sorter. In Outliner view, you can import ASCII text files to a slide from another application such as a word processor.

This text slide shown is one of many formats available. For example, you can include spreadsheet data, pie and bar charts, and clip art on any slide and in any color.

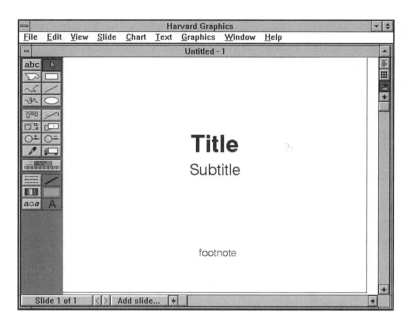

Figure 5.13

Harvard Graphics/Windows with a slide.

Harvard Graphics has built-in support for the Bitstream Speedo font format. You get five rather ordinary Speedo fonts, and you can add other Bitstream fonts if you have them in this format.

Bitstream fonts appear in the font list, but are not available to other Windows applications. You can treat them as graphic objects (which means you can rotate, flip, or resize them), and they will print as shown.

If you choose soft fonts or printer font cartridges for your text, you may get faster printing. You can also use your TrueType fonts and Type 1 fonts (if you've installed the Adobe Type Manager). They will print just as you see them. But these fonts don't act like graphics objects: if you rotate, flip, or drag to resize them, Harvard Graphics substitutes the closest matching Bitstream Speedo font.

Unlike full graphics applications, Harvard Graphics doesn't let you convert text to free-form objects for editing.

Create text art in another application and then import it. You can either paste it from the Clipboard using **Edit Paste**, or import it as a standard bitmap file (with the extension "BMP").

Harvard Graphics has three graphics special effects you can apply to any font: frame, drop shadow, and sweep. A *frame* is a background shading, and the *sweep* effect makes the text appear as the top of a stack of succeedingly smaller grayed-out copies.

When you place or edit text, you can display a ruler that gives you control over tabs and text position. A pull-down menu lets you select text font size, style and color. Figure 5.14 shows the text for a title line, with its ruler and the text dialog box dropped down in front of it.

Figure 5.14

Harvard Graphics, with Text dialog box.

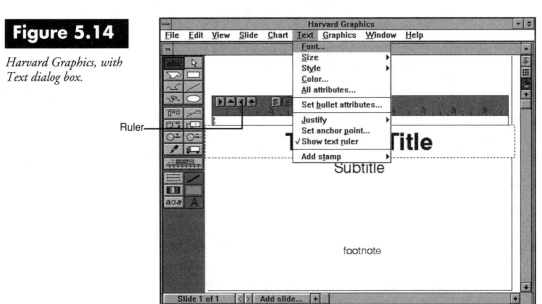

If you select the **All Attributes** command from the **Text** menu, you get the dialog box shown in Figure 5.15, which gives you control over all the font attributes at once. You get the same box by clicking on the text tool at bottom left of the Toolbar.

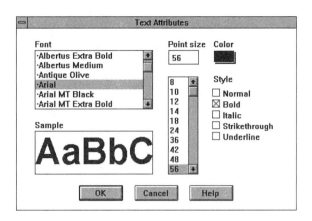

Figure 5.15

Harvard Graphics' Text Attributes dialog box.

Harvard Graphics for Windows has several other text-related services that may interest you. If you want to change the font for all text in your presentation, use the **S**lide Change presentation font command. Unlike PowerPoint, Harvard Graphics won't let you substitute a specific font for another wherever it occurs. You may not want to use this tool if you are using several fonts in your presentation; the result will be a single font in all places.

Figure 5.16 shows the Anchor Point dialog box (which you access by using the **T**ext Set anchor **p**oint command). The visual control in this dialog box lets you set what amounts to a visual origin for all text entry. When you indicate an origin angle by clicking on one of the nine boxes shown, all text you enter appears to start from that direction. In most cases, you'll want to use the Edit Select all command first, to select all text on the slide before you set the anchor point.

Finally, if you import or export to non-Windows applications that use different character sets, you can use the File Preferences command and select the **Import/export ASCII character set** option. It selects the "code page" that Harvard Graphics uses to map characters properly. Use it to choose Windows (ANSI character set), DOS (ASCII character set), and some foreign-language character sets.

Figure 5.16

Harvard Graphics' Text Anchor Point dialog box.

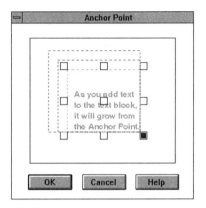

Here are a few problems and solutions that may help you with Harvard Graphics for Windows.

PROBLEM: I changed to another font using the Text Font command, but nothing happened. What do I do?

SOLUTION: Only the text you have selected will change. If you want to change all the text on this slide, use the Edit Select all command. That will put selection boxes around all text. Now, when you command any text changes, all characters will be modified.

If you only want to change specific text, first put a selection box around it: click on the arrow tool (top right on the toolbar), then hold the left mouse button down while you drag a dotted rectangle around the text you want to include. When you release the button, a box remains. Any text attribute changes you now make will only affect text that's in a selection box.

PROBLEM: I want to use that neat ruler to adjust my text, but it doesn't appear. Why not?

SOLUTION: It's optional. Select the Text Show text ruler line from the Command menu. A check mark will show at the left of that command line. Now, whenever you select text or add a new line, the ruler will appear above it.

PROBLEM: I want to use a special foreign language character, but it's not on the standard keyboard. How do I access one?

SOLUTION: There's a table that shows the available special characters on page 14–43 of the *Using Harvard Graphics for Windows* documentation. To enter each character, hold the **Alt** key down, and type **0** followed by the character's code. For example, the c with a cedilla (ç) is **Alt+0231**. Be sure to enter the digits using the numeric keypad only (with NumLock turned on, of course). The numbers along the top key row will not work.

(This list is the standard one, but because some fonts do not adhere to it, you can't be absolutely sure it's the one that will print. Print a trial page to be sure.)

You can also find money symbols and Greek characters in the symbols library. Enter them using the **File Symbol library** menu item.

PROBLEM: I have some text on my slide, and I thought it was supposed to be centered. But it appears off to one side. Is this normal?

SOLUTION: When you use the **T**ext Set anchor **p**oint I described earlier, that takes control over the text position and overrides the regular settings. To return to a straight text effect, choose an anchor point that is top-centered.

PROBLEM: I'm using a sharp-looking TrueType font in my presentation. I even gave it a drop shadow for a 3-D effect, and it looks fine. But when I tried to rotate it, a very plain font appeared instead. Yet Harvard Graphics indicates my original font is selected. How do I get my font to appear?

SOLUTION: Harvard Graphics substituted a Bitstream Speedo font the instant you rotated the text. But it "remembers" your original selection. If you present or print the slide, you'll get the Speedo font.

You have some choices: select an existing Speedo font that you like better, or buy and install a Speedo font that's a closer match. Or, simply forego the rotation. If you rotate the line back to zero, Harvard Graphics will again display and print the font you originally selected.

Looking Back and Looking Ahead

I've reviewed several of the most popular Windows graphics applications in this chapter. Many others are available (because this is an extremely competitive product category), but these are good examples.

Next, we'll review a couple of the most popular DOS-based word processing applications. They handle fonts in a sharply different way from the Windows-based products we've seen in these last two chapters.

Fonts in DOS Applications

After all my glowing descriptions of the virtues of Microsoft Windows, why include a chapter on DOS applications? The answer's simple: many more people use DOS *without* Windows than with it. There's a very good reason for that—money!

As you learned in Chapter 5, Windows gives you smooth, consistent font and printer control throughout all Windows applications. But to give you its many benefits, Windows needs more of everything: a faster computer, more memory, a lot more hard disk storage, and a graphics display.

DOS applications are more frugal, but less consistent. Each application is on its own to handle fonts—both on the screen and on the printed page. That means there's no universal solution to the font issue in DOS.

But there is some help; in this chapter, I'll discuss some auxiliary programs that let you use TrueType and Type 1 fonts in some DOS applications. I'll examine the two most popular DOS word-processing applications—WordPerfect and Microsoft Word—to see how they improve on this simple font scenario. I'll also look at two popular spreadsheets, Quattro Pro and Lotus 1-2-3.

Fonts That DOS Uses

DOS stands for "Disk Operating System"—and that's its main job: to provide a system to save and retrieve files from disks. DOS provides some other services, but it doesn't know how to create graphics—not even graphic images of fonts. (The so-called DOS graphics mode simply uses extended characters with lines and shades to simulate true graphics.)

How does DOS produce any characters at all? It's because your video display board has a built-in permanent bit-mapped font. DOS sends character codes to the display board, which uses them to select and display the bitmaps. (If you've forgotten what a bitmap is, take a look back at Chapter 1.)

This font is pretty boring; it's only one size, monospaced, and usually looks like Courier. An example is shown in Figure 6.1. (Your display may show bold characters a bit brighter, show italic a bit dimmer, and add underlines—but it shows no actual font shapes.)

Figure 6.1

This is the boring font displayed by DOS.

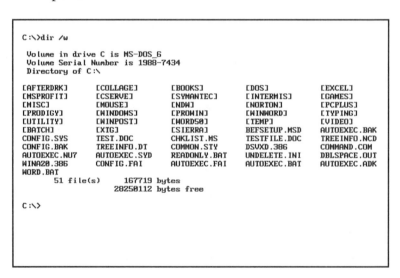

```
C:\>dir /w

 Volume in drive C is MS-DOS_6
 Volume Serial Number is 1988-7434
 Directory of C:\

[AFTERDRK]     [COLLAGE]      [BOOKS]        [DOS]          [EXCEL]
[MSPROFIT]     [CSERVE]       [SYMANTEC]     [INTERMIS]     [GAMES]
[MISC]         [MOUSE]        [NDW]          [NORTON]       [PCPLUS]
[PRODIGY]      [WINDOWS]      [PROWIN]       [WINWORD]      [TYPING]
[UTILITY]      [WINPOST]      [WORD50]       [TEMP]         [VIDEO]
[BATCH]        [XIG]          [SIERRA]       BEFSETUP.MSD   AUTOEXEC.BAK
CONFIG.SYS     TEST.DOC       CHKLIST.MS     TESTFILE.DOC   TREEINFO.NCD
CONFIG.BAK     TREEINFO.DT    COMMON.STY     DSVXD.386      COMMAND.COM
AUTOEXEC.NU7   AUTOEXEC.SYD   READONLY.BAT   UNDELETE.INI   DBLSPACE.OUT
WINA20.386     CONFIG.FAI     AUTOEXEC.FAI   AUTOEXEC.BAT   AUTOEXEC.ADK
WORD.BAT
         51 file(s)       167719 bytes
                        28250112 bytes free

C:\>
```

The same is true for printing: DOS sends characters to your printer, which contains at least one bitmapped font. It's no surprise that this font looks like the screen font—they're both monospaced, plain-vanilla fonts.

Most simple DOS applications rely on the fonts available in your display and printer. But for word-processing and other text-intensive uses, programs often provide truly graphic methods of displaying fonts. To use these enhancements, you must also have a video system that can display true graphics.

WordPerfect (for DOS)

Why is WordPerfect Corporation's WordPerfect for DOS the world's most popular word processor? Simple: it works on almost any PC and monitor, it's fast, it lets you produce many kinds of documents, it uses almost any printer imaginable, and it's supported extremely well.

So why look any further? Because except for its View Document mode, WordPerfect's display uses only the font available from DOS (see Figure 6.2). While you're entering text, you can't see your document with actual style and size fonts or with graphics. If you have a page with headlines, multiple fonts, graphics or a complex layout, you may miss having a fully-interactive graphics display.

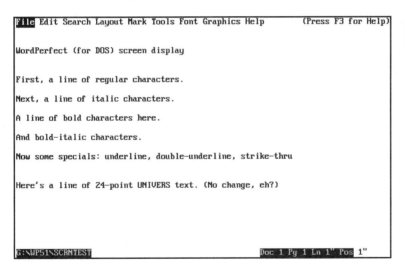

```
File Edit Search Layout Mark Tools Font Graphics Help        (Press F3 for Help)

WordPerfect (for DOS) screen display

First, a line of regular characters.

Next, a line of italic characters.

A line of bold characters here.

And bold-italic characters.

Now some specials: underline, double-underline, strike-thru

Here's a line of 24-point UNIVERS text. (No change, eh?)



G:\WP51\SCRNTEST                              Doc 1 Pg 1 Ln 1" Pos 1"
```

Figure 6.2

In WordPerfect for DOS, all fonts appear in the default system font on-screen.

WordPerfect Font Basics

Let's take a look at WordPerfect for DOS 5.1—the current release. When you start WordPerfect, you see at first a display showing nothing but a short status line at bottom right. It's as close to simulating a blank piece of paper in your typewriter as you can get. You just start typing.

Figure 6.2 shows the regular text-entry display with a few lines of characters, with various attributes. The line shown at bottom left supplies the document's file name.

In the basic editing view, all lines are shown in the font offered by your display board. Each character attribute is represented by a color (although you can't see them in this black-and-white figure). The bottom line is 24-point text, but on this display its characters take the same space as the 12-point text above it.

*WordPerfect has several display modes available. With some of them, you can use some of the available display colors in order to represent bold, italic, or underlining on-screen. Use Setup (**Shift+F1**) to make the change.*

At the top of the screen in Figure 6.2 is an enhancement new to version 5.1: a menu bar. (To reveal the bar, you press Alt+=.) With the command bar, you can also use a mouse or the cursor keys to select a pull-down menu.

You can use the keyboard function keys to enterWordPerfect commands. Until you learn most of the 42 basic commands, you'll probably rely heavily on the provided command guide that fits on the keyboard. After you press a function key, you're usually shown a series of numbered or lettered menus from which to select further menus.

Applying Text Attributes in WordPerfect
To set font attributes in WordPerfect, you highlight the affected text and then apply the attribute. Figure 6.3 shows how to choose italic text from the Font menu. Another method of

applying italics is to press Ctrl+F8 and select menus that
appear at the bottom of the display.

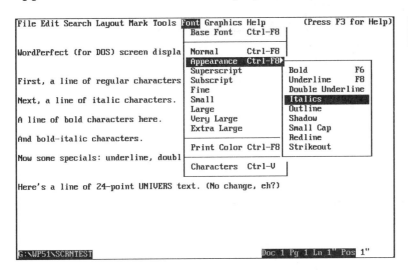

```
File Edit Search Layout Mark Tools Font Graphics Help        (Press F3 for Help)
                                  Base Font   Ctrl-F8
WordPerfect (for DOS) screen displa  Normal      Ctrl-F8
                                  Appearance  Ctrl-F8 ▶ Bold          F6
                                  Superscript            Underline     F8
First, a line of regular characters  Subscript             Double Underline
                                  Fine                   Italics
Next, a line of italic characters.   Small                 Outline
                                  Large                  Shadow
A line of bold characters here.      Very Large            Small Cap
                                  Extra Large           Redline
And bold-italic characters.                              Strikeout
                                  Print Color Ctrl-F8
Now some specials: underline, doubl
                                  Characters  Ctrl-V
Here's a line of 24-point UNIVERS text. (No change, eh?)



G:\WP51\SCRNTEST                              Doc 1 Pg 1 Ln 1" Pos 1"
```

Figure 6.3

Selecting a font attribute in WordPerfect.

Changing Text Size in WordPerfect

Figure 6.3 also shows you the available choices for font size:
fine, small, large, very large, and extra large. If none of these is
selected, you are using what's called the base font—a selected
font style in a specific size.

WordPerfect selects a base font for you, but you can change
it. Figure 6.4 shows the fonts available in the currently selected
printer. This printer has several built-in fonts; some are *fixed*
(available in only one or two sizes), and others are *scalable*
(available in any size). Usually you choose a base font in a
regular text size (typically 10- or 12-point).

Remember the five font sizes listed in Figure 6.3? These sizes
are proportional to the base font size. That's the only way we
can set font sizes in WordPerfect. Unlike some other word
processors, you can't specify a certain point size for selected
text.

133

Figure 6.4

*WordPerfect base font
selection.*

```
Base Font
  CG Times (Scalable)
  CG Times Bold (Scalable)
  CG Times Bold Italic (Scalable)
  CG Times Italic (Scalable)
* Courier 10cpi
  Courier 10cpi (Bold)
  Courier 10cpi (Italic)
  Courier 12cpi
  Courier 12cpi (Bold)
  Courier 12cpi (Italic)
  Line Printer 16.67cpi
  Univers (Scalable)
  Univers Bold (Scalable)
  Univers Bold Italic (Scalable)
  Univers Italic (Scalable)




 1 Select; N Name search: 1
```

You can change the percentages for each of the sizes at the
Setup: Print Options menu (Figure 6.5). Select Se**t**up from the
File menu (or press **Shift+F1**), then select **I**nitial Settings **P**rint
Options **S**ize Attribute Ratios. For example, let's say you chose
a 12-point base font. In Figure 6.5, Fine is set at 60 percent of
base (in this case, 60% of 12, or 7.2-point), and Extra Large at
200 percent (200% of 12, or 24-point).

Figure 6.5

Setting Size Attribute Ratios.

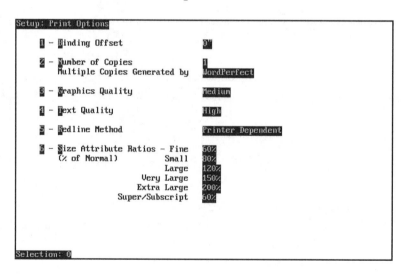

```
Setup: Print Options
    1 - Binding Offset                        0"

    2 - Number of Copies                      1
        Multiple Copies Generated by     WordPerfect

    3 - Graphics Quality                    Medium

    4 - Text Quality                          High

    5 - Redline Method              Printer Dependent

    6 - Size Attribute Ratios - Fine       60%
        (% of Normal)         Small        80%
                              Large        120%
                         Very Large        150%
                        Extra Large        200%
                      Super/Subscript      60%




Selection: 0
```

In the Problem/Solution section later in this chapter, there is a table that can help you determine the percentage to enter to get the font size you want.

I think this is a silly way to designate type sizes. But how can you argue with success? It does have the advantage of keeping all the sizes in proportion to each other if you change the base font size. When you later print your document, the result depends on the available fonts. A graphics printer can usually produce any size font; other printers may only have certain fixed sizes available.

WordPerfect and Text Fitting

Once you've entered some text, you may want to know how your page will appear when printed. WordPerfect has several ways to help you determine this.

Font Size and Line Length

First, even though all characters are the same size on-screen, changing the point size will change the line length. Figure 6.6 shows the effects of different point sizes on line length.

The lines of text in the base font and the 4-point font run off the screen, and you must scroll right with the cursor to see them. (Rest assured, however, that they will not run off the page when printed.) The larger fonts have much shorter lines, as you'd expect. The dotted line near the bottom shows the break between pages.

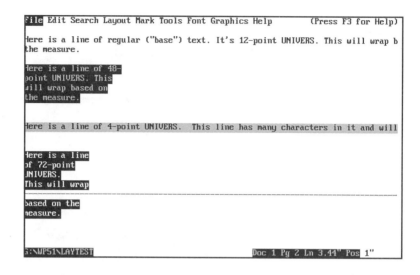

Figure 6.6

Line breaks for different point sizes.

View Document Mode

When you're ready to see your work as it will be printed, select Print from the File menu (or press Shift+F7), then select View Document. WordPerfect will compose a page using fonts that approximate the look of serif and sans-serif text, as shown in Figure 6.7.

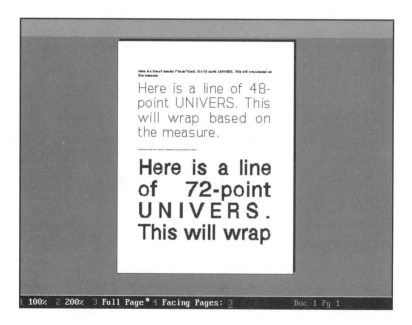

Figure 6.7

A WordPerfect View Document page.

This display is equivalent to "print preview" in other word processors. The squiggly line at the top, and an even thinner one in the middle, are the 12-point and 4-point lines, dwarfed by the larger lines. The line break is just where Figure 6.6 showed it would be—right after the word "wrap" in 72-point Univers.

Although you can see text and graphics in proper position on this page, you can't edit the text or adjust margins. It's just to look at.

WordPerfect and Printers

One exceptional capability of WordPerfect is that it can handle over 700 printers. You'll find everything from simple dot-matrix and daisywheel types to sophisticated laser printers.

When you install WordPerfect, you select the printers you'll be using, and a file that defines the available printer functions and fonts is created. An initial base font (the standard or default font) is selected for each printer. You choose among your printers in the Print: Select Printer menu, where you can also change various options.

One of the printer setup options is to substitute characters in one font for those in another. This lets you replace an unused character in your normal font with a special one you use often.

Besides their internal fonts, the printers you choose may have added font sources: daisywheels, cartridges, and soft fonts. When you add a printer, WordPerfect provides a list for you to indicate which add-on fonts are in use. When you use a soft font in a print job, WordPerfect automatically downloads it to the printer. I'll give you some details on this feature in the Problem/Solution section.

If your printer can print graphics, you can use any of the over 1,500 characters in the twelve included graphics fonts. I'll describe how to do that in the Problem/Solution section for WordPerfect.

Using TrueType and Type 1 Fonts with WordPerfect

Unless you have a PostScript printer, WordPerfect can't directly employ scalable outline font formats (such as TrueType or Type 1 fonts). Later in this chapter, however, I'll describe a couple of auxiliary programs that let you use such fonts with non-PostScript printers. The programs convert the character outlines into bitmaps that can then be sent to any printer capable of graphics.

WordPerfect Font Problems and Solutions

Here are some of the most common problems and questions that users have with WordPerfect fonts.

PROBLEM: I want to print a special character that I know exists. How do I put it in my text?

SOLUTION: WordPerfect has a special feature to enter special characters. Turn it on using the Font Characters menu item (or press **Ctrl+V**). Then enter the character, using its 3-digit code.

You'll find a list of codes in an appendix of the *WordPerfect Handbook*. You can also see a character map (a list of characters and codes) by running the Printer Program, also described in the *Handbook*.

PROBLEM: I want to use a character from one of the twelve WordPerfect fonts you described. How do I do that?

SOLUTION: First, your printer must be capable of printing graphics (unless it already has that character in one of its fonts). Next, you must turn on both text *and* graphics printing. That's because these fonts are graphics, and your other characters are probably text.

Probably you will also want the graphics quality high for the best character look. Select Se**t**up from the **F**ile menu (or press **Shift+F1**), then **I**nitial Settings **P**rint Options; you'll find the **G**raphics Quality and **T**ext Quality settings here. For best quality (and slowest printing) set them both *high*.

PROBLEM: I bought some soft fonts to use with my printer and WordPerfect. What do I do with them?

SOLUTION: First, install them into a subdirectory on your computer. The soft fonts may have an install program to make that easier.

Next, let WordPerfect know where that subdirectory is. Select **P**rint from the **F**ile menu (or press **Shift+F7**), then choose **S**elect Printer and select **E**dit to enter the path for downloaded fonts.

If your downloaded font is one of the standard sets, you'll find it listed for your printer in the soft fonts group. (It's in the same menu you got into above with the **E**dit command.) This time, select **C**artridges Fonts Print Wheels, and then select **Soft Fonts** for the list. Mark each font you have installed with a plus sign (+) to enable downloading.

PROBLEM: I want to use 18-point type for a headline, but I don't know how to set the size. Is there an easy way?

SOLUTION: No. First choose the five font sizes you're most likely to use. Then figure the percentage difference it is from the base font, and record those percentages on the **P**rint Options menu. Now you can select the relative size (from fine to very large) from the menu. (We talked about these percentages earlier in the chapter—turn back to Figure 6.5 for another look at the menu.)

You can assign any of these percentages to any of the five sizes WordPerfect provides. Select Se**t**up from the **F**ile menu (or press **Shift+F1**), then **I**nitial Settings **P**rint Options, and enter the Size Attribute Ratios for Fine, Small, Large, Very Large, and Extra Large (also Super/Subscript, if they're different from the default 60%).

Here's a table that will help. For base sizes from 8- to 12-point, specify these percentages to yield several common type sizes:

Table 6.1   **Assigning percentages to change type size in WordPerfect.**

To change this base font	*To this size*	*Enter this percentage*
8-pt	6-pt	75
	14-pt	175
	18-pt	225
	24-pt	300
	36-pt	450
	48-pt	600
10-pt	6-pt	60
	14-pt	140
	18-pt	180
	24-pt	240

To change this base font	To this size	Enter this percentage
10-pt	36-pt	360
	48-pt	480
12-pt	6-pt	50
	14-pt	117
	18-pt	150
	24-pt	200
	36-pt	300
	48-pt	400

For example, let's say you're using a 12-point base font, and you've decided to call the 18-point font "Very Large." You'd put the number 150 in the table next to "Very Large."

TIP

It's probably best to write down on a small card the percentages and sizes you entered, so that you know what's in each size setting. (WordPerfect doesn't show you.)

PROBLEM: I deleted some text in my document, and suddenly some font changes I made (or other formatting changes) were lost. Why did that happen, and how can I fix it?

SOLUTION: Whenever you add formats to text, WordPerfect puts invisible codes in your document. Sometimes it puts a *pair* of codes on either side of the affected text, to the bracket where format starts and ends. When you deleted text, you accidentally deleted one or more of the hidden codes.

To recover from this common difficulty, first make the codes visible. From the **E**dit menu, select **R**eveal Codes (or press **F11** or **Alt+F3**). The screen splits in half; the top part shows the regular text, and the bottom shows the text with the "secret" codes—indicated by square brackets.

TIP

*You can return to the normal display at any time by pressing **Alt+F3** or **F11** again.*

Your job (should you choose to accept it) is to locate the missing code or codes and correct them. A list of codes is in an appendix of the *WordPerfect Reference Manual.* Probably the easiest strategy is first to delete all suspect codes using the bottom display, then reapply the formatting.

Is this much fun? Not really.

PROBLEM: I have some Type 1 (PostScript) fonts, but I don't have a PostScript printer. Can I use them in WordPerfect?

SOLUTION: Yes you can. Two programs are available that add Type 1 font support.

PrimeType for WordPerfect, from LaserTools Corporation, is one. It includes 20 fonts and lets you use any Type 1 scalable font. (It also includes a copy of Adobe Type Manager in case you want to use these fonts in Microsoft Windows.)

PrimeType creates a special printer driver to add type services to any supported printer. Support is provided for LaserJet, DeskJet, and other Hewlett-Packard models, for IBM and Epson laser, dot-matrix and inkjet printers, and for a range of compatibles. (You can continue to use any PostScript-compatible printers in WordPerfect in the usual way.)

The second program is MoreFonts, from MicroLogic Software. It includes 28 scalable typefaces and gives you Type 1 support for the same classes of printers that PrimeType does. It also gives you special font effects such as patterns, outlines, shadows, and backgrounds.

PROBLEM: I have some TrueType fonts (the kind used by Microsoft Windows). Can I use them in WordPerfect?

SOLUTION: Yes. (Really—would I have put this rhetorical question in here if you couldn't?)

A program called TrueType for DOS by MoreLogic Software provides rasterizing and special effects for any TrueType font you have. It works only with WordPerfect and a couple of other DOS applications. To use its features, you run TrueType for DOS, and it loads and runs WordPerfect.

TrueType for DOS includes 36 TrueType fonts. It supports all Hewlett-Packard LaserJets, DeskJets, and compatibles, as well as similar Canon printers, and also Epson and IBM compatible dot-matrix printers. It creates a special printer driver for the selected printer that adds TrueType support. Once it's running, you select from the installed TrueType fonts in the regular WordPerfect Base Font menu list.

(TrueType for DOS also works with Microsoft Word—just ahead.)

Microsoft Word (for DOS)

Until Windows version 3 came along, Word (for DOS) was Microsoft's flagship word processor. First released in the early 80s, it has evolved steadily into a very competent DOS application.

Version 5.5 (the latest) gives you window-type screen effects in DOS. Where the previous version (5.0) had a list of commands at the bottom of the screen, this one has drop-down menus from a command bar. The screens and instructions in this book are for Version 5.5.

Word gives you a choice of two kinds of displays: *text* or *graphics mode.*

Text mode is something like draft mode in a Windows-based word processor. You see characters in the font your video board provides, just as in WordPerfect. If you have a color display, Word shows characters with special attributes (bold, italic, underlined, varying size) in your choice of 14 colors. (I'd show you an example here, but the colors don't reproduce well in black-and-white.)

In graphics mode, Word shows you characters that actually appear as italic, bold, underline, strikethrough, and several other attributes. It's shown in Figure 6.8. However, graphics mode doesn't show you a page as it will actually appear in print; all characters are the same size (the usual 12-point), and on this display a 24-point line looks like any other size text.

Figure 6.8

Word for DOS in graphics mode.

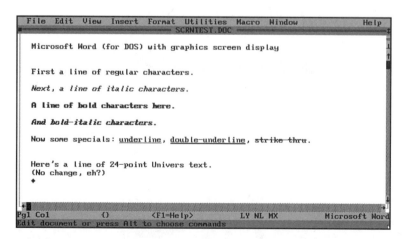

> *For all the figures about Word, I changed the screen colors from their original white-on-black to black-on-white because it prints better that way. I did that using the **V**iew **P**references **C**olors command. If you make a change, be sure not to choose white-on-white or black-on-black; they're very hard to read!*

To use graphics mode, you need a video adapter that can display graphics; color isn't required. You can switch back and forth between graphics and text modes by pressing **Alt+F9**.

Setting Font Attributes in Word

To choose font attributes in Word:

1. Highlight the text you want to change.

2. Select the Forma**t** **C**haracter command. A dialog box opens, shown in Figure 6.9.

3. Put the mouse pointer on each attribute you want, click the mouse button, then click on **OK**.

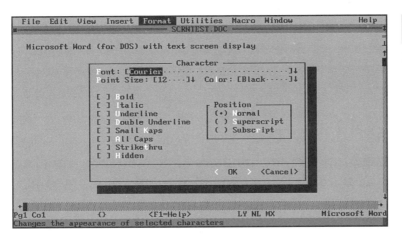

Figure 6.9

The Character dialog box.

It's possible to make all command menu selections using the **Alt**, **Tab**, **Spacebar**, *and* **arrow** *keys, but a mouse is quicker and less frustrating.*

4. To select a font from the available list, point and click on the down arrow at the right of the Font line. You'll see a second drop-down menu like the one in Figure 6.10.

5. Double-click on a font to select it, and you're back to Figure 6.9 again.

6. Point and click on the down arrow at the right of the Point Size line.

7. Double-click on the desired point size.

8. Click on **OK** to close the dialog box.

Word gives you an elaborate system of style sheets to allow you to create and apply styles for character, paragraph, and section formatting. Once you've decided how a particular document should be laid out, style sheets allow you to apply formatting consistently for every page, and for any new job.

Word and Printers

Word includes support for hundreds of printers. You install a printer driver for each printer you plan to use. Built into the driver is the information for all available fonts and character widths. Whenever you select a new printer, the font list changes to show what's provided with that model printer.

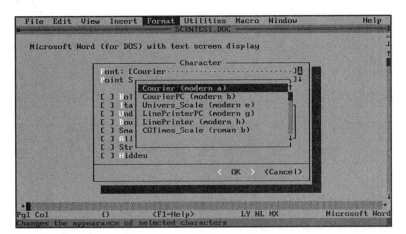

Figure 6.10

Font selection dialog box.

Suppported printers are listed in a large booklet, the *Printer Information for Microsoft Word.* For each printer, you'll find lists of fonts, sizes, and attributes available—either on a print wheel, built in, or on font cartridges.

Because Word was introduced when daisywheel and dot-matrix printers were the norm, those types are well-represented. Laser and inkjet printers are also included.

For printers that accept Adobe Type 1 fonts, Word provides a program to download them. I'll describe how to do that in the Problem/Solution section later.

Word and Text Fitting

When you enter text into Word—even in graphics mode—you get no indication of character style or size. Figure 6.11 shows three lines of text, in 4-point, 12-point, and 48-point; they have the same character styles and line length.

You get two ways to verify what will be printed: *Layout* view and *Print Preview.*

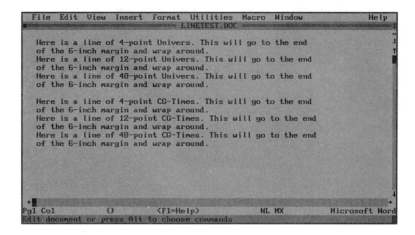

Figure 6.11

Word normal display with three sizes of fonts.

Layout View

Layout view lets you enter and edit text, and also visualize the printed page. It shows approximate text position, including columns, and shows position (but not content) of any graphics.

Use the **V**iew **L**ayout command on the menu bar to select layout view. The text on-screen changes to show the true line lengths based on the type size, as shown in Figure 6.12. Compare this to Figure 6.11, where the lines all have the same length; in layout view you get an indication of the number of characters on a line.

You also get a problem with layout view: a line of small type will often run off the page. To view this 4-point type, you'll have to scroll the screen far to the right.

Notice that even though there are very few lines on the page, the 48-point type doesn't completely fit. Because of its size (2/3-inch high characters), it runs onto the next page. (You can only see the first part of it here.)

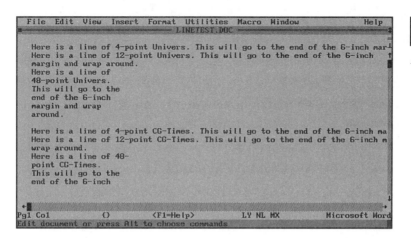

Figure 6.12

Layout view.

Print Preview Mode

Use the File Print Preview command to switch to Print Preview mode. It gives you miniatures of one or two pages, as Figure 6.13 shows. This is the preview of the text in Figure 6.12. The little squiggles at the top represent the lines of 4-point and 12-point type. Text is shown in a special (sans-serif) preview font, and there's no difference between Univers and CG-Times in the figure.

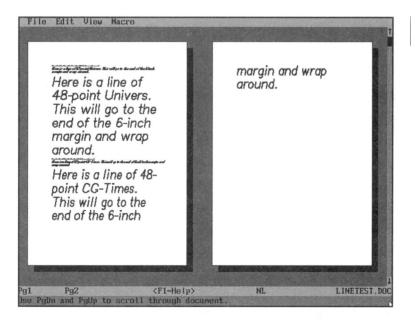

Figure 6.13

Text preview.

In Preview view, you see the position of all items on the page, including miniature graphics (if you want). This view includes margins, page numbers, and running heads. You can see one or two pages, and view the entire document page by page. This is the only view that simulates font styles and relative sizes. You can't edit while in this view.

Microsoft Word Font Problems and Solutions

Here are some of the most common problems and questions that users have with Word fonts.

PROBLEM: While I'm working on my document, I use Graphics mode so I can see the character formats. But Word seems so slow. Can I speed things up?

SOLUTION: Graphics mode is noticeably slower than text mode because Word must send a bitmap of each character to the display instead of simply a character code. If the slow response bothers you, use text mode until you want to check formatting, then switch to graphics mode.

You could also upgrade to a faster computer. You can get incredible bargains in hardware these days.

PROBLEM: I'm using text mode for a quick display, and I want to know what my character attributes are. I have a Hercules-type display (with graphics but no colors). I know I can find out by looking at the box I get using Forma**t** **C**haracter, but I'm tired of pulling it down every time. Is there an easier way?

SOLUTION: Sure: turn on the *ribbon*. It's a strip that appears just below the command bar and shows you the style, font, size, and attributes of the text at the cursor position. To display it, use the **V**iew Ri**b**bon command.

You can also select any of the formatting items directly from the ruler; to get an item to drop down a dialog selection box, just click on the **down** arrow.

PROBLEM: I'm using some small type, and (just like the example in Figure 6.12) the lines go way off to the right. How can I edit my copy that way?

SOLUTION: Word shows you text in lines that indicate where they will break when printed. Unless you need to verify the breaks, you're better off with the feature off. Choose **V**iew P**r**eferences and click on the **L**ine Breaks check box to turn it off.

PROBLEM: I have some Type 1 fonts I want to use with my laser printer. How do I do that?

SOLUTION #1: First, be sure you have a PostScript-compatible printer. If so, read carefully the *Downloading Procedures* section of the *Printer Information* book— especially the sections about downloading PostScript (Type 1) fonts, and downloading to a laser printer.

To use a Type 1 font, Word must have its associated Adobe Font Metrics (AFM) file that's usually supplied with the font. Word already has this info for ten of the most popular Type 1 fonts.

SOLUTION #2: You say you don't have a PostScript-compatible printer? Try using MoreFonts, from Micro-Logic Software. It includes 28 scalable typefaces and gives you Type 1 support for laser, inkjet, and dot-matrix printers. It also gives you special font effects such as patterns, outlines, shadows, and backgrounds.

PROBLEM: I have some TrueType fonts, and I want to use them with Word. Is there a way?

SOLUTION: Yes, use the same method I just described. You need an auxiliary program to do this. This one is called TrueType for DOS, from MicroLogic Software. It provides rasterizing and special effects for any TrueType font. (It also works with WordPerfect.) To use its features, run TrueType for DOS, and it loads and runs Word.

TrueType for DOS includes 36 TrueType fonts. It supports the same classes of printers that I described above for MoreFonts.

PROBLEM: I'm confused about what characters my printer actually can print. How do I find out?

SOLUTION: The surest way is to print a test document. There's a macro called "test_character" in the MACRO.GLY glossary that will print out the contents of any font you select. It requires a document file called CHARTEST.DOC. Both of these files are usually installed on your computer when you install *Word*.

To print a test document, run the macro, and answer the prompt questions. Here's how to access and run the macro:

1. Close all open documents.

2. From the menu bar, choose the **M**acro **E**dit, then click on the **O**pen Glossary button.

3. Select **MACRO.GLY** from the list of glossaries, and click on **OK**.

4. From the menu bar, choose **M**acro **R**un.

5. Select the **test_character** macro from the list of macros, and click on **OK**.

6. Answer the prompts. To interrupt the macro at any time, press the **Esc** (escape) key.

For more information, see the *Tips* section of your *Printer Information* book.

PROBLEM: I want to print a special character. I know it's in my font (because I printed out a test sheet using the directions you just gave me). But how do I insert one into my document?

SOLUTION: From the test sheet, find the 3-digit code for the character you want. While you hold down the **Alt** key, enter the code.

Don't be too surprised if the character that appears on your screen isn't the one you want printed. Try printing the page and verify you have the right character. If you do, just make a note to yourself describing how it appears on the screen; there's no way to change the display to match the printing.

PROBLEM #1: My daisywheel printer is printing too slowly. I'm in a hurry to get my documents out. Is there a way to speed the process?

PROBLEM #2: My daisywheel printer used to print both directions (bidirectionally). Now it prints in only one direction, making the printing slower. I want the speed back!

SOLUTION: You can switch your printer from high-quality to draft mode. That reduces the quality of printing, but also speeds it up dramatically.

While in high-quality mode, the printer may be performing micro-justification: spacing the characters out exactly right. When it does this, it may not print in both directions.

Use the **File Print** command, click on the **O**ptions button, and check (turn on) the **D**raft option. Look at a sample page to see if the results are good enough for the printing job you're doing.

PROBLEM: I need to control a special printer function that's not available from within Word. Is there any way to do this?

SOLUTION: You can include (*embed*) special printer control codes in your document. Using a supplied utility program, you can even create and modify printer drivers. (This is a very intense undertaking, and beyond the scope of this book; it's described in the *Printer Information* booklet.)

Quattro Pro (for DOS)

Borland's Quattro Pro (for DOS) version 4.0 is a spreadsheet application with an attractive 3-D effect windowed screen—complete with menu bar and toolbar. You can use your mouse to activate commands, or to move through the working spreadsheet using scroll bars along the screen edge.

Figure 6.14 shows a blank spreadsheet and an inset window that appears when you click on the Font toolbar button. With a little imagination, you might think you were using a Microsoft Windows application, except that Quattro Pro lacks multi-document features and direct links to other applications. (There's also a Quattro Pro for Windows.)

Figure 6.14

Quattro Pro font selection box.

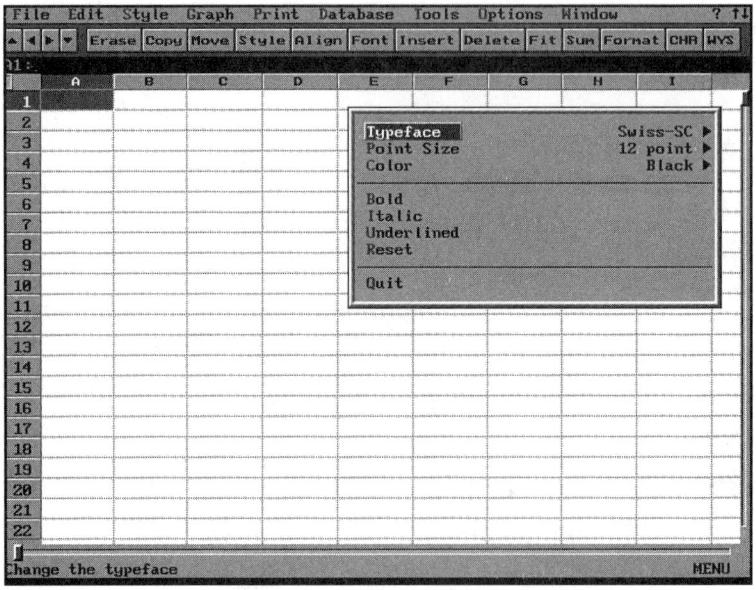

Quattro Pro has two distinct screen displays: the *WYSIWYG* mode shown here, and a *Character* mode that looks more like a DOS screen. (You remember that "WYSIWYG" stands for "What You See Is What You Get"—another way of saying it's a graphical screen.) WYSIWYG screens require an EGA or VGA display system on your computer. To show you the vast difference, Figure 6.15 shows the character version of the same info shown in Figure 6.14.

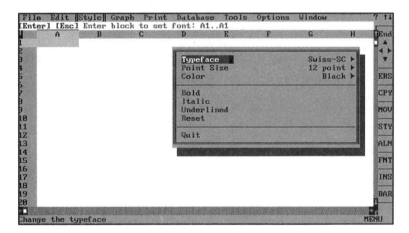

Figure 6.15

QuattroPro font selection (character display).

Choose WYSIWYG mode by selecting **WYSIWYG** from the Options Display Mode menu or choose Character mode by clicking on **CHR**. (Why would you ever want to use Character mode if you have a choice?)

As part of the installation, you choose which printer you'll be using. Quattro Pro installs a printer driver that is aware of the standard fonts and sizes available for that printer, as well as any font cartridges. You can also specify a second printer (for example, you might have a draft printer and a high-quality one).

When you install a font cartridge, you make Quattro Pro aware of it by using the command series **O**ptions **H**ardware **P**rinters **F**onts **C**artridge; the fonts cartridge menu is shown in Figure 6.16. (For this model printer, there are two cartridge slots: left and right.)

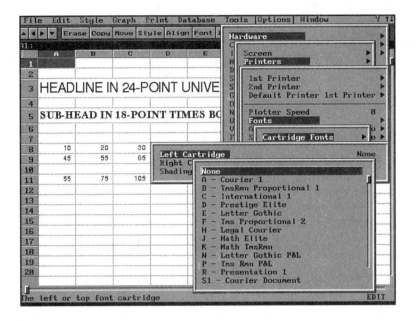

Figure 6.16

Quattro Pro fonts cartridge menu.

The H-P LaserJet I selected has the usual set of fixed fonts in a few text sizes (such as Courier), and also some scalable fonts in Times (serif) and Univers (sans-serif) faces. Figure 6.17 shows the scrolling box that appears when you select **T**ypeface from the box in Figure 6.14. In this case, I've chosen Univers bold because it's a good-looking face I can use for spreadsheet examples.

When you select a typeface size (in the box shown in Figure 6.14), Quattro Pro shows it on the screen in a style and size that looks much like the printed product. In Figure 6.18, a spreadsheet shows a grid of cells and several lines of type. Notice the height of cells in each row increases automatically to accommodate the type sizes. You can also zoom in (enlarge) the view to check details; the text still appears in WYSIWYG mode.

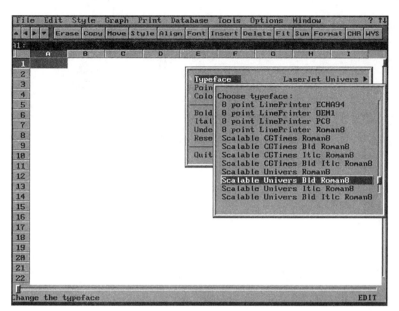

Figure 6.17

Quattro Pro printer typeface selection.

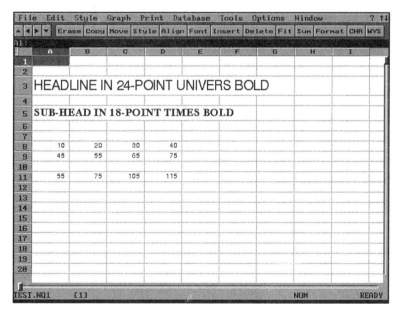

Figure 6.18

Quattro Pro typeface display.

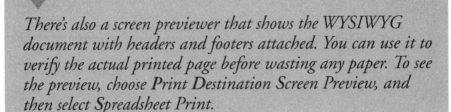

There's also a screen previewer that shows the WYSIWYG document with headers and footers attached. You can use it to verify the actual printed page before wasting any paper. To see the preview, choose Print Destination Screen Preview, and then select Spreadsheet Print.

Quattro Pro Fonts Problems and Solutions

Here are some hints that may help you with Quattro Pro.

PROBLEM: I want to use the great-looking WYSIWYG mode you described, but all I see is the DOS-style screen. How can I get the better display?

SOLUTION: First, you must have a graphics-type display system (EGA or VGA) to use WYSIWYG. If Quattro Pro couldn't determine your display type during installation, it chose Character mode because that will work on any display.

If your display wasn't recognized (or you upgraded to a better system), you can select WYSIWYG. Choose the **O**ptions command and select the **D**isplay Mode box.

PROBLEM: WYSIWYG mode is working, but it's too slow: when I make changes or select command boxes, it takes too long to display the screen. Help!

SOLUTION: If you have a very slow computer, you may want to move to Character mode to do most of your work (such as spreadsheet number entry), and switch to WYSIWYG mode to preview the page layout. That will also let you see graphs you may have created.

PROBLEM: I'd like to see more spreadsheet columns on-screen at the same time—without distorting my typefaces. Is there a way to do this?

SOLUTION: Some VGA display cards have modes that support as many as 132 columns at once. Choose the **O**ptions **D**isplay Mode command and select your card if it's listed there. There are also selections for generic EGA cards to show 43 spreadsheet rows at once, and generic VGA cards to display 50 rows.

PROBLEM: I have some Bitstream Speedo format scalable fonts. Is there any way to use them with Quattro Pro?

SOLUTION: Yes—and Quattro Pro has three included fonts from Bitstream. Most printers that can print in graphics mode, including laser, inkjet, and dot-matrix printers, can print these scalable fonts.

To use Speedo-format fonts you've bought elsewhere, you must convert them to the Quattro Pro format in the proper directory. That's described in an appendix in the *User's Guide*. (Borland suggests that you not use older-format Bitstream fonts; they are slower, and lower quality.) Once installed, these fonts appear in the font list for your printer.

PROBLEM: I want to insert a bullet (a special font character) in my spreadsheet text. How do I do that?

SOLUTION: Insert this string of characters in your text (followed by any other text you want):

```
'\bullet #\
```

The apostrophe indicates this is a flush-left text string, and the string between the backslashes (\) selects the kind of bullet. Replace the "#" symbol with a digit from 0 to 6 that selects one of seven bullet styles. That list is in the *Quattro Pro User's Guide*.

PROBLEM: I want to insert a special character from my font (such as Greek or international symbols). What's the procedure?

SOLUTION: Quattro Pro uses the standard DOS ASCII character set for the first 128 characters, and the "IBM graphics screen characters" for a second group of 128. First, find the character in the table shown in an appendix of the *User's Guide.* To enter the character, hold down the **Alt** key while you enter the character's three-digit code using the numbers on the numeric keypad with NumLock turned on. (If the character has only a two-digit code, enter a leading zero.)

There's a strong limitation: these characters only print when you've selected draft-quality printing, and not in graphics-quality. To select draft-quality, use the **O**ptions **G**raphics Quality command and select **D**raft.

Lotus 1-2-3 for DOS Release 3.4

For many years, Lotus Development Corporation literally owned the spreadsheet market. Especially for conservative corporate users, Lotus 1-2-3 has been the one to buy. Now, Lotus has stiff competition from high-quality DOS and Windows spreadsheets from other vendors—and even its own Windows offering.

Lotus DOS spreadsheet applications have been on a dual track, with support for both release 2 and release 3. With the latest release, 3.4, Lotus is expected to discontinue the older release 2 series over time.

Release 3.4 lets you create files that contain as many as 256 spreadsheets, and you can form *3-D ranges* that relate two or more sheets to each other. If you have a display such as EGA or VGA, you can use a graphics screen. Then 1-2-3 can show you a spreadsheet that looks much like it will when printed. (Otherwise, 1-2-3 will give you a DOS character-based display.)

1-2-3 Graphics: the Wysiwyg Auxiliary Program

To use graphics with 1-2-3, you must install an auxiliary program called Wysiwyg—"What You See Is What You Get." (Lotus calls programs that add extra spreadsheet features "add-ins.") With Wysiwyg you also get mouse support, as well as control over fonts and other publishing effects. You have the option to install Wysiwyg when you install 1-2-3. (That's also the time to choose which printers you're using.)

Figure 6.19 shows the basic worksheet display in Graphics mode. Along the right edge is a new graphics feature—an icon toolbar that Lotus calls "SmartIcons." You can activate these command functions by clicking with a mouse. The figure also shows the menu of spreadsheet commands at the top of the screen that appears when you enter a slash (/) keyboard character.

Figure 6.19 shows a completely different Wysiwyg menu that appears when you type a colon (:). (In this figure, the Format command is highlighted, and a submenu of format commands appears on the next line.)

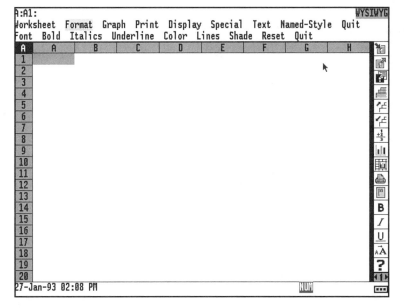

Figure 6.19

Lotus 1-2-3 spreadsheet display—Wysiwyg mode.

Using the Wysiwyg menu, you can format any part of the spreadsheet with a selected font and style, including bold and italic. You can also select some of these using the toolbar.

1-2-3 Font Sets

Your choice of fonts for any one spreadsheet is one of eight in a group called a font set. Each of the eight fonts in a font set is a particular face and point size. You get an initial or default font set that includes text fonts in Bitstream Speedo format, as well as a symbol font.

To apply a typeface format to characters in your spreadsheet, you enter **: Format Font** and select the font by number (1 to 8). Then highlight the range of spreadsheet cells you want to format. You can also choose bold, italic or underline by selecting commands in the **: Format** menu, or by clicking on the toolbar icons.

Lotus 1-2-3 Font Problems and Solutions

Let me help you navigate through the Lotus 1-2-3 font system.

PROBLEM: I want to use a Wysiwyg screen display, but I seem to have a text-type character display now. What's wrong, and how can I go to Wysiwyg?

SOLUTION: First, you must have a graphics display system on your PC. Next, make sure the Wysiwyg add-in is installed. 1-2-3 gives you the option to select your display type and install the add-in when you install the basic application.

To verify that Wysiwyg is installed and available, press **Alt+F10** (hold down the Alt key and press the F10 function key). From the menu that appears, select **Settings** and then **System**. A list of available add-ins appears, and **Wysiwyg** should be on the list.

If it isn't, install it by running the 1-2-3 install program again. (You can't simply copy it from the diskettes.)

WYSIWYG should automatically start if it's installed. If it doesn't, you can start it by pressing **Alt+F10** and selecting **Wysiwyg** from the displayed list.

PROBLEM: Wysiwyg is installed and running, but I still don't see my spreadsheet in Graphics mode so I can verify font and size. How do I turn it on?

SOLUTION: You can switch between Wysiwyg and Character mode at any time. Access the Wysiwyg menu by typing a colon (:). Then select **Display Mode** and choose between **Graphics**, **Text**, **B&W**, and **Color**.

B&W and Color choices are active only in graphics mode. They let you select whether you want a black-and-white or color display. Color is the initial, or default, setting.

PROBLEM: I want to use more than eight fonts in my spread-sheet. How can I do that?

SOLUTION: You can't; 1-2-3 restricts you to eight fonts (one font set) for each spreadsheet. Frankly, that should be plenty; you don't want your work to look like a font sample sheet!

But remember: each spreadsheet can have its own font group. If you have a title page or summary sheet that you want contrasting fonts for, create a different spreadsheet.

PROBLEM: Okay, I want a special "mix" of fonts for a spread-sheet. How do I get that?

SOLUTION: Figure 6.20 shows you the Wysiwyg font list for the default font set. You display it by entering the Wysiwyg command **: Format Font**. Each font is available in only one size. For example, SWISS12 is 12-point sans-serif (like Helvetica), and Dutch 8 is 8-point serif (like Times Roman).

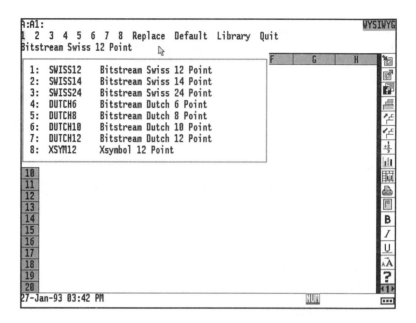

Figure 6.20

The 1-2-3 default font set list.

You can change any font, but only one at a time. Select **Replace** from the submenu (after **Format Font**), then select (by its number) the font you want to replace. You'll get a menu that lets you choose from SWISS, DUTCH, COURIER, SYMBOL, and OTHER (OTHER isn't available for all printers.) I didn't show that menu here, but it lets you select the family of fonts from which to choose a replacement font.

If you select SWISS, DUTCH, COURIER, or XSYMBOL, the main reason would be to choose another point size for one of these faces. They're like what's in the default menu. I chose OTHER instead, and Figure 6.21 shows what appeared.

This is a complete list of all fonts available for your printer. The right-hand column shows the shorthand "code" for the font. You can scroll through the list and choose what you need. I chose 14-point Century Schoolbook to replace font 7 (which had been DUTCH 12). Figure 6.22 shows the result.

You can continue selecting fonts in the group by number, and other fonts on the list, until you've made all the substitutions you want.

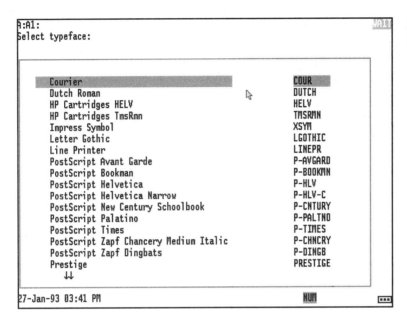

Figure 6.21

The 1-2-3 "OTHER" Font selection list.

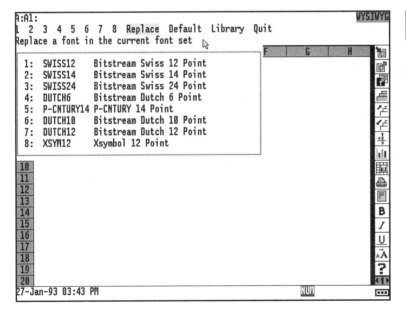

Figure 6.22

1-2-3 font group with substitution.

PROBLEM: I've made up this new font group, and I want to
save it for future use to keep my spreadsheets consistent.
How can I do that?

SOLUTION: When you save your spreadsheet (using **/ File Save**), the font set you're using is saved with it.

If you want to save a font set to use with another spreadsheet, you can put it in a *font library*. Use **: Format Font Library Save**, and choose an eight-character name for the font set. Don't forget the name! (Font sets are usually saved in the ADDINS subdirectory.)

To use a font set you've saved, enter **: Format Font Library Retrieve**, and select it by name from the file list that appears.

PROBLEM: I want even more fonts than the font list gives me. Where do I find them?

SOLUTION: During installation, 1-2-3 gives you three choices for the number of fonts you'll see. The smallest group is the default Swiss, Dutch, and Courier set; you can later select any size for a font set. The medium group is the one I've shown in Figure 6.21 (only part of it will fit in the displayed box).

Finally, there's a large font group Lotus suggests you use only if you have great need; it takes a lot of time to build and a lot of disk space. If you need to add this, reinstall 1-2-3 and select it. Expect to wait during installation while 1-2-3 works on the fonts.

Although Lotus uses Bitstream Speedo format fonts, I know of no way to install any that are not provided with 1-2-3.

PROBLEM: I'm using a small typeface, and I want to "zoom in" on a portion of my spreadsheet to make it easier to see. What's a good way?

SOLUTION: 1-2-3 gives you five different screen magnifications (assuming you're in Wsyiwyg mode, of course).

Figure 6.23 shows the menu that appears when you enter
: Display Zoom.

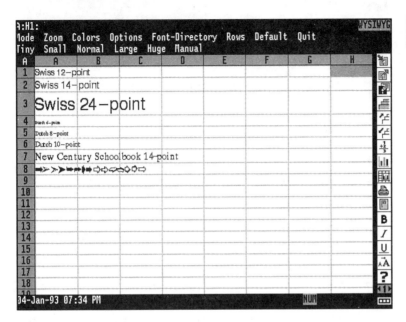

Figure 6.23

The 1-2-3 Display Zoom menu.

You get Tiny, Small, Normal, Large, and Huge. That's a
range of 63 to 150 percent of normal screen size. If the preset
choices aren't enough, you can choose **Manual**, for control
from 25 to 400 percent. Figure 6.24 shows what happens to
the fonts in my new font set when I select 400 percent! (Notice the symbol font at the bottom.)

Remember: Zoom affects only the screen display, and *not*
the size of printed characters!

PROBLEM: Sometimes it seems that Wysiwyg mode is too
slow. What happens if I don't use it?

SOLUTION: You will get slightly improved performance, and
that may help if you're using a very slow computer. Remember, you can switch to Text mode at any time by
using **: Display Mode Text**. Figure 6.25 shows how the
display looks after switching; you're back to the good old
DOS screen. (This is the same text I used in Figure 6.24.)

Figure 6.24

1-2-3 fonts at 400 percent display.

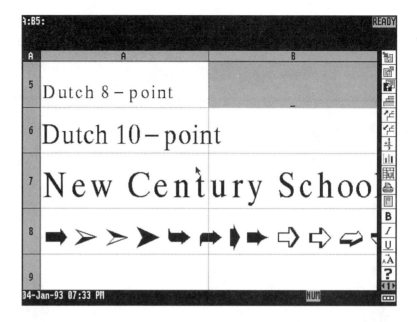

Figure 6.25

1-2-3 display in Text mode.

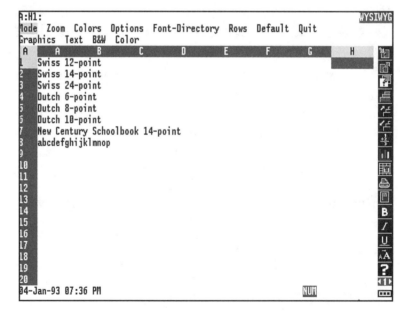

PROBLEM: I want to put a special symbol in a cell, such as an arrow. How do I enter those special characters?

SOLUTION: Most special characters are in the symbol font, which doesn't have regular letters and numbers. Begin by selecting the XSYM font (usually **: Format Font 8**). It's in the default font set; if it isn't in your font set, you'll need to substitute it for one that is there.

Now when you type a regular keyboard character, you'll get a symbol. To determine which character you'll get, look in the back of the *Lotus 1-2-3 Reference Manual* for a table.

PROBLEM: That entry system works for most of the characters in the symbol font. But I have a font with extended characters, and I want to use them. What's the method?

SOLUTION: If the character you want is in the font but not available as a keyboard character, you enter it as a function. In the cell, type the characters **@CHAR(#)**. Instead of the "#" sign, put the two- or three-character code for the character you want. The standard codes are in an appendix of the *Reference* manual, and the numbers can be from 32 to 255.

You can enter some extended characters using an alternate "compose" method that's a little tricky. Begin by pressing **Alt+F1** twice. Then type **0-** or **1-** (zero or one, followed by a hyphen). That selects the code group. Finally, enter a three-digit "compose" code from the table I just mentioned. (If the symbol has only a 2-digit code, enter a leading zero.)

For example, to enter a bullet (which is in group 1), you'd press **Alt+F1**, then type **1-007**.

Lots of fun!

PROBLEM: I have a spreadsheet with lots of rows, and I want to display more of them at once than 1-2-3 now lets me. Do I have a choice?

SOLUTION: Yes, if you're using Wysiwyg mode. Select the menu item **: Display Rows**, and then a number from 16 to 60 to choose the number of rows you want.

Once you've made a display change, to make it permanent (unless you change it later), select the menu item **: Display Options Update**.

Looking Back and Looking Ahead

Now that we've looked at some popular DOS applications, it's time to turn to one of the most thorny subjects of all: printers and how they handle fonts. I think you'll find some interesting ideas in the next chapter.

Four score
and seven
years ago..

Printers and Fonts

Here's some info about printers from a different angle. In Chapter 2, I took the long view: types of printers, how they work, and some ideas about making a purchase choice. Now I want to give you some specifics about printer problems and solutions.

Can Your Printer Print *Anything*?

What do you do if your printer doesn't print anything at all? Let's face it: who cares what fonts you're using if you can't print?

Here's a checklist that will probably resolve that problem. Your computer and printer link together in a long chain, where any item out of place can block everything. This list traces down that chain.

Before we do any problem solving, we'll do a simple test to help you decide where the problem lies. Let's find out whether your printer is printing from DOS.

First, boot your computer to run DOS. (Don't start Windows running even if you use it.) Then, print a list of directory contents. To do so, enter one of these lines at the DOS command prompt (then press **Enter** after the command):

DIR > LPT1   (for a parallel printer)

or

DIR > COM1 (for a serial printer on port 1)

If the "chain" of necessary connections from your computer to your printer is unbroken, you'll get a printed directory of the current disk drive. In this case, go right to step 7 in the checklist (if you're trying to print from a Windows application), or try the Windows test (next) to see if the problem is originating in Windows. If you didn't get a printed directory, start at step 1 of the checklist that follows.

If you can print from DOS, then test Windows printing. The following simple test from within Windows is equivalent to the one we did for DOS.

Start Windows and double-click on (select) the **Notepad** icon (usually found in the Program Manager's **Accessories** group). Select **File Open** from the menu bar and select a short text file with the extension TXT (or you could simply type in a line of text).

Now, select **File Print** and the text should print. If it is printing, the problem is probably with the specific Windows application that wouldn't print. (See Chapter 4 for information on troubleshooting specific applications.) If it's not printing, exit the Notepad and proceed to step 5.

Step 1: Is Your Printer Plugged into a "Live" Power Receptacle and Turned On?
Sounds silly—but it's a common problem: no power where you need it (and think you have it). If your printer doesn't have a "ready" or "on" light, plug a lamp or tester into the socket to check for power.

Is there a blown fuse, a bad power cord or (egad!) a switch that isn't turned on?

(I remember once—long ago, when I was a college student playing TV technician—wasting an hour using fancy test equipment to repair a dead television; that is, until the service manager pointed out there was a broken wire in the power plug!)

Step 2: Is There Paper in the Printer, and Is It Properly Loaded?
Most printers have a hidden switch that "feels" the paper to see if it's loaded in the right position; if it isn't, the printer refuses to print. Sometimes there's a paper-out indicator that tells you (sometimes there isn't).

Are you using a printer that's usually been sprocket-fed (with those holes along the edges of the paper), and you've switched to single sheets? If so, you may need to make an option setting or move a lever; check the user's guide to be sure.

Step 3: Is the Printer Properly Connected to the Computer?

That means that the cable is the right kind—either parallel or serial—and that it is completely attached to both the printer and the computer.

These descriptions refer to a "standard" IBM-compatible PC; yours may vary.

Parallel printers: The connector on the back of the computer for a parallel printer (called the parallel "port") is trapezoid-shaped (like a rectangle with one side too short); it has 25 little holes for pins. The printer cable has a matching connector with 25 little pins. The other end of the cable looks about the same size, but it has a little plastic bar in it with 37 little shiny metal tabs (very hard to count). The printer has a connector with a slot in it that accepts the bar. Figure 7.1 shows a parallel port and the end of the cable that connects to it.

Serial printers: The connector on the computer serial port looks just like the one for a parallel port, *except it's reversed*: it has 25 little pins in it instead of holes. (The serial cable has a matching connector with 25 little holes.)

Some serial port connectors have nine pins instead of 25; they're referred to as "AT-type" ports. You can buy a serial printer cable that has a matching connector, or you can use an adapter that lets you use a cable with a 25-pin connector. There's no difference in performance.

The other end of the serial cable *usually* has a connector (with 25 little pins) that plugs into the printer. A few printers need special cables that have their own unique connectors. Figure 7.2 shows a serial port printer connection.

Figure 7.1

Parallel printer connection.

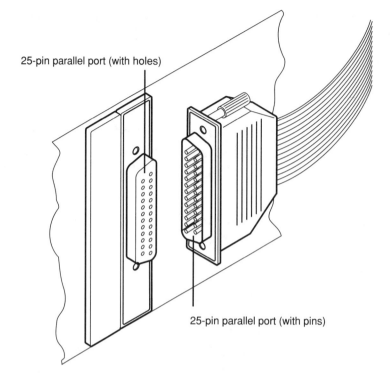

25-pin parallel port (with holes)

25-pin parallel port (with pins)

Figure 7.2

Serial printer connection.

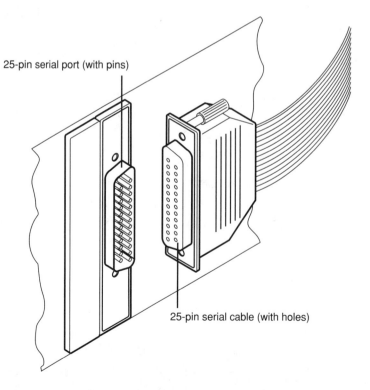

25-pin serial port (with pins)

25-pin serial cable (with holes)

Very few printers need special cables; sometimes the cables look exactly like regular ones, but have different internal wiring. (One pesky example is an older series of Radio Shack parallel printers.) Consult your user's guide if you have any doubts.

Have you been following this? OK—here's a test: It's possible to plug the printer end of a serial cable into the computer's parallel port accidentally. But then the other end wouldn't plug into the printer.

(If you're using a graphics printer—especially a laser printer—you should always use a parallel connection if it's available. It transfers the printing information much faster than a serial cable can.)

Finally, make sure all connectors are completely attached. They usually have little screws or clips that pull them together. If the screws aren't turned down all the way, they can hold the connectors together without pulling the little pins into their sockets. The connectors may *look* like they're connected when actually they have a small space between them!

But be gentle! Those little pins bend easily, and those little screws can be cross-threaded. They're a real nuisance to repair.

Step 4: Is the Printer Properly "Configured?"

If you're using a parallel connection and your printer has both serial and parallel ports (many do), be sure the printer is using (not just plugged into) the parallel port. Check the printer manual to see if you need to set a switch or make a menu selection to activate (turn on) the parallel port. There's no configuration needed for the computer's parallel port.

If you're using a serial connection, you need to both activate the printer's serial port *and* set its communication speed (sometimes called the *baud rate*). Check the printer manual. In most cases, you'll get the fastest printing by using the fastest rate (highest number) available—usually 9600 baud or *bps* (bits per second). Other typical rates are 1200, 2400 and 4800—sometimes even 19,200 bps.

For a serial port, you'll need to configure the computer also; that's covered in the next step.

Step 5: Is Your Computer Port Properly Configured?

If you're using a parallel port and running DOS applications, you should have a line in your DOS AUTOEXEC.BAT file that reads:

```
MODE LPT1:,,b
```

To find out what's in your AUTOEXEC.BAT file, return to the root directory of your system by typing CD\ and pressing Enter. Then, type TYPE AUTOEXEC.BAT and press Enter.

In this line, include the two commas. (This example is for DOS version 5.0; for most earlier versions of DOS, you'd substitute a "p" for the "b" shown here.) To enter the line in the AUTOEXEC.BAT file, you can use the DOS EDIT program (available in version 5.0 and later), or you can use the Windows Notepad. (See the documentation for each program to learn more about editing files like AUTOEXEC.BAT.)

If you have more than one printer, it will be identified in DOS as LPT2 or LPT3. You should separate commands for each printer.

You don't need this line if you're *only* using Microsoft Windows applications (but it doesn't hurt). You must reboot the computer to activate the settings.

If you use the Mode command from the command line, it is not necessary to reboot the computer.

If you're using a serial port and DOS applications, you'll need to know two things: the speed of the printer port (for example, 9600) and the computer port that's in use (COM1, COM2, COM3 or COM4). If there's only one serial port on your computer it's usually (not always) COM1.

You will need a line in your AUTOEXEC.BAT file that reads:

```
MODE COM1:96,n,8,1,b
```

This is an example for DOS version 5.0, for the COM1 port, and a speed of 9600. Notice that you use only the first two digits of the speed (96, not 9600). This example will be correct just as I show it for most printers. (If you want to know what the other settings mean, check your DOS user's guide for more details.)

You must reboot the computer to activate the settings.

If you're using Microsoft Windows, serial port setups are in the Control Panel. For a serial printer, click on the **Control Panel/Ports** icon, and double-click on the COM port you're using (**COM1**, **COM2**, **COM3** or **COM4**). A dialog box like the one shown in Figure 7.3 appears, letting you set up the selected port. You can set the port to match your printer. Here are the usual settings:

Baud Rate (speed)	**(set to match your printer)**
Data Bits	**8**
Parity	**None**
Stop Bits	**1**
Flow Control	**Hardware**

Figure 7.3

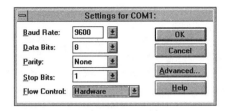

Windows control panel for serial ports.

Step 6: Is There a Printer Driver Installed for Your Printer?
DOS applications vary widely in the way they handle printers and drivers. I'll use Microsoft's Word (for DOS) as an example. Check your user's manual for other applications to see how they do it.

To check for your printer, use the **File** Printe**r** Setup command. In the **P**rinter File box, you can see which *printer driver* is installed. (Printer drivers—the files that run the printer—have the extension PRD.)

To choose a different printer, select it in the Printer **N**ame box. If the printer you're using isn't listed, you'll need to run the SETUP program again (the same one you used to install Word). It's on the Setup diskette—the first one in the set. This program will prompt you to insert one of the Printers diskettes.

If you've installed a new printer, use the **File** Printe**r** Setup command, select the printer in the Printer **N**ame box, and be sure the correct port for this printer appears in the **C**onnect To box.

For Windows applications, open the Windows **Control Panel** and double-click on the **Printers** icon. You'll get a list of installed printers, as shown in Figure 7.4. If the one you want to use is on the list, you can make it the *default printer* (the one that applications will use unless you tell them otherwise). Either double-click on the printer's name in the list, or click on the Set as Default Printer button.

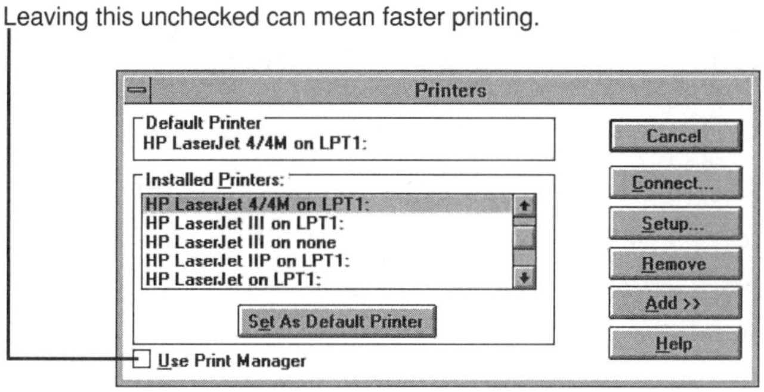

Leaving this unchecked can mean faster printing.

Figure 7.4

Windows Control Panel Printers dialog box.

If your printer (or a close equivalent) isn't in the list, install a driver for it. Click on the **A**dd>> button, and a list of supported printers appears (as shown in Figure 7.5). Choose yours from the **L**ist of Printers at the bottom of the dialog box, choose the **I**nstall button, and follow the directions. Sometimes Windows will ask you to insert a numbered diskette from its installation set to add the driver.

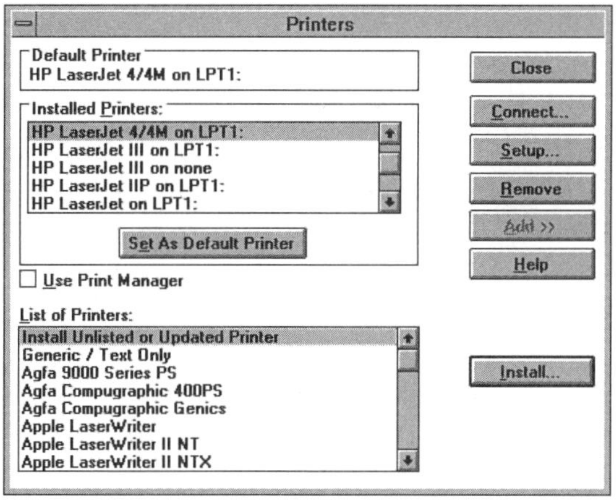

Figure 7.5

Windows Add Printers dialog box.

If your printer isn't listed, try choosing one that's similar. Read the printer manual or check with the manufacturer to see if there is a way your printer can *emulate* (pretend to be) a listed model. Be careful not to choose a PostScript driver unless your printer is actually PostScript compatible.

Your printer vendor may have a Windows driver available. In that case, get a diskette with the driver on it. Then choose

Install Unlisted or Updated Printer (the first item in the **List** of Printers) and follow the directions to install the new driver.

When you have the driver installed, choose the **S**etup button, and specify the options you want for your printer. This includes items such as paper size and source and installed fonts and font cartridges. (I'll get back to this for some specific printers a bit later.)

Are we having fun yet? Great—on to the next step!

Step 7: Is Your Computer Port (for the Printer) Connected to a Printer Driver?

Most DOS applications give you a method of selecting the printer you intend to use and choosing the active port; that selection enables the printer driver. There's no easy way to show you an example here because DOS applications vary widely. See the documentation for your specific application to learn how to ensure that the driver is printing to the correct port.

CAUTION

If the port you intend to use isn't listed, you may have a setup or equipment failure: go for help to a computer dealer or a friend who knows a lot about hardware!

Checking the connection in Windows is easy. While in the **Control Panel**, click on the **Printers** icon. Choose your printer from the list of Installed **Printers**, then choose the **Connect** button; you'll get a list of the available serial and parallel ports, like the one in Figure 7.6.

Choose the printer port you're using by selecting it and choosing **OK**. In Windows version 3.1 it's allowable to have two printers selected for the same port, and just plug in the one you want. (It wasn't allowed in version 3.0.) Now click on **Close** to exit the Printer controls.

A few applications—especially high-level graphics programs (often with PostScript output)—provide their own printer drivers. In that case, follow the installation directions carefully.

Check this box to bypass DOS for faster printing.

Figure 7.6

Windows Printer Connect dialog box.

If you see a checkbox in the Connect dialog box marked Fast Printing Direct to Port, go ahead and select it. That allows Windows to bypass DOS when it prints—speeding up the process considerably.

Did you find anything wrong with Windows while trying steps 6 or 7? If so, you've probably fixed the problem; try the printing test using Notepad again. If that doesn't work, try steps 6 and 7 again.

Step 8: Have You Selected an Available Printer from Within Your Application?

You'll usually find the printer commands in the File menu. For example, you might select File Printer Setup or File Setup Printer. Selecting a command like this provides a list of all installed printers, with the currently selected one already highlighted. If one isn't highlighted, that means no printer is selected in this application, and you should choose one.

For DOS applications, the approach may be different. See the documentation that came with the program.

Some Windows applications give you a choice of either the default printer or a specific printer for this one print job or session. Figure 7.7 shows an example from CorelDRAW! version 3.0. When you select an alternate printer, it doesn't change the default for any other Windows application. That saves a lot of confusion when you switch between applications and print jobs.

Figure 7.7

Application dialog box for multiple printers (CorelDRAW!).

Print Setup
Printer
◇ Default Printer
(currently HP LaserJet 4/4M on LPT1:)
◆ Specific Printer:
HP DeskJet 550C Printer on LPT2:
Orientation ◆ Portrait ◇ Landscape
Paper Size: Letter 8 1/2 x 11 in Source: In Tray
OK Cancel Options... Network...

If You Still Can't Print

Let's say you've checked all the steps, and your DOS or Windows application still can't print. It's time to repeat the DOS and Windows printing tests you tried at the very beginning. If your system still fails to print a directory, go over all the steps carefully one more time. If that doesn't cure your printer ills, you may have an equipment failure. It's time to call for some expert help.

Other Problems with Printers

The checklist you've just completed was meant to solve the problem of not getting any printing; it doesn't mean you're getting the best printing. Read on to get some pointers on specific kinds of printers and their drivers. First, the basic question: do you have a printer?

If you haven't purchased a printer and you want to know which kind to buy to get the best use of fonts, read Chapter 2 to get some ideas about how printers use fonts (and some tradeoffs). There have never been more good choices at excellent prices than now.

Following are font solutions for the three major types of printers: laser, ink- and paintjet, and dot-matrix.

Working with Laser Printers

First, I'm going to discuss information you may need if you have a laser printer. I'm going to use Hewlett-Packard's new LaserJet 4 as an example. It's a high-quality, mid-priced unit with a good (and representative) range of features. It also has some new and impressive functions. I'll talk about those, too.

QUESTION: How do laser printers "talk" to my computer— and why do I care?

ANSWER: Most laser printers communicate with your computer in what's called *PCL*: Printer Control Language, developed by Hewlett-Packard (H-P). (A printer that emulates an H-P printer uses PCL.) You can probably guess why the Windows laser printer driver is named "HPPCL."

A PCL printer can print characters in either portrait or landscape orientation, and lets you put bitmapped graphics anywhere on a page. PCL printers have internal fonts—often a mix of fixed-size bitmapped fonts and scalable outline fonts.

The second category of laser printers is called *PostScript*. PostScript printers include built-in scalable fonts (usually 35 or more) that can be printed at any angle on the page (not just portrait or landscape). Pages with complex text and graphics often print best on a PostScript printer.

You can buy a PostScript version of the H-P LaserJet 4; it costs several hundred dollars more than the PCL model. You can also buy plug-in cartridges to add PostScript capability to other laser printer makes and models.

An H-P LaserJet 4 has two new features that will probably be included in many printers. First is a language called *HP-GL*: H-P Graphics Language. That extends PCL to print lines and basic graphic shapes quicker and with better quality. Second is a built-in TrueType font rasterizer. Instead of Windows creating TrueType fonts' images, it's done in the printer for faster results.

QUESTION: How do I install my new laser printer?

ANSWER: Use the checklist I started this chapter with. If you've already done the connections part, go to steps 6 and 7 to learn how to install and connect a driver for the printer.

One small hint: take another look at Figure 7.4. You'll see a checkbox labeled, Use Print Manager. That enables what used to be called a "spooler": a program that takes your print job from the application that created it and passes it to the printer. That releases the application to do something else before the printing is complete. Problem is, the application sends the print job to the Print Manager, which then must send it to the printer. For many printers, it actually can take twice as long to print. I suggest you don't check this box, and leave the Print Manager disabled.

QUESTION: How do (non-PostScript) laser printers provide fonts—and why do I care?

ANSWER: You get fonts from six possible sources: internal bitmapped fonts (in fixed sizes), internal scalable fonts, plug-in cartridge fonts, downloaded soft fonts (bitmapped fixed size), downloaded scalable fonts, and finally, downloaded bitmaps (graphics). Note that internal fonts are also called resident fonts, for obvious reasons.

You care because each font source has various tradeoffs. I've summarized them in very general terms in Table 7.1.

Table 7.1   Font sources for laser printers.

Font Type	Source	Sizes	Advantages	Disadvantages	Screen Fonts
Internal bitmapped	Printer	Few	Fast printing	Few font or size choices, some only portrait orientation	Loaded in computer separately
Internal scalable	Printer	All	Fast printing	Few font choices	Loaded in computer separately
Cartridge	Printer cartridge	Some	Fast printing, no printer memory use	Reduced font choices, cost	Loaded in computer separately
Soft fonts	Computer	Some	Low cost	Storage space, download time, printer memory	Loaded in computer separately
Scalable fonts	Printer or computer	All	All sizes, many fonts, any orientation	Download time, printer memory, cost	Created in computer automatically
Graphics	Computer	All	All sizes, any orientation	Page creation time, printer memory	Created in computer automatically

QUESTION: How do I use the internal bitmapped fonts if there are any?

ANSWER: When you select the printer in Windows, the printer driver "knows" those fonts exist. You'll see them appear in the application's font lists. Windows also displays screen fonts that are similar to the printed ones.

A DOS application also will have a printer driver that "knows" about the built-in fonts in the same way.

QUESTION: How do I use soft fonts or font cartridges?

ANSWER: Let's use the H-P LaserJet 4 as an example. Figure 7.8 shows the Control Panel dialog box that appears after you select the **Printers** icon and choose **S**etup. To make Windows aware that you've installed a font cartridge, just select it in the list of Cartridges near the bottom. That makes the selection of fonts and available sizes for that cartridge appear in every application using the printer. The printer driver makes matching screen fonts (of the proper size and spacing) available at the same time.

Figure 7.8

Control Panel Setup dialog box for Printers.

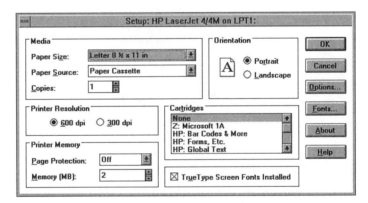

If you're installing soft fonts, certain scalable typefaces, or support for font cartridges that weren't listed, go one step further. Click on the **F**onts button shown in Figure 7.8, and you'll get the Font Installer box shown in Figure 7.9. Then click on **A**dd Fonts, and insert the diskette with the fonts or support files when prompted by the Add Fonts dialog box.

The Font Installer works with the printer driver. When you use one of the soft fonts, the driver sends them to the printer (and sometimes sends matching fonts to the screen) automatically.

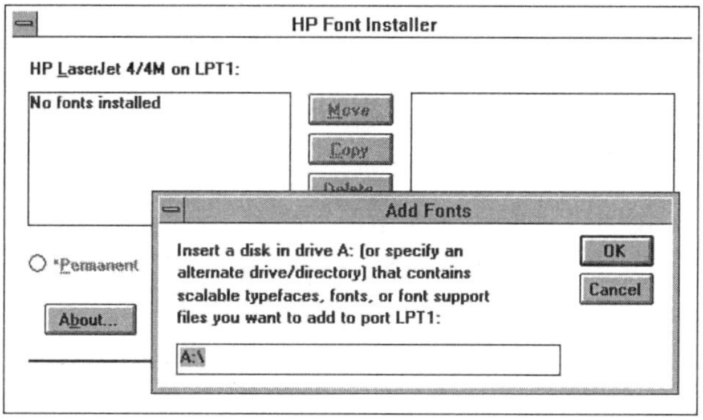

Figure 7.9

Printer Font Installer dialog box.

You can download fonts to the printer on a *permanent* or *temporary* basis. A permanent font stays in the printer's memory until you shut it off or reset it. It must be downloaded before it can be used. A temporary font is downloaded just before a print job that uses it, and is deleted from the printer's memory as soon as the job is done. You can choose how you want to download each soft font in the printer driver.

If you're using a DOS application, the application itself (or an add-on program) must download soft fonts to the printer as needed. (Soft fonts are usually provided in a very limited range of sizes.) H-P provides a program with its soft fonts to download them to the printer before running a print job. Read the H-P literature to find out more about that.

QUESTION: How do I use the printer's internal scalable fonts?

ANSWER: The H-P LaserJet 4 (for example) has 45 built-in scalable fonts—35 in the Agfa Intellifont format, and 10 in TrueType format. These scalable fonts are much more convenient than the bitmapped fonts of some other models, because they give you any size you need.

CAUTION

Be sure the printer is turned off before plugging in or removing a font cartridge. That prevents damage or printer errors.

Many other laser printers don't have built-in scalable fonts, and this section won't apply to them.

When you install the Windows printer driver for the H-P LaserJet 4 printer, all applications are informed immediately about all the built-in scalable fonts. But there are some catches!

Take a quick look back at Figure 7.8; notice (at the bottom right) a check box that says, "TrueType Screen Fonts Installed." Let's assume, for the moment, that it isn't checked (the fonts aren't installed). In that case, the Windows font list in an application will list each of the scalable fonts with a "W1" after it. (The W1 means a font has the character set used by Windows Version 3.1.) If you use one of these, Windows will substitute a screen font that is as close as it can find to the printer font.

There's no guarantee of a good match between screen and printer, but the page will print with the font you selected.

If you install the TrueType "screen fonts" and check the TrueType Screen Fonts Installed box, the fonts with the "W1" tags disappear. When you select the TrueType fonts equivalent to those built into the printer, Windows will display the TrueType font. For the ten built-in TrueType fonts, Windows will tell the printer to use them to create the page, and won't download them. You'll get faster printing that way.

H-P makes the so-called TrueType screen fonts available to LaserJet 4 owners on a diskette. (It may be shipped with the printer.) These are actually regular TrueType fonts you could use with any printer. For the LaserJet 4, they're used only for screen display for the ten built-in TrueType fonts, and are downloaded to substitute for the 35 Intellifont fonts. To install them, you open the **Control Panel**, select the **Fonts** icon, and choose the **A**dd button, as I described in Chapter 5.

(If you want the printer to use the internal Intellifont fonts, you could install Intellifont for Windows, a font rasterizer available from H-P. But it probably won't make a big speed difference.)

If you're using a DOS application with a printer that has scalable fonts, its printer driver must know what fonts are provided, and the width of each character. Typically, DOS applications don't show matching screen fonts.

QUESTION: What are graphics fonts, and why are they used?

ANSWER: Anything that isn't built into the printer has to come from the computer. Some applications can create a page with text in many orientations, sometimes combined with special effects and graphic images (art). If the application and the printer driver can determine that the exact font is available in the printer, the printer can create the characters itself.

But if not, the computer must send a bitmap of the entire page—bit by bit, including the fonts—to the printer. This is the usual case with Windows and TrueType or Type 1 (ATM) fonts, because most printers don't have these scalable fonts built in. (The LaserJet 4 handles TrueType fonts differently; see the later question that addresses this.)

In other words, graphics fonts are not "graphic" per se, but are actually any scalable fonts the computer sends to the printer in graphic form. Printing time is slower than for built-in fonts because of the download time.

PROBLEM: I have a complex printing job with graphics or lots of fonts on each page. The printer gives me an error or "locks up" when I try to print. What can I do about it?

SOLUTION: Because the printer needs enough internal memory to store an entire page, you may have problems printing a page with lots of type or graphics. Either only part of the page will print, or you'll get an error on the printer's display that indicates a memory "overflow" error.

You have four choices: switch your font selections to ones built into the printer (not always what you want), print less on the page (not a great idea either), add more printer memory (costs money), or reduce the resolution of your print job.

Take a look back at Figure 7.8. You'll notice a Printer Resolution choice of **6**00 or **3**00 dpi—the number of dots per inch. Most laser printers only have 300 as a maximum resolution, and the driver offers 150 and 75 as well. If you can't print a complex page because you're out of printer memory, you can set the resolution to 150 or 75. The image will be coarser (you'll be able to see the dots more easily).

If you need good quality printing of complex pages, the only real solution is to add printer memory. The LaserJet 4 has 2 megabytes (MB) of memory standard; many have as little as 512 kilobytes (KB), or 0.5 MB. Check your printer documents to find out how to add memory.

A complex print job on a 300-dpi resolution printer typically requires 2 to 4 MB of memory. The LaserJet 4 can hold as much as 32 MB (if you choose to add it)!

QUESTION: How does the LaserJet 4 handle TrueType fonts?

ANSWER: Because the LaserJet 4 has a built-in TrueType rasterizer, it creates bitmaps for these fonts internally. When you use a TrueType font, Windows downloads an *outline* form of the font to the printer. That means quicker printing for any TrueType font, not just the built-in ones.

QUESTION: What's the best way to buy fonts—on a cartridge, or on diskette?

ANSWER: If the font you want isn't built into your printer, you have to supply it. When you plug in a cartridge, you make fonts directly available to the printer. That means very fast printing speed. That's a fine solution if you're willing to spend the money, and you can find a cartridge with the right fonts and the right sizes.

On the other hand, a huge variety of scalable fonts is available on diskette at reasonable prices. You install the fonts you need on the computer hard disk, and delete them if you're through with them.

Some newer font cartridges are available with a surprisingly large number of fonts—some even scalable. One kind of cartridge lets you download fonts to it from the computer.

QUESTION: I want to use Type 1 fonts with my laser printer. How can I do that?

ANSWER: For a regular (PCL) laser printer, install a Type 1 font rasterizer. For Windows, you'd use the Adobe Type Manager (ATM). There are DOS products that allow you to use Type 1 fonts. I'll discuss them in Chapter 6.

QUESTION: If I buy a PostScript-compatible printer (or plug in a PostScript cartridge), what are the advantages over a regular (PCL) printer? Disadvantages?

ANSWER: Two major advantages. First, your printer can accept downloaded Type 1 fonts in outline form. Then any print job can use them in any position on the page, and in any size. Second, PostScript printers can generally produce better-looking and more complex print jobs. (That advantage is being eroded by more sophisticated PCL printers such as the LaserJet 4.)

The main disadvantage is cost. Not only does the printer itself cost more, but you'll need more printer memory to hold the complex image created. There are different "flavors" or versions of PostScript; make sure you use the proper driver for your printer.

If you plug in a cartridge to convert your PCL printer to PostScript, you'll also need more memory—lots more in some cases. Check that out before you commit to a cartridge purchase. Also, a cartridge conversion is usually much slower than a similar printer with built-in PostScript.

Working with Ink- and Paintjet Printers
You might consider these the "poor person's laser printers." They offer the same kind of resolution (300 dots per inch

or dpi), and are small and quiet. Some models offer color printing at a very reasonable cost.

I'll use the new Hewlett-Packard DeskJet 550C as my example printer. Excellent inkjet-type printers are also available from Canon and other manufacturers.

One feature sets the 550C apart: it has both a black and a color ink cartridge. You get the best of both: color or solid black on the same page. Other printers are black or color only. (Black images on most color inkjet printers are simulated with a mixture of colors, resulting in a muddy, dirty-colored "black.")

QUESTION: How do I install my new inkjet printer?

ANSWER: Use the checklist starting at the beginning of this chapter. (To install just the Windows driver, skip to step 6). But before you do, read the next paragraph.

H-P provides a setup program on diskette with the 550C for Windows called HPSETUP; it installs H-P's printer driver and three included scalable fonts. (A booklet with the printer explains how to run this program.) You then use the Windows Control Panel Printers **S**etup to select options, install fonts, and create bitmapped screen fonts.

When you choose the **Printers** icon from the **Control Panel** and click on **A**dd>>, you'll see a dialog box as in Figure 7.10. Select your printer model from the list, or install a new driver (as I described earlier).

Figure 7.10

Control Panel Printers selection dialog box.

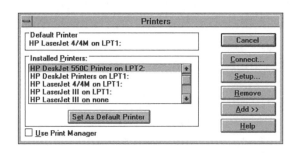

An inkjet printer may have several other options. Figure 7.11 shows those for the 550C. There are intensity, dithering, ink, and color printing controls. The only one relevant to font printing is the **I**ntensity control; set it for the clearest characters and good contrast without making the background dark.

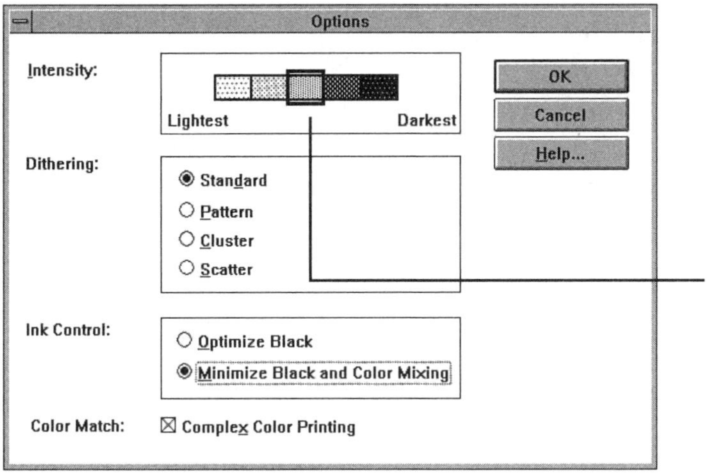

Figure 7.11

H-P 550C Windows driver options.

Adjust this setting to control the quality of the fonts printed with an inkjet or paintjet printer.

DOS applications probably won't even have a printer driver for a newer color printer like the 550C. It's worth asking your application vendor if they can supply one. If not, you'll probably have to use a driver for an older or less fancy printer, such as the DeskJet 500 or 500C.

QUESTION: What do I need to know most about inkjet printer cartridges?

ANSWER: An ink cartridge is really both an ink reservoir and a "squirt gun" used to create an image. It's a precision device (even though it's disposable). If it's stored at the wrong temperature or is too old, it may not work right.

To install one, you take it from a sealed storage container and clip it into the printer. The printer has a built-in cleaner to keep the cartridge from clogging up, and a storage position to keep the ink from drying out. Be sure not to shut off the printer before the cartridge is "parked" for storage. Follow the manufacturer's recommendations about cartridge storage.

An earlier model H-P printer (the 500C) had an accessory case (called a "garage") to store open spare cartridges. If your printer has something like this, be sure to use it. Once a cartridge is clogged, it may be impossible to clean. (And they're not cheap!)

QUESTION: What do I need to know about paper?

ANSWER: Paper is more critical for an inkjet than for any other kind of printer. That's because ink tends to spread out. If you print a page on soft or textured paper, the ink tends to absorb or break up, giving the image a soft or rough look.

For the best-quality image, you must use special coated paper. It's expensive—but worth it for color images. The difference is really noticeable.

For ordinary correspondence, you can still use regular bond paper; its image is just not as crisp as a laser printer's would be.

If you're using the H-P version of the DeskJet Windows driver, Figure 7.12 shows you some of the setup choices. Most are obvious, but notice there's a **M**edia selection. That adjusts the printer for best ink flow for the paper you're using. It lists not only regular and coated paper, but also transparency media. You'll need to change this setting whenever you change media.

Figure 7.12

H-P 550C Windows driver setup.

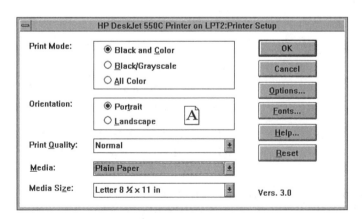

Drivers for DOS applications may not have as many controls for printer setup, but it's worth a look. Use whatever printer setup command it offers and check for media settings.

QUESTION: What kind of fonts does an inkjet printer use?

ANSWER: An inkjet printer is a graphics printer, much like a laser printer. For example, the DeskJet 550C contains seven internal bitmapped fonts in various sizes and orientations, and can use downloaded scalable fonts and plug-in font cartridges. Using a Windows printer driver, the 550C can access any font available to Windows applications, including TrueType and Type 1 (if you have ATM).

To install more printer fonts in Windows, use the installer that's part of the printer driver. Click on the **F**onts button shown in Figure 7.12. In the next dialog box, choose to install printer fonts. Then you'll see a dialog box as in Figure 7.13.

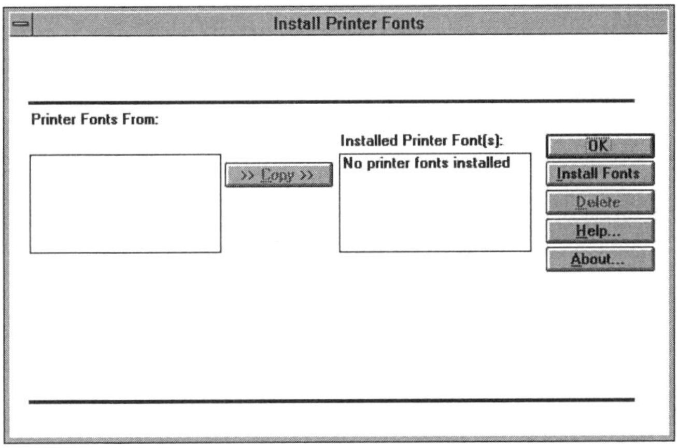

Figure 7.13

The Install Printer Fonts dialog box.

Hang in there—now it gets a bit tricky!

H-P's driver for Windows doesn't support cartridge soft or internal fonts. If you want to use them, you must install an inkjet driver supplied by Microsoft with Windows. Then using the Control Panel Printers **S**etup, you can select internal fonts or tell the driver which cartridge is in use.

But the Microsoft Windows driver currently used for the 550C is actually for the DeskJet 500 model, which doesn't support internal or cartridge landscape-oriented fonts. And it doesn't support any of the 550C's color options.

To recap, if you want color, use H-P's Windows driver; you can use the scalable fonts provided, but not the internal or cartridge ones. If you don't want color but *do* want to use the internal fonts, use the Microsoft Windows driver. Either way, you can use any of the TrueType or other scalable fonts provided by Windows for all printers. Simple or what?

If you use downloaded soft fonts, you may need extra printer memory to use several fonts at once. H-P's DeskJet 550C lets you plug a memory cartridge into its "font cartridge" slot. Other model printers may also have memory expansion options; read your user's guide to find out.

DOS applications vary widely on installing fonts. Look back at Chapter 6 for an explanation of fonts in several popular applications. It's possible that one of the add-on programs that provide Type 1 or TrueType font support will serve your needs.

One way to select a font when using a DOS application is from the printer's control panel. For the 550C and many similar printers, you can select internal or cartridge fonts in portrait or landscape orientation.

Working with Dot-matrix Printers
It's difficult to make general comments about dot-matrix printers because there are so many different kinds. Some have multiple built-in fonts, others accept downloaded soft or scalable fonts.

I'll use a very common and popular printer—the Panasonic KX-P1124—as my example.

QUESTION: How do I install my new dot-matrix printer?

ANSWER: Use the checklist at the beginning of this chapter. (To install the Windows driver, go to step 6.)

QUESTION: What choices do I have when I install a dot-matrix printer?

ANSWER: When you install the Windows driver for your Panasonic 1124 printer, you can open the **Control Panel**, choose the **Printers** icon, and choose your printer. Then when you choose the **Setup** button and select **O**ptions, the dialog box shown in Figure 7.14 appears. You get intensity, print quality, and dithering controls.

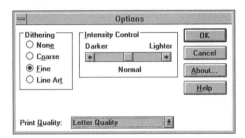

Figure 7.14

Panasonic 1124 Windows Driver Options.

The intensity control sets the force at which the dot pins strike the ribbon to make an image. For a new ribbon, you'll get the best fonts with this control set to **Lighter**. As the ribbon wears, move the slider progressively toward **Darker**.

The higher the print quality, the slower the printing. That's because the printer has to make multiple passes across the paper to create the more complex image required for higher-quality text or graphics. (Dithering affects only graphics images, and not text.)

QUESTION: What kinds of font choices do I get with a dot-matrix printer?

ANSWER: It depends considerably on the printer. For example, the Panasonic 1124 has several built-in bitmapped fonts in various sizes. Some printers may let you download soft fonts (often available only from the manufacturer). Others may have font cartridge slots. Older printers may have only one simple built-in font— usually something like Courier.

When you install the Windows driver for the 1124, its built-in fonts are available to every application.

Nearly all modern dot-matrix printers can operate in graphics mode. While in that mode, a printer accepts codes from the computer containing patterns of dots exactly the way they are to be put on the page. It's up to the computer to figure out the patterns that comprise characters or pictures.

Using the printer's graphics mode and its built-in font manager, Windows lets you use TrueType fonts; even this relatively simple Panasonic printer can print any of those fonts you have available. With ATM or another add-on font manager, you can use other font formats as well. Windows prepares a bitmap of the page (including all type and graphics) and then downloads it line-by-line to the printer as a graphic image.

Other printers may have more complex controls, and even a font installer such as the one for the H-P inkjet printer. Some dot-matrix printers support color, downloaded soft, and even scalable fonts. In these cases, the printer may have special fonts available from the vendor. It may also be able to accept memory expansion to hold extra fonts.

DOS applications aren't usually as capable. They let you choose internal and cartridge printer fonts. Add-on font products I discuss in Chapter 6 will allow some applications to use Type 1 and TrueType fonts for dot-matrix printers, using their graphics mode.

Looking Back and Looking Ahead
In this chapter, I've given you some ideas about printers that may help you get the best font printing results. There are tips

for both Windows and DOS users. Using my detailed trouble-shooting checklist, you may be able to bring a non-performing printer back to life.

In the next chapter, we'll approach the thorny issue of sharing text—and fonts—between different applications and different computers. I'll also discuss the role commercial printers and service bureaus can play.

Exchanging Documents

There is only one sure way to get your document to the reader the way you intended: make a photocopy of it and hand it to them; all else is conditional. Document exchange is complex and fraught with difficulties.

But there's a great need. Let's say you work on a document on your home computer, put it on a floppy, and bring it to the office to finish. Or you want a service bureau to create your presentation transparencies. Or you get a document from a Macintosh and want to use it on your IBM-compatible PC.

A service bureau (at least for desktop publishing) is somebody who takes over where your resources leave off. At minimum, it might be the local PC store that lets you use their laser printer. Or, it might be the local print shop that has PC's with desktop-publishing software where you can finish your document layout. More likely, it's an outfit that runs your document through a typesetter to produce a publishing-quality page; it may print the document as well. Or, it could be a shop that takes your graphics or presentation files and produces overheads or slides.

Service bureaus are often national operations; you send your file via telephone modem to their office, and they ship back the processed images. (Have your credit card ready!)

Or—the possibilities are almost endless.

For your document to remain the same when you move it to another computer, all these items have to match:

- the set of characters (including any special ones)
- the character design (styles, weight and hinting)
- widths of all characters
- character spacing (including kerning)
- line spacing
- the page layout (including graphics or other objects)

Not only are these elements necessary for correct printing, you'd probably want the displayed documents to agree as well.

(You can probably understand why large companies try to enforce consistency by insisting that everybody use the same word-processor applications and computers. They don't want to deal with these issues.)

Now I'll explore how your documents can keep their integrity in an imperfect world. I'll start with simple concepts, and work toward complex situations.

Exchanging Documents between Different Computers Running the Same Word Processor

PROBLEM: I use Word for Windows both at home and at work. When I copy my documents on a floppy and bring them into the office, they don't display the same. I want them to. (I'm using TrueType fonts.)

SOLUTION #1: Make sure you're using the same version of Word for Windows in both places. There's some difference in formatting abilities between version 1 and version 2.

If you must use two different versions of WinWord, you can use Version 2 to convert a version 1 file to a version 2 file. That occurs automatically whenever you open a document file (although you're asked if you want to make the conversion). (But you can't use version 1 to convert a version 2 file back again.)

Are you using the same version of Windows? (If you're trying to use TrueType under version 3.0, you're out of luck: that version didn't even accept TrueType). Upgrade to Windows 3.1.

To check your current version of Windows, use the Help About Program Manager command in the Program Manager (or the Help About File Manager in the File Manager). Either one shows you the version number.

SOLUTION #2: Be sure you've selected the same printer for printing on both computers. If someone creates a text file using a particular font, and later you open the file with a different printer selected, a font could be listed that was available to the original printer, but not to the current one.

If a specified font is not available, Windows substitutes the closest match it can find from the other fonts it has. Also, if you select a style that's not available in the font you're using, Windows constructs one. To construct italic, it tilts the characters; for bold, it makes all the character lines thicker. These made-up characters are not as good as ones designed as part of the font, but they work.

PROBLEM: I use Word for Windows both at home and at work. When I copy my documents on a floppy and bring them into the office, they don't print the same. I want them to. (I'm using TrueType fonts.)

SOLUTION #1: Are you using the same (and latest) printer drivers in both places? Some early versions either didn't use TrueType or didn't handle them correctly. Printer drivers have a revision number that you can read by clicking on the Control Panel Printers icon and selecting Setup About. You'll see a dialog box with the number.

Another way to check is to use the Windows File Manager to view the printer driver file date code. If it's an old date, an upgrade may be available. It may be a bit difficult to identify the driver file for your printer. They are all in the \WINDOWS\SYSTEM directory, with the extension DRV (for driver). As an example, the H-P DeskJet driver is called HPDSKJET.DRV and the H-P LaserJet driver is HPPCL.DRV (or something similar).

Windows uses a library file of universal printer functions called UNIDRV.DLL that many printer drivers rely on. If you install the latest version, it will probably improve printing speed for most laser printers. (An update for this file is included in Microsoft's H-P Font Set and is automatically installed with the fonts. It's also included with laser printer driver updates from Microsoft.)

To get the latest Windows printer drivers, contact Microsoft customer service. If you have a very new printer, or one with unusual features, you might do better calling your printer vendor. Check the printer manufacturer's forum on CompuServe; that's often the first place a new driver appears.

SOLUTION #2: Are you using the *same* TrueType font at both sites? Different vendors make fonts that have almost the same names, but aren't exact duplicates—especially popular styles like Century Schoolbook and Times Roman. If you're using TrueType fonts, the display and printed page should match. But it's sometimes hard to spot subtle differences in line length or kerning.

The only way to assure you're using the same TrueType fonts is to verify that the font files are identical. They're usually in the

CAUTION

To install new printer drivers, always use the Windows Control Panel, and don't simply copy files to directories. (Installation involves more than simple file transfer.) Click on the Printers icon then select your printer from the list. Click on the Remove button to remove the old driver, then the Add>> button to install the new one. (You'll be prompted to insert a diskette with the driver.)

\WINDOWS\SYSTEM directory, with the extension TTF. Using the Windows File Manager, you could verify that the files have the same date and size in each PC. For example the Arial TrueType font is ARIAL.TTF, bold is ARIALBD.TTF, italic is ARIALI.TTF, bold-italic is ARIALBI.TTF; for Times New Roman, it's TIMES.TTF, and so on.

SOLUTION #3: Word for Windows doesn't automatically change the font name it finds in a file. That means the font name you see on the toolbar may not be available in your PC. If it isn't, it won't appear in the font list when you scroll through it. (A true case of "now you see it, now you don't.") If you're using only one font and want to change it to one you have, use Edit Select All to select all text. (Or, use Control 5— hold the Control key down and press the number 5 in the numeric keypad.) Then choose the new font from the toolbar or using Format Character.

SOLUTION #4: Windows matches the fonts in the document with those on your PC that have exactly the same names. If the fonts in both places are TrueType fonts, it's easy. But if you *don't* have the matching TrueType font—and you *do* have a soft font with the same name—you'll get that soft font.

If you want Windows to make another substitution, you may be able to use your printer driver's font installer to change the name. For example, a font installer is built into H-P printer drivers. Figure 8.1 shows what you get when you choose the **Printers** icon from the **Control Panel** program group, choose the Setup button, and choose Fonts. If any fonts were available, you'd click on the Edit button to make font substitutions.

CAUTION

Don't attempt to remove a TrueType font by deleting its TTF file. For one thing, there's a second information file for each font with an FOT extension; for another, the Fonts manager applet needs to be informed which fonts are active. It makes entries in the WIN.INI file to keep track. Use the Control Panel Fonts control to add or remove fonts.

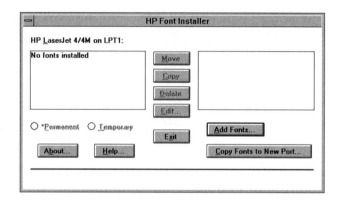

Figure 8.1

*The H-P Font Installer
dialog box.*

SOLUTION #5: You can also edit the font names that are
embedded in font files to control substitutions. Read
Chapter 9 for some advanced font editing applications
that let you do that.

SOLUTION #6: Lacking an exact font match, Windows
checks a section in the WIN.INI file called
[FontSubstitutes] to find a substitute font. (Windows
surrounds a section title with square brackets, as I've
shown here.)

The Windows 3.1 WIN.INI substitution section starts out
looking like this:

    [FontSubstitutes]
    Helv=MS Sans Serif
    Tms Rmn=MS Serif
    Times=Times New Roman
    Helvetica=Arial

For example, if your document file uses a font called
Helvetica, Windows will display it using the available
TrueType font named Arial. That's true *only* if Helvetica isn't
available. Using the Windows Notepad, you can add to this
list.

(If Windows can't find a substitute specified, it tries to find
the closest match according to an internal priority list of

attributes it keeps for all fonts. Read your *Windows User's Guide* for more details.)

Printing a Document on a Different Printer

PROBLEM: I'm using TrueType fonts when I'm on the road using a portable dot-matrix printer; at the office I have a fancy PostScript-compatible laser printer. I can't get the same printed results.

SOLUTION: You can use TrueType on both your dot-matrix and your PostScript printers (and on almost any other Windows-supported printer). TrueType is device-independent; that means it should print much the same on every device. That should give you matching fonts and a similar page layout.

You must set up your laser printer driver correctly to get the results you want. Figure 8.2 shows an example setup for an H-P PostScript laser printer. You get it by selecting the **Printers** icon from **Control Panel**, clicking the Options button, then choosing **Advanced**.

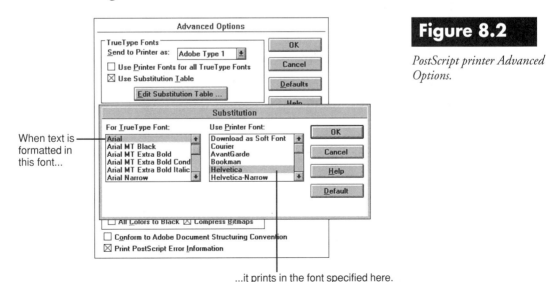

Figure 8.2

PostScript printer Advanced Options.

When text is formatted in this font...

...it prints in the font specified here.

TrueType fonts are usually downloaded to a PostScript-compatible printer just as though they were Type 1 fonts. And TrueType fonts that are much like Type 1 designs often have similar character spacing; that was part of the plan. That makes for a good match on the printed page.

Look at the top portion of Figure 8.2. Don't check the box Use **P**rinter Fonts for all TrueType Fonts; if you do, only the printer's internal Type 1 fonts will be used. Also, don't check the box Use Substitution **T**able unless you want to use a mixture of fonts, such as TrueType and internal ones.

Don't forget to include the template file associated with your document file, to assure layout and font style consistency between sites. For example, template files for WinWord have the extension DOT, and are often in a separate directory from documents. To find the template associated with an open document, used the command File Summary Info Statistics. The dialog box will show the template's complete file name and path, as well as a lot of other info about your document.

Printing the Same Document on Two Different Printers

PROBLEM: I'm using Type 1 fonts with Adobe Type Manager *and* some TrueType fonts when I'm on the road; at the office I use only a PostScript-compatible laser printer. How do I get consistent printed results?

Figure 8.2 also shows the Substitution dialog box that appears when you click on Edit Substitution Table. Use this dialog box to select how you want the Windows PostScript printer driver to treat each one of your TrueType fonts. You'll probably want to download them as soft fonts (the first choice in the list). That way, TrueType prints as TrueType, Type 1 as Type 1. In the highlighted example, whenever the TrueType font Arial appears in a document, the internal Type 1 printer font Helvetica will be substituted.

When you check Use Substitution Table in the **Advanced Options** dialog box, the font substitutions you specify in the Substitution dialog box take effect.

Again, don't forget to include the associated template file when you copy the document file, to assure layout and font style consistency.

Printing a File from Two Different Word Processors

PROBLEM: I use Word for Windows (or another Windows word processor), but I have an associate who uses Word for DOS (or another DOS word processor). What do I do with the files I get from that source?

SOLUTION #1: Choose File Open and then List Files of Type to select the incoming file extension. (You may have to use a file-importing command in your application). Figure 8.3 shows the Word for Windows Open dialog box, with **All Files** (*.*) selected, and files with any extension will be displayed in the file list at left.

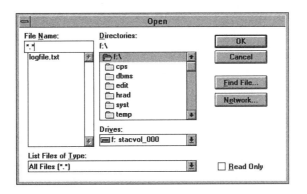

Figure 8.3

The Word for Windows dialog box for opening files.

When you select a file and click on **OK** (or double-click on the file name), and Word for Windows doesn't recognize it as its own document file type, it displays the Convert File box, shown in Figure 8.4. Word for Windows analyzes the document file, and usually proposes the most appropriate conversion. If you know the right one, select it from the list yourself. (Your word processor may handle this a little differently.)

Figure 8.4

The Word for Windows Convert File dialog box.

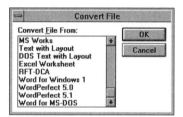

NOTE

If Word for DOS (or whatever word processor your associate uses) isn't listed, you may not have installed the related converter when you installed Word for Windows or your Windows word processor. To install a converter, you'll need to see your documentation.

Font references in one word-processor document format are usually passed along to the other format when the file is converted.

SOLUTION #2: Templates and style sheets help you maintain layout consistency. When transferring files with colleagues, include the template file or style sheet file associated with your document, so the file converter translates your templates and styles with the document.

PROBLEM: I want to send my Word for Windows files (or files from another Windows word processor) to a friend who uses WordPerfect for DOS (or another DOS word processor). What's the approach?

SOLUTION: Use a converter to save instead of open your file. Figure 8.5 shows Word for Windows' File Save As dialog box. (Again, if the word processor you want isn't shown, install it. Some software companies provide a few seldom-used converters by mail-order request. They are also available on the CompuServe Information Service.)

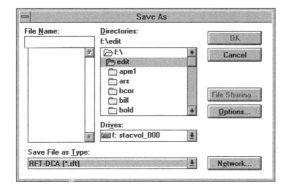

Figure 8.5

The Word for Windows Save As dialog box.

If no converter is available, you can save the document in a universal exchange format such as the RFT/DCA shown in the figure. Most word processors can open such a file, and extract text and most formatting.

PROBLEM: I want to exchange documents with someone who has a word processor I never heard of before. It doesn't accept a universal file format, and there is definitely no converter available from the company that publishes my word processor. Am I left without a solution?

SOLUTION: 'Course not. Several file conversion utility programs are available from other vendors. Software Bridge, for example, is a popular DOS application from Systems Compatibility Corp. that converts between dozens of word processor types. (It also handles databases and spreadsheets.) Even if there's no support for a word processor, you may be able to exchange a formatted text file using what's called "smart ASCII."

Such a product can be a lifesaver when you need to resurrect documents for reuse, and they're stored in an obsolete or arcane format. Software Bridge also handles documents to and from the Macintosh platform, as well as font mapping for various formats.

When all else fails, you can probably exchange files in ASCII format. These documents consist of nothing but standard codes for characters and line-endings (like a typewriter "return" key). Except for line-endings, there are no formats of any kinds—and no font references either. Almost every word processor can accept such a file.

If you're curious, ASCII stands for American Standard Code for Information Interchange. Another code type you might see is ANSI, or American National Standards Institute. That's an extended variant of ASCII.

In WinWord, for example, you can save an ASCII file by using the command File Save **As** or Save File as **T**ype, and select Text only or Text only w/line breaks from the list.

As an absolute last resort, you can select a very simple printer in your word-processor and then "print" to a file. (In Windows, for example, this kind of printer is called Generic/ Text Only.) The resulting file will consist of ASCII characters and line-endings. Unfortunately, it will have a line-ending at the end of each displayed line instead of just one at the end of each paragraph. That means the text won't "wrap" to fill a paragraph in the destination word processor unless you delete all the extra line-endings.

PROBLEM: Using Word for Windows, I have converted between word-processing files, but some of the characters aren't right. What's going on, and how can I correct it?

SOLUTION: In some cases, it's possible to specify both character and font substitutions for converted files. For Word for Windows, a file called CONVINFO.DOC explains how to do this; you'll find it in the WinWord program directory. (This information is not in any printed documents.)

You may find small errors in character conversion—especially with special extended characters. The DOS, Macintosh, and Windows platforms use slightly different character sets.

Preparing Files for a Service Bureau

Most electronic typesetting from PC-based documents is done using PostScript. Service bureaus commonly use a Macintosh for final review, and a Linotronic typesetter that "prints" directly to film negatives. IBM-compatible PCs are relatively rare in publishing, as is TrueType. But both are quickly becoming more popular.

PROBLEM: I have a friend (or am using a service bureau) that uses a Macintosh with System 7 operating system and Microsoft Word 5.0. I want to send some documents on diskette for review. Is there a way?

SOLUTION: Assuming you're using Word for Windows, select File Save As from the menu, and then Save File as Type to choose Word 5.0 for the Macintosh. (Your diskette file will now be in Macintosh document format, but still in DOS file format.)

Other word processors will often have similar translations available but may not save as much formatting information as the Word-to-Word transfer.

To accept your DOS diskette, your friend's Mac must have a SuperDrive diskette drive—standard on recent models. It will also need Apple File Exchange (included in recent operating systems) or another program such as DOS Mounter (by Dyna Communications). They allow the Mac to read the DOS diskette and put it in an acceptable format. Then Word for the Mac can access it as a document file.

Because your friend uses System 7 (the first Mac operating system to support TrueType), you may be able to specify the same TrueType fonts on both platforms. If necessary, agree on a font substitution and change your document's fonts to be in agreement before translation.

To be compatible with Type 1 fonts used on a Mac with System 6 or earlier, you can switch to Type 1 for your document. Or, find a TrueType font with a style and name similar to the Type 1 font; you may find it to be a very close match.

PROBLEM: I've created a document that I want published. I want the document to look the same as displayed and as printed on my laser printer. What's the best approach?

SOLUTION #1: Call your service bureau contact to find out what kind of word processing or page layout program documents they can output. Convert your document to that format. If the service bureau doesn't use a format you can convert to, you could save your document in a universal exchange format such as ASCII, DCA/RFT, or RTF.

Because service bureaus commonly use Word for the Mac, you could convert to Word for DOS. Using a file exchange utility, the service bureau can convert the diskette and then Word for the Mac will accept the Word for DOS format. Most other Mac word processors will accept one of the universal formats. (Some formatting may be lost or distorted.)

Make sure the service bureau has the same fonts you're using. Use Type 1 (you can also specify TrueType if the Mac is running System 7). Otherwise, the fonts may not look like the ones you used.

SOLUTION #2: You can do a direct PostScript transfer—*if* you don't expect the service bureau to do any viewing or editing. With this method, your document is converted to a "snapshot" of itself in the PostScript page description language; because PostScript provides an absolutely standard translation, it doesn't matter what fonts and formatting you start out with. This technique should enable the service bureau to output an exact duplicate of your file.

In Windows, use the Windows **Control Panel** and select the **Printers** icon to display the dialog box shown in Figure 8.6. Install the driver for the Linotronic model your service bureau uses—even if you don't own one.

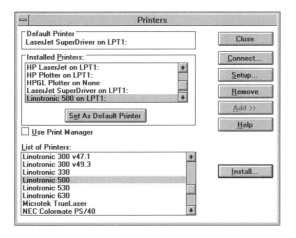

Figure 8.6

Control Panel's Printers dialog box for PostScript printers.

Click on **Connect** to specify the output to be a file instead of a printer port, as Figure 8.7 shows. Select **OK**. You can use the Setup button to change page orientation.

In your Windows application, use the File Print Setup (or equivalent) command to choose the printer you just installed for your document. Then, when you print your document, Windows asks you to specify a file name. Type in a name, then choose **OK**. The service bureau should be able to print your file with no problem.

Your application may offer an alternative method of printing to a PostScript (.EPS) file. See the documents for the program.

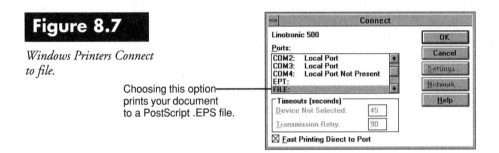

Figure 8.7

Windows Printers Connect to file.

Choosing this option prints your document to a PostScript .EPS file.

If you specify one of the standard 35 fonts available in most PostScript printers, you'll probably get an excellent match on the Linotronic. If not, you need to be sure the service bureau has exactly the same Type 1 font you used. (Products like Ares FontHopper, described in Chapter 9, can do font conversions across platforms. But it may be a violation of your license to supply a converted font to your bureau—*even* if it's only used to print your job.)

If you normally use a PostScript printer, your application may provide an easier way to print to an .EPS file. See your documentation.

PROBLEM: I "printed" my document to a file, but the file is so large it won't fit on a diskette. How can I manage this problem?

SOLUTION #1: PostScript files can be very large. You will probably need to "print" large documents as many files (perhaps a chapter each). Break your document into smaller pieces using your application, then print each to a PostScript file.

SOLUTION #2: Request a single PostScript "header" file for your entire document. In Windows, open the **Control Panel** and select the **Printers** icon. Select your service bureau's PostScript "printer" (for example, the Linotronic) and click on the Setup button, then the **O**ptions button to display the Options box (as in Figure 8.8). Make sure you've selected to send the document to an Encapsulated PostScript File, entered a **N**ame, and unselected Send Header with Each Job. Now, click on the Advanced box, select File, and enter a name for your header file. Finally, click on **S**end Now to create the header file. Click on all the Cancel buttons until you're out of the Control Panel applet.

> *Ordinarily, every PostScript document sent to a printer has a header section that describes fonts in use and other setup information. For a single document, the header is the same for every file. To reduce the size of the files, you can put the header in a single file of its own.*

Include this header file with the document files when you send them to the service bureau. Be sure the **Options** box called **Send Header with Each Job** is not selected; otherwise you'll defeat the purpose. (This solution saves file space because only one header file is created for your entire job, instead of one for each file.)

Figure 8.8

Use this dialog box to create a PostScript header file.

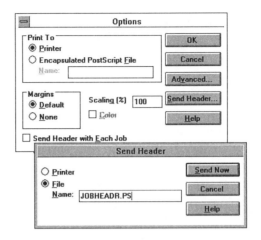

PROBLEM: I'm about to prepare a Windows document for the service bureau by printing it to an EPS file, but I've decided at the last minute to use the fonts available in the Linotronic to substitute for some TrueType fonts in my document. Where can I make the substitutions?

SOLUTION: Before you print to the disk file, go to the **Sub-stitution** dialog box shown in Figure 8.2 (which you reach by choosing the **Printers** icon from **Control Panel**, choosing **Options**, choosing **Advanced**, turning on the Use Substitution **T**able check box, and finally choosing Edit Substitution Table). Substitute the fonts you want. You don't have to substitute every TrueType font.

One other option is shown at the bottom of Figure 8.2: Conform to Adobe Document Structuring Convention. You might want to check this to ensure the document settings are in a standard PostScript format. That might make the document more compatible with some service bureau equipment. (It also prevents your control over some advanced options.)

PROBLEM: I have made a presentation using PowerPoint, and I want to put a show together using 35mm slides (or overhead transparencies). How do I get them?

SOLUTION #1: Make the overheads yourself. If you have a color inkjet printer, such as H-P's DeskJet 550C, you can print color transparencies using special plastic film sheets. The special media available from H-P is quite expensive; you'll want to make a test print on paper first.

If you don't have the media, you can take your paper prints to a copy center for duplication on a color copier loaded with transparency film. Call around first to make sure they have the film. Expect to pay several dollars for each copy!

I have also made slides myself, using a 35mm camera pointed at a video display. With a little care, the results can be quite good. I suggest you use a flat-screen monitor, if available. Avoid motion and vibration for both the monitor and camera—use a good tripod.

Put the monitor in a dim room and set contrast and brightness slightly lower than you'd use for viewing. Be careful to avoid reflections from room lighting. I like to use a "long" lens—90 to 150mm—to reduce the effects of display curvature and focusing errors. Use an exposure of *no shorter* than 1/4-second; that's to avoid variations in screen brightness. You'll want to use a shutter-release cable on your camera. You should use "slow" film, say 64 speed, for the best image quality and to keep the lens aperture in mid-range. Have fun!

SOLUTION #2: Send your file to a service bureau and let them make the slides or transparencies. You can ship your files on a diskette, but for faster service, most bureaus accept them on-line via modem. They may also offer special communications programs to automate the process.

Microsoft provides a special "printer" driver with PowerPoint that you can use to create graphics files for Genigraphics—a national imaging service. You install the driver in Windows and simply "print" your presentation to a file. Using a specialized communications program, you can send files to a regional service center for quick reproduction. An enclosed booklet gives you directions.

Other agencies can also give you slides, transparencies, prints, and flip charts in a hurry. AutoGraphix is one that offers support for leading graphics applications, and there are several other companies. You'll find addresses for AutoGraphix and Genigraphics in the Appendix.

SOLUTION #3: Put your show on electronically. For a small group, you can display an animated presentation on your computer's monitor. For larger crowds, use a projection TV connected to a special video adapter in your PC.

You can also buy an LCD (Liquid Crystal Display) projection panel that sits on an overhead projector and connects to your PC using an adapter. Acting as an electronic transparency, it generates either monochrome or color images. (Color panels are very pricey—and allow some very effective displays!)

Looking Back and Looking Ahead

In this chapter, I've given you solutions to some of the dilemmas involving word processors, documents, changing fonts, and printer interchange. I've also hinted at some other combinations, but there are too many to cover completely.

In the next chapter, I'll explore some solutions that can help you meet your needs for fonts nobody's even discovered yet.

Making a Good Font Even Better

As the song goes, you can't always get what you want. It's as true with fonts as with many other important life issues. How hard do you have to try to get what you need? That's the answer I'll try to give you.

One part of the "it exists" font dilemma is that too many may exist on your system to keep track of them easily. You may need a better way to manage fonts.

You may have bought a font in TrueType, Speedo, Intellifont, or one of several other formats. But it's not compatible with your current environment, and you want to convert it to another format. Or you may have a font you once used on your Macintosh computer, and now want to move it to your IBM-compatible PC.

Even with literally thousands of fonts available, perhaps you have needs that can only be met with a custom set of characters. You might want a set of graphics symbols, or you might even want to convert your own handwriting to a font set!

I'll explore some of the solutions to these special needs here.

Organizing Fonts

There was a time when you only had a handful of fonts: a serif, a sans-serif, a script and perhaps a symbol font. But now you have dozens or even hundreds! Every time you open a Windows text application, you spend the first five minutes scrolling through the font list to find what you need. There must be a remedy.

(Sorry, you DOS users—there aren't any neatly packaged font organizing solutions for you.)

QUESTION #1: Is it possible to have too many fonts?

QUESTION #2: My large fonts list slows down my Windows applications.

QUESTION #3: I'd like to organize my fonts in handy "volumes" or groups. Each group might contain the cluster of fonts I use for a particular job. Or it might contain a certain kind of font—for instance, all my Arial or all my sans-serif designs. How can I do that?

ANSWER: Glad you asked. If you have so many fonts you're confused about when to use them—or can't even remember what they're called—that's too many to be useful. Now if you could only cluster them into easy-to-remember groups that you could associate with an application or job....

At least two or three products are available to add this feature to Windows. One is a new release from Microsoft called the Font Assistant; it's included with their new H-P/TrueType Font Pack. As you'd expect, it works only with TrueType fonts.

Figure 9.1 shows the main window for Font Assistant. It contains three lists: Font **Group(s)**, Fonts in Active Group(s), and Font Samples. In this case you're seeing font sample lines for the font group called "all fonts" (all the fonts on the PC). Font Assistant put this list together by scanning the WINDOWS/SYSTEM directory for all the FOT files related to each TrueType font.

To create a font group, click on the Create button, and you'll see a window (as Figure 9.2 shows). Select the fonts you want from the master list at left, and click on Add to Group; the fonts are added to the list at right. The descriptive name you give the group appears in the Font Group list (top left of Figure 9.1). Choose OK when you're done.

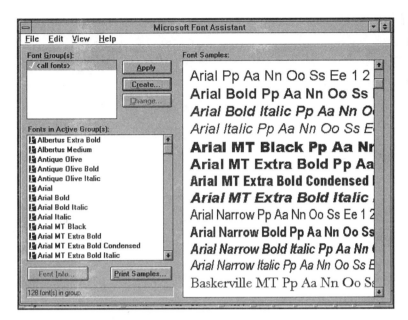

Figure 9.1

Microsoft Font Assistant and font samples.

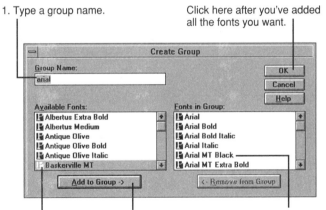

Figure 9.2

Font Assistant group creation.

Here's the real payoff of Font Assistant: decide which font groups you want to use currently and double-click on them in the Font **G**roup(s) list shown in Figure 9.1. A check mark then appears next to them, and *only* fonts in those groups will appear in text applications. Now, instead of a bewildering forest of fonts, you choose only the relevant ones.

Font Assistant also lets you install new fonts; it simply starts the Control Panel's Fonts applet for you.

Another font-cataloging product is FontMinder from ARES Software. Figure 9.3 shows its main window, including three lists similar to Font Assistant's. FontMinder calls its groups *Font Packs*. FontMinder asks you for the Directories to Search for font files, as Figure 9.4 shows. Because FontMinder handles both TrueType and Type 1 fonts, these files may be in several directories. (You can't combine TrueType and Type 1 fonts in the same Font Pack.)

Figure 9.3

ARES FontMinder.

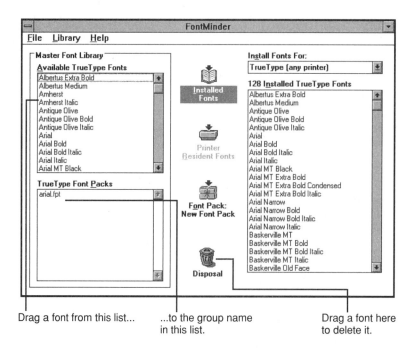

Drag a font from this list...   ...to the group name   Drag a font here
                                     in this list.   to delete it.

FontMinder provides a drag-and-drop display, so you can select fonts from the list using a mouse and simply drag them into the Font Pack list (see Figure 9.3). You can also delete fonts easily this way: just drag them to the disposal (waste can) icon. The can lid opens conveniently as you drag.

Learning About the Fonts on Your System

QUESTION: I want to display and print samples of my fonts so I know what I really have. What's the easiest way to do that?

ANSWER: If all you want is a quick look at a font, the Windows Fonts icon in the Control Panel will let you select one and see a few of its characters on-screen. (The characters are usually **AaBbCcXxYyZz** and maybe a digit or two.) You see only one size, and you can't print anything.

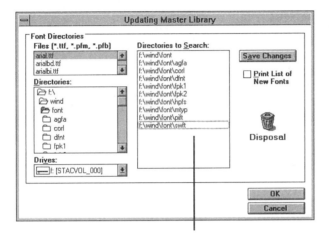

Figure 9.4

FontMinder font directory selection.

Searching for fonts in these directories

If you want more (and who wouldn't?), you can use Font Assistant (an application I just described). Figure 9.5 shows a sample for one selected font; in this case, Arial. (Font Assistant uses a font description system called PANOSE; fonts that have that description have a decorated "P" to the left of their names.) Click on the **P**rint Samples button, and you'll get a printed set of font characters as they appear. You can also get a printed list of a few characters of multiple fonts.

FontMinder doesn't give you font sample printouts, but it does print lists of available fonts—in Courier, of course.

QUESTION: Can I find out more about a font—such as its name, and where it's stored in my PC?

ANSWER: If it's a TrueType font, it usually has two files: one with a TTF extension and another with an FOT extension (created by the Windows Font installer). The FOT files are always in the WINDOWS\SYSTEM directory.

Figure 9.5

Font Assistant single font sample.

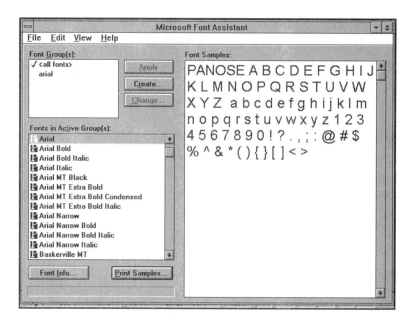

You want more? Microsoft's Font Assistant maintains a third small file in the WINDOWS\SYSTEM directory for each TrueType font, called a FIF (Font Information File). Figure 9.6 shows what Font Assistant knows about Arial, for example. It shows not only where it's stored and what size the TTF file is, but also any embedding and copyright notices. There's also a line listing typefaces you might use as alternatives to this one.

Figure 9.6

Font Assistant font information.

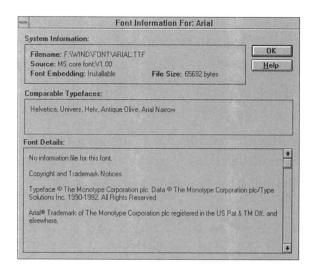

FontMinder also gives you a little font information, as you see in Figure 9.7.

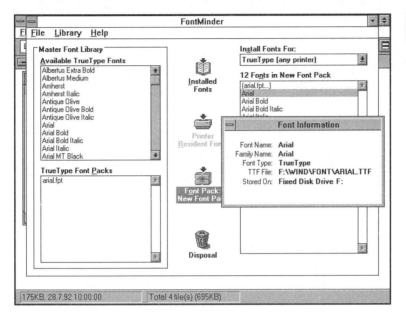

Figure 9.7

FontMinder font information

Creating Font Special Effects

What's a *special effect*? It's anything we do to a character beyond changing its spacing, size, or style (bold, italic and so on). Use your imagination!

QUESTION: I don't need much: just a bold headline on a contrasting background with a shadow for 3-D effect. What's the fastest way?

ANSWER: If you're using Word for Windows, don't forget the MS WordArt applet, available through the Insert **O**bject command. You'll find it on similar menus within Excel and PowerPoint. With WordArt, you can do all you asked for, and also curve headlines up or down or bend them in a semicircle. Its major limitation is its headline fonts; you can use only the lackluster nineteen it provides.

QUESTION: I want to make a line of type fit a shape; for example, I might create an outline of an airplane or car, and put its name inside the outline. Is there a simple package that can do that?

ANSWER: Adobe TypeAlign, available in DOS and Windows versions, makes type fit any curve or shape. It adjusts the characters automatically to fill the space.

QUESTION: How about a full-featured font manipulation utility that gives me full artistic license? I want to distort character shapes, add patterns, fit curves—the works!

ANSWER: If you want more than WordArt and TypeAlign give you (and you're using Windows), you'll need an add-on application such as Bitstream's MakeUp. Figure 9.8 shows a small example of its many features. I selected a TrueType font (named "Stop"), typed in the phrase, selected shadows and patterns, and then dragged the entire line into the distorted shape I wanted.

Figure 9.8

Bitstream MakeUp line editing.

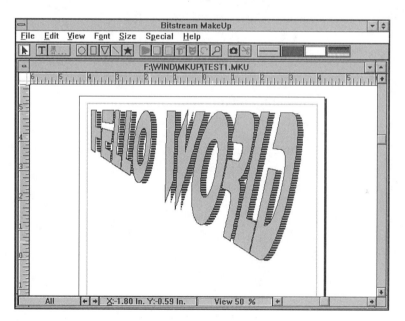

QUESTION: I don't want to simply distort a line of text, I also want to modify the shapes of characters. What's the method?

ANSWER: Let's take *MAKEUP* one step further. Figure 9.9 shows the feature you need. I've selected the "D" and displayed it as an editable outline (using **Edit B**reak Text and **Edit E**dit Object). You can see where I've dragged the Bézier curve control points to modify the original shape—just as I did using Arts & Letters in the Chapter 5 example.

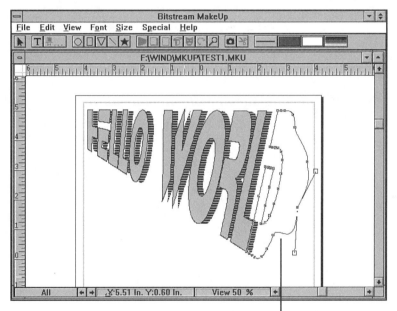

Dragging points to modify a letter

Figure 9.9

MakeUp character editing.

You can edit the Bézier curve outlines of either a character or the envelope (the outline for the entire line of characters). You can use color or gray-scale palettes for lines and fills. TrueType, Type 1 and Bitstream Speedo format fonts are all available.

MakeUp version 1.1 can be an OLE (Object Linking and Embedding) server; you can embed its graphics in most Windows applications. It imports and exports a variety of either bitmapped or vector-based graphics or backgrounds, including its own clip art.

QUESTION: I don't have MakeUp, but I still want to use some font special effects. Any options?

ANSWER: Do you have any of the graphics programs I discussed in Chapter 5? Each of them lets you edit fonts graphically. CorelDRAW! has some very advanced character-editing features that even let you create your own font (if you have a serious amount of patience)!

Converting Font Formats

CAUTION

Don't expect perfection from a converted font. There are at least two reasons. First, the system used to define the outline shapes differs between TrueType and Type 1; there's no direct translation. Second, the method for defining hinting is also different, and doesn't translate easily either. On the other hand, you should expect the character spacing ("metrics") to be faithfully copied.

QUESTION: So you have this huge library of Type 1 fonts, but you don't want to install Adobe Type Manager (ATM), and you'd prefer to have only TrueType?

ANSWER: A simple and direct way to translate Type 1 to TrueType—or TrueType fonts from the Macintosh platform to the IBM-PC compatible world—is with ARES Corporation's new FontHopper. It's an inexpensive application with a single purpose: cross-platform font conversions.

Take a look at Figure 9.10. It's from another ARES product: FontMonger, a popular Windows font-conversion application. Both letter "d's" are Garamond bold-italic; the left one is from a TrueType font (from Microsoft's HP Font Set), the right one is from the Type 1 font generated by FontMonger. Not bad, eh?

You can also use this application to rename fonts and change style settings so they appear in font lists the way you want. If you do, you'll lose all hinting. New hinting is automatically created for any new or modified font; the original hinting is ignored. See the program documentation for details about using FontMonger.

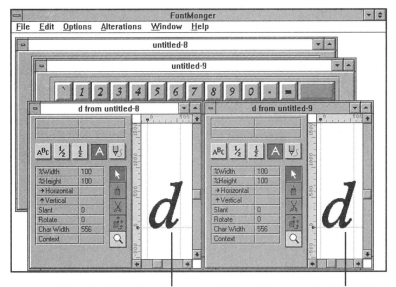

Figure 9.10

ARES FontMonger font conversion.

The original TrueType font   A Type 1 font converted to TrueType

FontMonger accepts and generates several font formats, including TrueType and Type 1 for either the IBM-compatible PC or Macintosh. But that's not all; I'll visit FontMonger again when I discuss creating and editing fonts.

One or two other products are also marketed for font conversion; this is a growing market.

Creating and Editing Fonts

So nothing suits you—not one of the thousands of available fonts? Are *you* hard to please!

Or perhaps you have a creative soul waiting to express yourself on type design (and you have the patience of a saint—you'll need it!), or you may want to store an image or symbol as a font character. Perhaps you want to create an original banner for a newsletter or a product logotype. You're a candidate for a *font editor* application.

QUESTION: How can I edit some characters in a font I own to "fine-tune" or personalize them?

ANSWER: Figure 9.11 shows a selected letter from a font displayed in outline form with Bézier control points. This is FontMonger in its editing mode. You can modify any aspect of the shape. You can also apply slant, rotation and scaling effects. If you want to personalize from the ground up, you can create a completely new font, character by character—using scanned or bitmapped images (or an existing font) as your template, or simply hand-drawing.

Figure 9.11

FontMonger character editing.

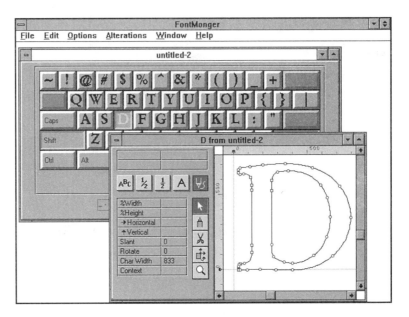

QUESTION: How can I "mix-and-match" characters from two different fonts? (I have a font used commonly for text and another that has some special symbols I'd like to also include without pasting special symbols.)

ANSWER: In Figure 9.10, you saw that FontMonger could have more than one font file open at once. In that case, you can easily copy a character from one font and paste it into an unused character position in another one.

QUESTION: I want to make a unique font consisting of my own handwriting. When I type a document, it will be just as though I wrote it, but much more consistent. How do I create this masterpiece?

ANSWER: You need an industrial-strength typeface design application. First, produce a legible example of both the upper case and lower case of each character (difficult enough if you have my handwriting). Next, scan each one into a separate bitmapped file (with a BMP extension). Now you're ready for Altsys Fontographer—a Windows application for font creation and editing.

Begin by selecting **File New Font.** Figure 9.12 shows the dialog box I've filled out for my new font. Notice I've selected script type and italic style (consistent with a handwriting font), and added my own notice in the box at the bottom.

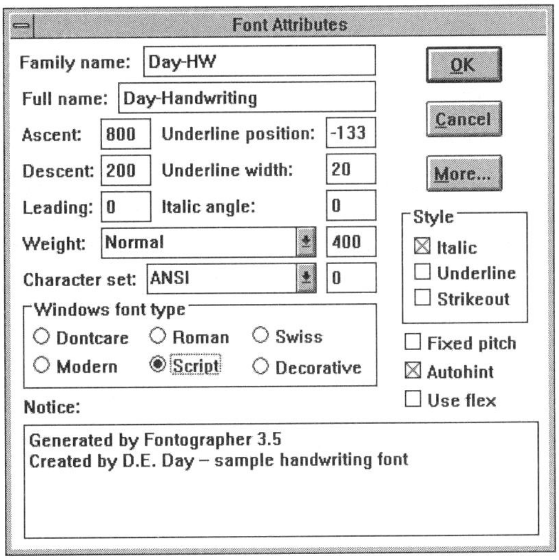

Figure 9.12

ARES Fontographer new font setup.

A window will open with boxes for every possible character. Click on one of them; I'll use the lowercase "d" for my example. Now, choose the menu item **File Import** and select the BMP file you created for that letter. Select the BMP file from the directory that contains your "d". Finally, select the **Path Trace Background** command. Figure 9.13 shows the result.

Figure 9.13

FontMonger character with autotrace.

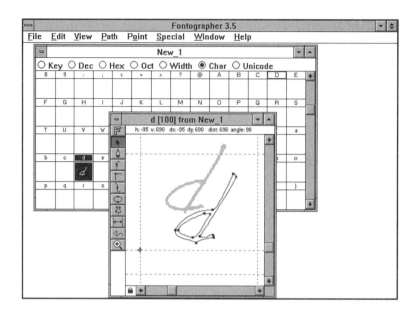

This figure shows two images (which I've offset from each other for clarity). The gray image is the background bitmap from the file I scanned in previously. The outline (with its control points) was created by Fontographer's *autotrace* function. Now you're ready for the "cleanup" stage. You'll want to adjust some lines because autotrace isn't perfect, and because handwriting isn't either. Then, add some leading and trailing extension lines so this letter will connect exactly with all the others. And it's done.

Won't this be fun to do for every letter?

CorelDRAW! has similar features for editing and creating fonts (as I described briefly in Chapter 5). It's harder to use, but if you already have this application, give it a try.

QUESTION: The handwriting example sounds interesting, but I have a more practical business application: I want to include a logo as a symbol in a commonly-used font. Where do I begin?

ANSWER: Use Fontographer as you did for the handwriting example. The difference is, you'll choose the command File Open Font this time. Open your text font;

Fontographer accepts either Type 1 or TrueType format. Choose an unused character position, and import the BMP file created from a scan of your logo. Do an autotrace, a cleanup, and save the font; now the character is just a keystroke away.

CAUTION

Save any font you modify under a new name, simply to preserve the original font without changes.

QUESTION: Can I use Fontographer to adjust attributes of my regular fonts?

ANSWER: Sure, but it's too expensive to buy for just that use alone. Figure 9.14 shows the Font Attributes dialog box for an Agfa Garamond font (which is open on the window in the background). You can change any item and then save the font. Notice that **Autohint...** is turned on; Fontographer will create hinting to replace the font's original hinting.

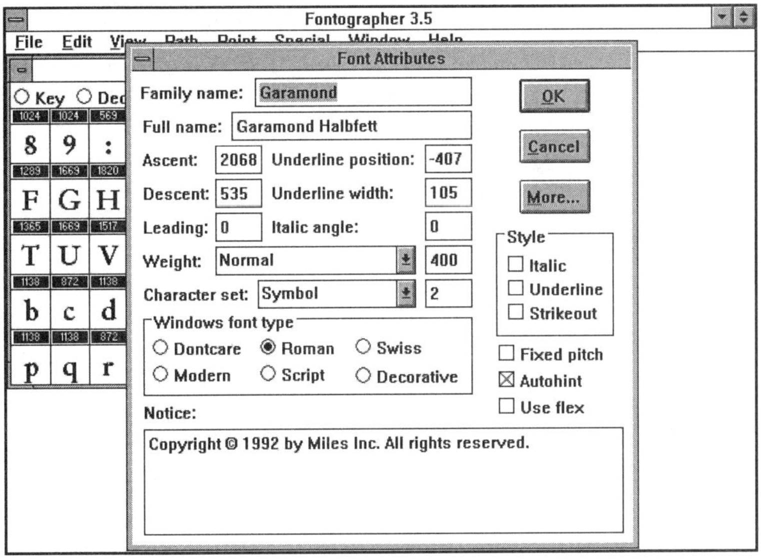

Figure 9.14

Use Fontographer to modify font attributes.

To simply change some font attributes, you might do better with one of several widely available shareware packages. For example, there's a freeware product called RenameTT that allows you to change the name of any TrueType font. It's a DOS-based application written by Rufus Hendon; I got my copy from CompuServe.(There's also a similar Windows-based application that he sells.)

Legal Aspects of Using Fonts

Now, a look at an often-ignored aspect of font use. Way back in Chapter 1, I described the enormous amount of work involved in creating a quality font. It involves inspiration and a sense of esthetics, design skill, a knowledge of printing and computer technology, and (probably most of all) persistence and patience. You might reasonably expect that a type design would be fully protected by law.

You might be wrong!

> *Please understand that I'm not offering legal advice; I'm trying to make you aware of the issues. If you'd like to know more, you might want to contact a group whose charter is to explain ethical use of software and police offenders:*
> *Software Publishers Association*
> *1101 Connecticut Avenue NW—Suite 901*
> *Washington, DC 20036*

For example, someone could print a copy of each character in a licensed font, and then scan the copies into a font-generation program. Perhaps they would make a few cursory editing changes. They could then produce and sell a new font file that would look almost exactly like the source. (It would be missing the original hinting and kerning values.) That might be legal to do, because a type *design* is not protected.

Here's a case where what may be legal isn't always ethical. Regardless of the law, it doesn't seem proper to me for anyone to make a copy of someone else's work and profit by it. It's the *reselling* that's the problem—not modifying a font you own for your own use.

It is possible for a manufacturer to patent a font design, but it's expensive and not often done. The *name* of a font is often copyrighted. When a vendor releases a font that is close in design to one already known, they will often give it a name that is very close to the original, but not exactly the same. That implies the similarity without violating the copyright.

What is clearly protected by law is the computer file that contains or *embodies* a font. For example, if you make a copy of your font diskettes and give or sell the copy to someone else, that's illegal. But it gets stickier than that. Read the fine print of the license that came with your fonts. You'll discover that you don't "own" the fonts in any way; by paying for them, you've only obtained a license to *use* them.

What use have you been licensed for? That depends. You can use the fonts to make as many documents on your printer as you like, and to publish the documents as well. (In other words, you can produce character images in any way you like—and for any purpose.

Some licenses allow you to use a font on one computer, and on any number of printers attached to it. Others let you use one high-quality and one low-quality printer—or even only one printer. You may have other restrictions.

You can make a backup copy of your font file, but only to protect you from file loss or damage, not to give to someone else.

What if you have a font in one format, and use a program to convert it to another format? It's probably OK to use one *or* the other format; but it's definitely **not** OK to use both at the same time (on two PCs). You've been licensed only for the use of one "instance" of a font. In other words, the converted file retains all the legal limitations of its source.

If you want to use the same font in several PCs in your office, you could buy several copies, of course. But you may also be able to buy a *site license*, which authorizes multiple copies of the same font. This is also what you might need if you have a network of computers sharing fonts.

What if you want your work printed by a service bureau because it has high-quality typesetting machines—but they don't have the fonts you've used? You could send them a laser-printed document for reproduction, but that would defeat the whole purpose. You could also send them a file containing graphics (bitmaps) for each page, but the file could be enormous and slow to image. The bureau could buy the fonts for your single printing job—a nuisance and possibly a big expense. You could send copies of your font files with the document itself—but that violates nearly every font license. Should you do it?

This may be a case of what's ethical isn't always legal: your intent is simply a reasonable use of a font to produce your printing job. (If the service bureau later used your font to typeset jobs from other clients, that would be *both* unethical *and* illegal.)

It's clear that fonts can be—and often are—copied illegally. What should discourage you from joining the throng? I suggest two reasons: quality and cost. If people avoid paying for fonts, that reduces the incentive to develop quality fonts; that hurts everybody. And frankly, the cost of a good font is far lower than it was even a year ago; it may not be worth the risk, even when the chance of getting caught is small.

My Font Is Buried in the Document
One recent technical enhancement really muddies the waters: font *embedding*. Some TrueType fonts are now permitted to be copied from your PC into a document file that uses them. When you give the document to someone else, they can display and print it using the embedded font. For the first time,

the font—with all its impact on meaning and all its artistic and decorative effects—can be as portable as your document file. This provides true consistency among users because your reader can now experience the effect of type style with your message.

If a font is allowed to be embedded in a document, the font vendor can no longer expect to license it for only a single PC. Wherever any copy of that document goes, so goes the font. Since an embedded font is stored in the document, it's very likely someone could extract it and use it for other documents. That's probably illegal, but I don't think it's even become an issue yet. It will.

Looking Back (and Still Looking Ahead)

In ways, this was the most enjoyable chapter to indulge in. It presented the "leading edge" of font applications. These are the tools that allow you artistic freedom and better control over the art form that is typography.

There's a lot of room for improvement. You'll see better applications that are easier to use which do more and tell you more. They'll be here soon, because for the first time, fonts are Big Business. With the blooming of TrueType, it's a growing market—and an intensely competitive one.

I hope I've helped you overcome some of the tricky aspects of using fonts. I also hope you have some fun.

Just ahead, you'll find a glossary of some terms I've used in the book and a listing of some of the many product vendors and manufacturers related to the font industry.

If you have any thoughts or comments about any of this material, I'd be glad to hear from you. Write me at the address shown on the diskette offer in the back of the book. Or contact me on CompuServe; my number is 76234,3233.

Font Product Suppliers

This is a list of the many vendors who provide fonts or related programs and equipment. You'll find the contact information for each, and a brief description of some of their most interesting products. I have discussed many of these products in more detail elsewhere in this book. Those I've talked about are marked with an asterisk (*).

This is *not* a complete listing of all vendors, and does not show all products (or all features) of the products listed. (That would be a book by itself!)

A product-to-manufacturer cross-reference follows the listing of manufacturers and their products.

Manufacturer and Product List

ATI Technologies, Inc.
3761 Victoria Park Avenue
Scarborough, Ontario, CN M1W 3S2
416/756-0718

* Graphics UltraPro: high-performance video board; multiple emulation modes; optimized for Windows; includes Crystal Font technology for high-quality font display.

Adobe Systems Inc.
1585 Charleston Road
P.O. Box 7900
Mountain View CA 94039
800/833-6687

* Adobe Type Manager (ATM): Type 1 font rasterizer program for Windows; includes 23 basic Type 1 fonts matching those in PostScript printers.

Super ATM: Type 1 font rasterizer program for Windows, with automatic font substitution; replaces fonts in document not available on system with alternates; allows display, editing, and printing; retains original font references; uses "Multi-Master" font technology; announced but not shipped for Windows.

* TypeAlign: Special-effects program for Type 1 fonts in Windows; selectable kerning, distortion and rotation; fits line of type to any curve or shape; produces EPS- or AI-format files for export; requires ATM.

* Adobe Type Library: Over 1,600 high-quality fonts in Type 1 format; many original designs; includes international, ornaments, and symbols; some sold as font sets.

Type Sets packages: Coordinated groups of Type 1 fonts selected for various applications; letters, spreadsheets, overheads, newsletters, invitations; includes ATM.

Type Set Value Pack: Thirty assorted Type 1 fonts; text, ornamental and symbol fonts; ATM included.

Plus Pack: Twenty-two popular Type 1 text fonts; matches fonts in PostScript printers (added to ATM fonts comprises complete basic printer set).

Type On Call: CD-ROM type library with most of Adobe Type Library of Type 1 fonts; fonts are locked—purchase unlocking codes by telephone using credit card; immediate access to any font needed.

PostScript and type cartridges: Plug-in cartridges for H-P LaserJet Series II printers; adds PostScript language capability or fonts.

Agfa Division, Miles Inc.
200 Ballardvale Street
Wilmington, MA 01887
800/424-8937
508/658-5600

> Agfa Type Library: Hundreds of fonts in TrueType and
> Intellifont format (used by Hewlett-Packard in some
> printers).
>
> Desktop Styles: Collection of 39 popular TrueType fonts;
> matches Intellifont fonts and metrics used in H-P LaserJet
> III printers.
>
> Discovery TrueType Pack: Text, headline and extensive
> "clip-art" (symbol) TrueType fonts; 46 fonts, including
> 1,000 clip-art images; eight font application document
> templates for word processors.

Aldus Corp.
411 First Avenue South
Seattle, WA 98104

> * PageMaker for Windows: Sophisticated desktop publish-
>   ing program for Windows; page creation and layout using
>   "pasteboard" metaphor; integrated basic word processor;
>   wide variety of font and type controls; position, size, and
>   display graphics; handles any mix of text and graphics on
>   page; handles color graphics and spot-color (process color
>   separations via add-on software); optimum for design-
>   intensive documents such as brochures; also handles long
>   documents.
>
> Freehand for Windows: Drawing program.
>
> Persuasion for Windows: Presentation management
> program.

AltSys Corp.
269 Renner Road
Richardson, TX 75080
214/680-2060

* Fontographer for Windows: Font creation and editing program for Windows; produces Type 1, TrueType, and bitmap fonts, as well as EPS graphics files; allows editing character outlines as Bézier curves; allows setting or importing metrics; imports bitmaps for editing or autotracing as outline; generates hints automatically; modifies font attributes. (This product was available originally only for Macintosh.)

(Note: AltSys designed and wrote Aldus FreeHand.)

Ares Software Corp.
P.O. Box 4667
Foster City, CA 94404
800/783-2737

* FontMinder: Font organizing and management program for Windows; handles both TrueType and Type 1 fonts; drag-and-drop interface; enables user to install and de-install fonts, create font packs (fonts grouped by use or type), manage multiple Type 1 printer sets, and print sorted listings of available fonts.

* FontMonger: Font converter and editor program for Windows; converts between Type 1, Intellifont, and TrueType formats (among others); generates automatic hinting; enables user to edit character outlines as Bézier curves, relocate and merge characters between fonts, and export characters as graphics.

* FontHopper: Font translation program; translates fonts between Macintosh and IBM-PC platforms; TrueType and Type 1 formats.

Autographix Overnight Slide Service
63 Third Avenue
Burlington, MA 01803
800/548-8558

> Imaging services for slides, transparencies, prints, posters, and flip-charts.

Bitstream Inc.
215 First Street
Cambridge, MA 02142
800/522-3668

* FaceLift for Windows: Font rasterizer for Windows; handles both Type 1 and Speedo formats (replaces ATM; required for Speedo fonts); allows font customizing and special effects (outlines, fills and shadows); includes 16 popular fonts in Type 1 and Speedo formats.

* FaceLift for WordPerfect: Font rasterizer for WordPerfect word-processor; similar functions to FaceLift for Windows (above); includes same 16 fonts.

* MakeUp: Creates font special effects for Windows; creates graphic from line of text; allows flipping, stretching, and rotating of text; enables user to fit text to shape or curve, or inside shape; shadow, 3-D, perspective, and other effects; color or gray-scale in solids and washes; allows blending between graphics and text, importing and exporting to many graphic file formats, and auto-sizing in document; OLE server; includes 5 typefaces in Type 1, Speedo, and TrueType formats; over 200 clip-art images.

* Bitstream Type Library: Over 1,000 quality fonts in Type 1, Speedo, and TrueType formats.

  L'il Bits: Informal TrueType font collections for Windows; includes Flintstones, Star Trek, and Winter Holiday; text and decorative characters and symbols.

Casady & Greene
22734 Portola Drive
Salinas, CA 93908
800/359-4920

> Fluent Laser Fonts (Libraries 1 and 2): Collections of text, display, and symbol fonts; both TrueType and Type 1 formats.

> Eastern European Library: Collection of 26 text and script fonts; support Albanian, Croatian, Czech, English, German, Hungarian, Polish, Romanian, Slovenian, and Slovak; both TrueType and Type 1 formats; over 500 kern pairs per font.

> Glasnost Cyrillic Library: Collection of 17 text and script fonts; support Russian, Byelorussian, Serbian, Ukrainian Bulgarian, Macedonian and English; over 500 kern pairs per font.

CompuServe Information Services
5000 Arlington Centre Blvd.
Columbus, OH 43220
800/848-8990

> On-line information service: includes forums for all major software and hardware vendors; direct manufacturer and customer service support; customer and user discussions; downloadable files of software upgrades, shareware and freeware programs.

Computer Support Corp.
15926 Midway Road
Dallas, TX 75244
214/661-8960

> * Arts & Letters: Full-featured graphics editor for Windows; Bézier-curve-based image editing; large clip-art library included.

Corel Corp.
1600 Carling Avenue
Ottawa, Ontario, CN K1Z 8R7
613/728-8200

   * CorelDRAW!: Renowned graphics editor for Windows;
     Bézier-curve-based image editing; very large clip-art
     library included; includes draw, chart, photo editing, and
     presentation applications; included CD-ROM version has
     250 TrueType and Type 1 fonts, and extended clip-art
     library.

Digital Typeface Corp. (DTC)
6900 Shady Oak Road
Eden Prairie, MN 55344
612/943-8920

     DTC Type Library: Hundreds of quality fonts in Type 1
     format; division of Lasermaster Corp.

FontBank Inc.
2620 Central Street
Evanston, IL 60201
708/328-7370

     Type Companion: Collection of 250 Type 1 display fonts;
     large, inexpensive set of quality headline fonts (sometimes
     usable as text fonts); wide variety of special-use faces;
     intended for Windows and ATM (required, not in-
     cluded); same set available in TrueType for Macintosh
     (should be available for Windows in the future).

FontHaus Inc.
15 Perry Avenue
Norwalk, CT 06850
800/942-9110

     FontHaus Type Library: Unique and original font designs
     from many sources; mostly Type 1 format; small (but
     growing) TrueType selection.

251

Frame Technology Corp.
1010 Rincon Circle
San Jose, CA 95131
408/433-3311

* FrameMaker for Windows: Composite word processor/
desktop publisher for Windows (also available for several
other platforms); full-featured word processor; advanced
page layout using frame metaphor; complete font and
type controls, formatting and kerning; templates for
characters, paragraphs, pages and complete documents;
graphics manipulation, position, and view; long document control, including multi-file documents; conditional
text document creation; hypertext document creation;
OLE client.

Genigraphics
Two Corporate Drive—Suite 340
Shelton, CT 06484
203/925-1921

Imaging services for slides and transparencies; multiple
regional service centers; on-line file transfer service with
available communications program.

Hewlett-Packard Co.
P.O. Box 15
Boise, ID 83707
208/323-2551

* LaserJet 4: High-performance laser printer; 600 dpi, 8
pages per minute with resolution enhancement (RET);
includes 10 TrueType and 45 Intellifont resident scalable
fonts.

LaserJet II, III: Laser printer; 300 dpi, 8 pages/min.

LaserJet IIp, IIIp: Laser printer; 300 dpi, 4 pages/min.

* DeskJet 550C: Low-cost, full-color ink-jet printer; 300 dpi resolution, simultaneous black and CMY color cartridge use.

DeskJet 500: Low-cost black-and-white ink-jet printer; 300 dpi resolution.

LaserTools
1250 45th Street
Emeryville, CA 94608
800/767-8004

* PrimeType for WordPerfect: Font rasterizer for Type 1 fonts in WordPerfect; supports both DOS and Windows versions (using included ATM); supports all WordPerfect-supported printers; includes 20 quality text, display, and symbol fonts in Type 1 format (uses any Type 1 font).

Logitech, Inc.
6505 Kaiser Drive
Fremont, CA 94555
800/231-7717

ScanMan 256: Hand scanner and software; max 256 gray scale, 400 dots per inch; graphics or line art scanning; maximum 4-inch scan width (extended with auto-stitch software); TWAIN-compatible driver; outputs bitmap files in several formats.

Lotus Development Corp.
55 Cambridge Parkway
Cambridge, MA 02142
617/577-8500

* Ami Pro: Respected word processor for Windows.

* 1-2-3 for DOS: Best-selling spreadsheet program for DOS.

* 1-2-3 for Windows: 3-D spreadsheet program for Windows.

Micrografx, Inc.
1303 Arapaho
Richardson, TX 75081
214/234-1769

* Designer Plus OLE: Comprehensive graphics editor for
  Windows; Bézier-based image editing; large high-quality
  clip-art library included; optimized for technical illustration; Windows OLE server.

* Draw Plus OLE: Graphics editor for Windows; inexpensive, full-featured; Bézier-based image editing; includes
  32 TrueType fonts, 18 Bitstream and Nimbus-Q fonts;
  includes clip-art library; Windows OLE server.

MicroLogic Software
1351 Ocean Avenue
Emeryville, CA 94608
415/652-5464

* TrueType for DOS: TrueType font rasterizer for DOS
  applications; can be used with WordPerfect, Word or
  Works for DOS; allows user to add patterns, outlines,
  shadows, and backgrounds to text; includes 36 TrueType
  text, decorative, and symbol fonts.

  MoreFonts for DOS: Type rasterizing and special-effects
  program; use with Type 1 fonts; can be used with
  WordPerfect and Word for DOS (also works with Windows applications); create outlines, patterns, shadows, and
  reverse type; includes 28 scalable text, display, and symbol
  typefaces; increases printing speed.

Microsoft Corporation
One Microsoft Way
Redmond, WA 98052
800/426-9400
206/882-8080

Windows: Graphical environment for PC platform; includes manager and rasterizer for TrueType fonts; includes "core" fonts from Monotype; requires DOS.

MS-DOS: Microsoft Disk Operating System; DOS for IBM-PC compatible personal computers; required for Windows.

* Excel: Highly-regarded spreadsheet program for Windows.

* PowerPoint: Competent presentation manager program for Windows.

* Publisher: Competent and economical desktop-publishing program for Windows.

* Word for Windows: Comprehensive word processor for Windows.

* Word for DOS: Comprehensive word processor for DOS.

TrueType Font Pack: Collection of 44 TrueType fonts; high-quality fonts from Bigelow & Holmes and Monotype; text, decorative, symbol, and icon fonts; extends Windows' basic font set.

TrueType Font Pack 2: A second collection of 44 TrueType fonts; quality text, headline, decorative, and symbol (icon) fonts; extends Windows font set; includes Font Assistant TrueType font manager; includes Flying Fonts screen saver.

Hewlett-Packard Font Set: Collection of 35 TrueType fonts; quality text and decorative fonts from Agfa; fonts match style and metrics of H-P LaserJet 4 fonts; includes upgraded Windows laser printer driver; includes Flying Fonts screen saver.

* Windows Printing System (WPS): TrueType font-rasterizer cartridge and program for Windows; add-on cartridge product for H-P LaserJet models; increases printing speed by rasterizing in printer.

Monotype Typography Inc.
53 West Jackson Blvd.—Suite 504
Chicago, IL 60604
800/666-6897
312/855-1440

> Monotype Type Library: Hundreds of high-quality fonts in Type 1 and TrueType formats; some sold as font sets.

> FoneFonts: Monotype type library on CD-ROM; hundreds of fonts in Type 1 format; fonts are locked—purchase unlocking codes by telephone, using credit card; immediate access to any font needed.

> Desktop Solutions: Selected typeface sets grouped for applications.

> TrueType Value Pack: Collection of 57 high-quality TrueType fonts; intended to extend Windows' "core" font set (duplicates most fonts in Microsoft TrueType Font Packs 1 and 2); text, display, script, and symbol fonts.

NISCA Inc.
1919 Old Denton Road—Suite 104
Carrollton, TX 75006
214/242-9696

> NISCAN Spectra: Full-color portable scanner; color, 256 gray shades, maximum resolution 400 dots per inch; photo images, graphics, or line-art scanning; eliminates image distortion from hand scanning; creates bitmapped files in several formats; requires Windows.

Software Publishers Association
1101 Connecticut Avenue NW—Suite 901
Washington, DC 20036

> Manufacturer's association charged with educating the public about ethical use of software products and policing offenders.

Software Publishing Corp.
3165 Kifer Road
Santa Clara, CA 95051
408/986-8000

  * Harvard Graphics for Windows: Presentation graphics
    program for Windows; text and charting tools; pre-
    designed styles; presentation show application; output to
    high-quality slide or overhead printers.

    Harvard Graphics for DOS: Presentation graphics pro-
    gram for DOS.

SWFTE International, Ltd.
Box 219
Rockland, DE 19732
800/237-9383

    TypeCase I and II: Collections of TrueType fonts; inex-
    pensive, wide variety; text, decorative, and symbol fonts;
    not all have kerning pairs.

    TypeCase TrueType Font Variety: Large collection of
    TrueType fonts on CD-ROM; includes all TypeCase I and
    II fonts; all fonts available (no unlocking needed).

Systems Compatibility Corp.
401 North Wabash—Suite 600
Chicago, IL 60611
312/329-0700

  * Software Bridge: File conversion program for DOS;
    converts between 58 formats for word processors,
    spreadsheets and databases; allows conversion between
    DOS and Macintosh formats.

Ventura Software Co.
9745 Business Park Avenue
San Diego, CA 92131
619/673-0172

Ventura Publisher: Comprehensive desktop publishing program for Windows; page creation and layout using "frame" metaphor; position, size, and display graphics; handles any mix of text and graphics on page; handles color graphics and spot-color (process color separations via add-on software); optimum for long documents such as textbooks; also handles short, design-intensive documents.

WordPerfect Corporation
288 West Center Street
Orem, UT 84057
801/227-4000

* WordPerfect for Windows: Word processor for Windows; extensive printer support.

* WordPerfect for DOS: Best-selling word processor for DOS; extensive printer support.

Zenographics
4 Executive Circle—Suite 200
Irvine, CA 92714
800/366-7494

* SuperPrint: Multi-format font rasterizer/printer driver set for Windows; handles Type 1, Speedo, Intellifont, and other font formats; enables user to build matching screen fonts in selected sizes; high-speed, accurate printing; includes laser, dot-matrix, and other printer drivers.

Z-Script: PostScript interpreter for SuperPrint; allows PostScript output to be printed on PCL-type printers; announced but not released.

Product Name Cross-Reference

1-2-3 for DOS	Lotus Development Corp.
1-2-3 for Windows	Lotus Development Corp.
Adobe Type Manager (ATM)	Adobe Systems Inc.
Ami Pro	Lotus Development Corp.
Arts & Letters	Computer Support Corp.
CorelDRAW!	Corel Corp.
Designer plus OLE	Micrografx Inc.
DeskJet 550C	Hewlett-Packard Co.
Desktop Solutions	Monotype Typography Inc.
Desktop Styles	Agfa Division, Miles Inc.
Discovery TrueType Pack	Agfa Division, Miles Inc.
Draw Plus OLE	Micrografx Inc.
Eastern European Library	Casady & Greene
Excel	Microsoft Corp.
FaceLift for Windows	Bitstream Inc.
FaceLift for WordPerfect	Bitstream Inc.
Fluent Laser Fonts	Casady & Greene
FoneFonts	Monotype Typography Inc.
FontHopper	Ares Software Corp.
FontMinder	Ares Software Corp.
FontMonger	Ares Software Corp.
Fontographer for Windows	AltSys Corp.
FrameMaker for Windows	Frame Technology Corp.
Freehand for Windows	Aldus Corp.
Glasnost Cyrillic Library	Casady & Greene

Harvard Graphics for DOS	Software Publishing Corp.
Harvard Graphics for Windows	Software Publishing Corp.
Hewlett-Packard Font Set	Microsoft Corp.
LaserJet 4	Hewlett-Packard Co.
L'il Bits	Bitstream Inc.
MakeUp	Bitstream Inc.
MoreFonts for DOS	MicroLogic Software
MS-DOS	Microsoft Corp.
NISCAN Spectra	NISCA Inc.
PageMaker for Windows	Aldus Corp.
Persuasion for Windows	Aldus Corp.
Plus Pack	Adobe Systems Inc.
PowerPoint	Microsoft Corp.
PrimeType for Windows	LaserTools
Publisher	Microsoft Corp.
ScanMan 256	Logitech Corp.
Software Bridge	Systems Compatibility Corp.
Super ATM	Adobe Systems Inc.
SuperPrint for Winows	Zenographics, Inc.
SuperQueue	Zenographics, Inc.
TrueType Font Packs	Microsoft Corp.
TrueType for DOS	MicroLogic Software
TrueType Value Pack	Monotype Typography Inc.
Type Companion	FontBank Inc.

Type On Call	Adobe Systems Inc.
Type Set Value Pack	Adobe Systems Inc.
TypeAlign	Adobe Systems Inc.
TypeCase	SWFTE International, Ltd.
TypeCase TrueType Font Variety	SWFTE International, Ltd.
Ventura Publisher	Ventura Software Co.
Windows	Microsoft Corp.
Windows Printing System (WPS)	Microsoft Corp.
Word for DOS	Microsoft Corp.
Word for Windows	Microsoft Corp.
WordPerfect for DOS	WordPerfect Corp.
WordPerfect for Windows	WordPerfect Corp.
Z-Script	Zenographics, Inc.

Glossary

3-D Spreadsheet format in which a cell can reference another spreadsheet; also can refer to a special shading effect applied to characters to give them the illusion of depth.

alias Alternate name (for a font).

angle Degree of tilt of the vertical lines of a character (see *italic, oblique*).

ANSI American National Standards Institute character code system; used by Windows; includes 256 possible character positions (see *ASCII*).

applet Program with single or limited functions, usually in Windows.

application Program intended to serve a particular need, e.g. word processor, graphics editor.

ASCII American Standard Code for Information Interchange; character set used by DOS applications; includes 128 possible character positions, often extended to 256 positions (see *ANSI*).

ATM Adobe Type Manager; font manager program for Type 1 fonts in Windows.

attribute Identifying characteristic of a character or font, e.g. size, style, color.

baud Rate of serial data transfer (see *bps*).

Bézier curve Mathematically-defined system used to store and edit fonts and graphics shapes.

bidirectional Printing in both directions, left-to-right followed by right-to-left without first returning to the left margin.

bit   One element or "dot" of a font or graphic; also, one element of binary data.

bitmap   Font or graphic comprised of a pattern or "map" of bits.

black   Extremely bold character or font.

BMP   One file extension for a bitmapped graphic.

bold   Character or font with thicker lines than a regular one (see *light, medium, heavy, black*).

boot   To restart a computer from the beginning, loading all programs freshly into memory (also "boot-up").

bps   Bits per second; rate of serial data transfer (see *baud*).

broken   Character or font with pits or cuts to suggest age or wear; lends an "antique" effect.

bullet   Character to left of text that denotes beginning of a new topic; is often a bold circle, but may be any shape or graphic.

byte   Number comprised of eight bits; a number specifying a single character (see *bit*).

CD-ROM   Compact Disk Read-Only Memory; a compact disk used to store programs, graphics or other computer data; may also contain music elements.

clip art   Pre-drawn art or icons, often provided with a graphics program for free use.

code   One or more special characters included in a file to control printer functions or select special printable characters; also jargon for "program."

COM   Serial communications port, as in DOS.

condensed   Characters or font with characters that are more narrow and "high" than regular ones.

Control Panel   Windows group of applets to control various system aspects, such as fonts and printers.

control point Point on a Bézier curve that can be moved to alter the shape of a character or graphic element.

daisywheel Disk with raised letters on flexible "petals" struck by a hammer while spinning in impact printing; also, a printer that uses a daisywheel to carry its printable characters.

DDE Dynamic Data Exchange; a method provided by Windows to allow applications to exchange information using links between the applications (see *OLE*).

decorative Font or character with artistic characteristics used to embellish text, e.g. illuminated, broken, or cursive characters.

display Font or character intended for use in large sizes, such as headlines.

DLL Dynamically Linked Library; collection of program functions in a file that can be accessed by Windows applications as needed.

DOC File extension for a document file; since many word processors use this extension, does not imply a single file format.

DOS Disk Operating System; a program group that allows access to disks, displays and other devices; required for most applications and for Windows (see *MS-DOS*).

dot-matrix Printer that uses a set of pins impacting through a ribbon onto paper to produce characters or images.

download To load a font set or characters to a printer prior to using them.

dpi Dots per inch; the number of dots on each square inch of paper, or on a video display; a higher number implies greater quality and accuracy (see *resolution*).

driver Program that allows applications to link with or use a device, e.g. a printer driver or mouse driver.

dropped capital   Character that is much larger than the rest of text, and is inserted as the first character of a paragraph ("dropped in") for visual effect.

EGA   Extended Graphics Adapter; a standard for video display, now superceded by VGA (see *VGA*).

elite   A typewriter character size of about 10 points (12 characters per inch). (See *pica*.)

embedding   Placing a font in a document so it can be used by the recipient on another PC; also, placing a graphic or other object in a document so that it references the application that created it.

EXE   Extension for an executable DOS file (program).

expanded   Font with characters wider than usual; also a line that has wide spacing between characters.

extended   See *expanded*.

extended set   Characters in a font in addition to the ones available from the keyboard, usually including diacritical marks and foreign-language symbols.

extension   One to three-character addition to a DOS file name, usually indicating the type of file, e.g. DOC, EXE.

FON   File extension for a Windows bitmapped font file.

font   Set of characters having similar design, sometimes meaning a character set of only one style and size.

font cartridge   Plug-in assembly for a printer, extending the number of available fonts.

font manager   Program that handles font functions such as creating printer and screen fonts from a scalable outline.

FOT   File extension for a Windows file that references a TrueType scalable font file.

frame   A defined area for text or graphics in a document (see *pasteboard*).

glossary   Storage location or system for storing character strings for reuse.

graphics mode   Printer mode where all text and other document elements are sent and printed as graphics (see *Text mode*).

graphics printer   Printer that allows printing in Graphics mode (see *Graphics mode*).

GUI   Graphical User Interface; system of interacting with a user using graphics and icons instead of simply using text messages, e.g., Microsoft Windows.

head   Printer component that carries pins or printwheel across a page for printing (see *daisywheel, dot-matrix*).

heavy   Character or font with much thicker lines than a regular one (see *light, medium, bold, black*).

hinting   Process in scalable font to increase the visual quality of characters at small sizes; dynamically alters the shape of a character according to its size (see *scalable font*).

illuminated   Character or font with artistic embellishments such as flowers; often used as a dropped capital (see *dropped capital*).

Intellifont   Format for Agfa fonts, used in some H-P printers; also, the name of the Windows font-manager program available to rasterize such fonts.

internal font   Font stored permanently in a printer.

italic   Character or font with vertical lines angled to the right, usually with flowing and curved lines (see *oblique*).

Kb   Kilobyte (abbreviation).

kerning   Adjusting the spacing between characters on a line; can be automatic (application-controlled) or manual (user-selected). (See *kerning pairs, track kerning*.)

kerning pairs   Pairs of characters in a font that are kerned (placed closer together) automatically when they occur together in a line (see *kerning, track kerning*).

kilobyte   A thousand bytes, abbreviated Kb; formally, 1,024 bytes (see *byte*).

landscape   Horizontal (wider than high) page orientation for printing (see *orientation, portrait*).

laser printer   Printer that employs a laser light beam (or other light source) to create printed images using xerography.

leading   Space between text lines; distance between the bottom of one line and the bottom of the next, usually specified in points (see *point*).

light   Character or font with thinner lines than a regular one (see *medium, heavy, bold, black*).

line spacing   Same as *leading*.

linking   Connecting a graphic or other element in one application with another application, often used to connect a graphic with the application that created it for later editing (see *OLE, embedding*).

LPT   DOS designation for a line printer port (see *COM, port*).

Mb   Megabyte (abbreviation).

media   Form of storage for an application or document (see *CD-ROM*).

medium   Character or font with normal-thickness lines (see *light, heavy, bold, black*); also a person who professes to communicate with deceased individuals.

megabyte   A million bytes, formally 1,048,576 bytes, abbreviated Mb; storage designation for a diskette or hard disk (see *byte, kilobyte*).

metrics   Defining aspects of a font, usually relative size and relative spacing; sometimes also the size and file attributes.

monospace   Characters or font with equal spacing between characters, e.g. Courier (see *proportional*).

MS-DOS   MicroSoft Disk Operating System (see *DOS*).

narrow   Characters or font with characters that are more thin and "high" than regular ones.

Nimbus-Q   Font format developed by URW, seldom used.

oblique   Characters or font with vertical lines angled to the right; usually refers to a sans-serif font that has been changed to italic style simply by tilting (see *sans serif, oblique*).

OLE   Object Linking and Embedding; a set of features provided by Microsoft Windows so applications can easily link to share text, graphics, or other elements ("objects"); creates a reference in an element to the application that created it (see *DDE, embedding, linking*).

orientation   Page alignment for printing (see *landscape, portrait*).

outline font   Font stored as a set of lines and curves so it can be scaled to be produced in any needed size (see *proportional font, scalable font*).

parallel   Printer connection; fastest communication to printer (see *serial, port*).

parity   Information added to check the accuracy of communication; may be used for printer or memory.

pasteboard   A visual area in which text or graphics can be freely placed; layout metaphor used by PageMaker (see *frame*).

PCL   Printer Control Language; complex system of codes devised by Hewlett-Packard to control printers and fonts; used in LaserJet and compatible printers (see *PDL, PostScript*).

PDL   Page Descriptor Language; system of commands and codes used to define appearance and placement of text and graphics on a printed page, e.g., PostScript.

permanent font   Font downloaded to a printer and stored in its memory for all ensuing print jobs; lost when the printer is shut off (see *temporary font*).

pica   Unit of type measurement; one pica equals 6 points, or about 1/6 inch (see *point*); also used to describe a typewriter character size of about 12 points (10 characters per inch). (See *elite*.)

pixel   One element of a graphic; equivalent to one bit of a bitmap with color and brightness information.

plotter   A specialized printer using pens to form text and graphic images.

point   Unit of type measurement; equals about 1/72 inch (see *pica*).

port   A connection that links an external device to a computer, e.g., printer port.

portrait   Vertical (higher than wide) page orientation for printing (see *orientation, portrait*).

PostScript   Page Descriptor Language used in documents and printers; allows high degree of control of text and graphics elements (see *PCL, PDL*); may also refer to PostScript Type 1 fonts (see *Type 1*).

PostScript cartridge   Plug-in assembly for a printer that converts it to accept PostScript documents (see *PostScript*).

preview   Mode provided by a word processor for a document to allow viewing pages as they will be printed; often used by DOS applications that do not have WYSIWYG displays (see *WYSIWYG*).

printer font   Font contained in a printer (see *permanent font*).

proportional   Characters or font with space between characters that varies according to the character (see *monospace*).

pt   Abbreviation for point (see *point*).

RAM Random-Access Memory; temporary memory used by a computer or printer to store programs and associated information while in use (see *ROM*).

rasterize Convert a scalable outline character to a bitmap for display or printing (see *font manager*).

regular Normal face style, as opposed to bold or italic (see *roman*).

render See *rasterize*.

resolution Ability of a printer or video display to show detail; expressed as the number of dots per square inch, and sometimes including dot size.

RET Resolution Enhancement Technology; a technique adopted in Hewlett-Packard LaserJet printers to improve the perceived resolution of an image by changing dot size (see *resolution*).

ROM Read-Only Memory; permanent memory used by a computer or printer to store programs and data (such as fonts) so that it is always available (see *RAM*).

roman Regular face style, as opposed to bold or italic; usually refers to serif faces (see *regular*).

RS-232 Computer or printer serial port type; formally E.I.A. RS-232; used by virtually all consumer computer serial ports (see *port, serial*).

sans serif "without serif"— characters lacking embellishment on the ends of lines; or fonts without serifs, e.g., Helvetica or Arial (see *serif*).

scalable font Font stored as a set of lines and curves so it can be scaled to be produced in any needed size (see *outline font*).

screen font Bitmapped characters or font generated for display purposes; may be in limited sizes, and may or may not match printed characters (see *printer font*).

script   Characters or font with design elements like hand-writing, with flowing, graceful lines and linked characters (see *decorative font*).

serial   Printer connection; relatively slow communication to printer (see *parallel, port, RS-232*).

serif   Embellishments on the ends of lines (can be bars, balls, curls, or other ornamental figurations); characters or font with serifs (see *sans serif*).

shareware   Programs or other computer materials (e.g., fonts, icons, and graphics) distributed at no charge, with the understanding that the user will pay for them if they continue to be used.

soft font   Font downloaded to a printer when needed; usually in bitmapped format (see *scalable font, bitmap*).

Speedo   Font format developed by Bitstream.

style   Characteristic of a font, e.g., bold, italic.

symbol font   Font comprised of symbols or icons rather than alphabetic or numeric characters.

System 7   Operating system used in Macintosh computers; makes TrueType fonts available to applications.

template   Cluster of information or "recipe" used to format characters, paragraphs, pages or documents.

temporary font   Font downloaded to a printer just before the print job it is used in, and then immediately discarded (see *permanent font*).

Text mode   Printer mode where all text and other document elements are sent and printed as characters (see *graphics mode*).

track kerning   Kerning that adjusts automatically for character size and style; may also refer to any kerning that affects an entire line.

TrueType   Scalable font format devised by Apple Computer and licensed by Microsoft for use in Windows; an aspect of the TrueImage PDL (see *PDL, scalable font*).

TTF   DOS file extension for TrueType fonts.

Type 1   Scalable font format devised by Adobe for use in PostScript printers (see *PostScript*).

Type 3   Scalable font format like PostScript Type 1 format, but without hinting; used by some font vendors before hinting techniques became available; no longer in wide use (see *hinting, Type 1*).

typeface   Design for a collection of characters that are closely alike in design; includes all normal styles (regular, bold, italic, bold-italic), and may include others; does not imply size.

vector font   Font comprised of lines and curves, with no interior fill; often used by plotters.

VGA   Video Graphics Adapter; a standard for video display consisting of 640 pixels wide by 480 pixels high, or about 72 dpi on a common monitor; also available in Super VGA (800 by 600 pixels) and higher resolutions (see *dpi, EGA*).

weight   Character or font line thickness; a regular character has a lighter weight than a bold one.

W.P.S.   Windows Printing System; hardware/software system developed by Microsoft to add TrueType rasterizing to H-P LaserJet printers.

WYSIWYG   What You See Is What You Get; a widely-used acronym for an application's ability to display a document as it will be printed.

Index

Symbols

1-2-3 for DOS (Lotus Development
  Corporation), 160, 253
  adding fonts to font list, 166
  display modes, 163
  font sets, 162
    changing fonts, 163-164
    saving to font libraries, 165-166
  special characters, 169
    extended, 169
  spreadsheets
    adding fonts, 163
    adding rows to displays,
      169-170
    zooming displays, 166-167
  Text mode, 167
  Wysiwyg, 161-162
    requirements for running,
      162-163
1-2-3 for Windows (Lotus
  Development Corporation), 253
3-D, 263
  ranges, 160

A

Adobe Systems Inc., 245
  fonts, installing in Windows, 47

PostScript-compatible printers,
  16, 28-29
    downloaded scalable outline
      fonts, 30-31
    font managers, 32
  PostScript Type 1 fonts, *see*
    PostScript Type 1 fonts
Adobe Font Metrics (AFM) files, 151
Adobe Type Library, 246
Adobe Type Manager (ATM), 14,
  40-41, 65-66, 246, 263
  fonts, *see* PostScript Type 1 fonts
  included in
    Ami Pro, 67
    Designer Plus OLE, 113
    FrameMaker for Windows, 88
    PageMaker for Windows, 93
    PrimeType for WordPerfect,
      142
Adobe TypeAlign, 232
  included in Designer Plus
    OLE, 113
advanced properties, 89
Agfa Division, Miles Inc., 247
  Agfa Type Library, 247
  Intellifont font format, 12
  font manager, 41
Aldus Corporation, 247
  PageMaker for Windows, 93-97

aliases, 90, 263
AltSys Corporation, 248
  Fontographer for Windows,
    237-239
Ami Pro (Lotus Development
  Corporation), 253
    kerning TrueType fonts, 69
    overlapping characters on-screen,
      70-71
    printing reverse characters, 69
    specifying PostScript fonts for
      style sheets, 71-72
    using fonts, 67-68
AMIFONT.DLL file, 70-71
angles, 88, 263
ANSI (American National Standards
  Institute), 214, 263
applets, 263
    Character Map, 50-51, 65
    Control Panel, 47-50, 63-64, 69,
      75-76, 81, 180-182, 264
    Notepad, 69, 75-76
    Print Manager, 57
    Setup, 48, 86
applications, 263
    1-2-3 for DOS (Lotus), 160-170
    Adobe Type Manager (ATM),
      65-66
    affecting Excel screen fonts, 86
    Ami Pro (Lotus), 67-72
    Arts & Letters (Computer
      Support), 102, 105-108
    Character Map (Windows),
      50-51, 65
    Control Panel (Windows),
      47-50, 63-64, 69, 75-76, 81,
      180-182, 264
    CorelDRAW! (Corel Systems),
      108-112
    DECOMP decompression utility
      (Lotus), 71-72

Designer Plus OLE (Micrografx),
  112-114
Draw Plus OLE (Micrografx), 112
Excel (Microsoft), 82-87
file conversion utility, 213-214
Font Assistant (Microsoft),
  226-227, 229-230
font managers, 31-32
FontHopper (Ares Software), 234
FontMinder (Ares Software),
  228-229, 231
FontMonger (Ares Software),
  234-236
Fontographer for Windows
  (Altsys), 237-239
FrameMaker for Windows (Frame
  Technology), 87-91
Harvard Graphics for Windows
  (Software Publishing), 120-126
MakeUp (Bitstream), 232
MoreFonts (MicroLogic
  Software), 143, 151
Notepad (Windows), 69, 75-76
PageMaker for Windows (Aldus),
  93-97
PowerPoint (Microsoft), 115-120,
  221-222
presentation, 115
PrimeType for WordPerfect
  (LaserTools), 142
Print Manager (Windows), 57
Publisher (Microsoft), 91-93
Quattro Pro (Borland), 154-160
RenameTT freeware, 239
Setup (Windows), 48, 86
shareware, 272
Software Bridge (Systems
  Compatibility), 213
TrueType for DOS (MicroLogic
  Software), 143, 152
TypeAlign (Adobe), 232

vendors, 245-261
Ventura Publisher (Ventura
	Software), 97-99
Windows (Microsoft),
	see Windows
Word for DOS (Microsoft),
	143-154, 180
Word for Windows (Microsoft),
	51, 72-77, 204-209
WordArt (Microsoft), 74, 93, 231
WordPerfect for DOS
	(WordPerfect), 131-143
WordPerfect for Windows
	(WordPerfect), 77-82
Ares Software Corporation, 248
	FontHopper, 234
	FontMinder, 228-229, 231
	FontMonger, 234-236
Arial font, 40
artistic text, 109
Arts & Letters (Computer Support
	Corporation), 250
	character special effects, 107
	text
		converting to freeform, 108
		editing, 108
	using fonts, 102, 105-107
ASCII (American Standard Code for
	Information Interchange), 263
	format, exchanging files in, 214
ATI Technologies, Inc., 245
	Ultra Graphics Pro, CRYSTAL
		fonts, 46
ATM, *see* Adobe Type Manager
attributes, 263
	bold, adding to text, 82
	changing, 132-133, 145-146, 239
	viewing, 150-151
Autographix Overnight Slide
	Service, 249

B

base fonts, 133
baud, 177-178, 263
Bézier curves, 263
	control points, 265
	editing, 233
bidirectional printing, 263
bitmapped fonts, 17-18
	internal, for laser printers
		sources, 187
		using187-188
bitmaps, 27, 264
	soft fonts, 29-30
bits, 264
bits per second (bps), 177, 264
Bitstream Inc., 249
	Bitstream Type Library, 249
	FaceLift type manager, 14, 40,
		42-43
	MakeUp, 232
	Speedo fonts, 12, 113, 121,
		159, 272
black characters/fonts, 264
BMP file extension, 237, 264
bold, 264
	attributes, adding to text, 82
	characters
		creating by computer, 6
		thickness/weight variations, 9
booting, 264
Borland Quattro Pro, 154-160
bps (bits per second), 177, 264
broken characters/fonts, 264
bullets, 264
	inserting in Quattro Pro
		spreadsheets, 159
buying fonts, 12-14
	cartridges versus diskettes,
		192-193
	deciding which to buy, 14-15
bytes, 264

C

Canon
    ink-jet printers, 22
    laser printers, 21
cartridges
    font, 13-18, 29, 266
        buying fonts on, versus buying
            diskettes, 192-193
        fonts appearing in font dialog
            boxes, 59-60
        sources for laser printers, 187
        using with laser printers,
            188-189
    inkjet printers, 195-196
    PostScript, 270
Casady & Greene, 250
CD-ROM (Compact Disk Read-
    Only Memory), 264
    disks, buying fonts on, 13
    storing graphics, 104-105
CDCONFIG.SYS file, 112
centering text, 125
character formats, 89
Character Map (Windows), 50-51
    viewing font files, 65
characters
    angles, 88
    bitmaps, 27
    black, 264
    bold, 6, 264
    broken, 264
    bullets, 159, 264
    condensed, 264
    converting between word-
        processing files, 214-215
    decorative, 265
    display, 265
    distorting shapes, 232
    dropped capitals, 266
    editing in fonts, 236
    extended, 169

foreign language, 125
formatting individually in
    Excel, 85
from WordPerfect fonts, 139
graphics
    custom, sources for shapes, 111
    editing, 111, 119-120
    oblique, 110
    special effects, 107
Greek, 125
heavy, 267
illuminated, 267
italic, 267
    oblique, 6
jagged edges, 52
light, 268
logos as, 238-239
medium, 268
mixing-and-matching from
    multiple fonts, 236
monospace (fixed space), 10-11
narrow, 269
oblique, 269
overlapping
    in narrow spreadsheet rows, 87
    on-screen, 70-71
proportional, 10-11, 270
regular, 271
reverse, printing, 69, 75-76
roman, 271
script, 272
spacing in Macintosh documents
    in Ventura Publisher, 99
special, 50-52
    1-2-3 for DOS, 169
    disappearing, 53
    entering in text, 138-139, 153
    inserting in Quattro Pro
        spreadsheets, 159-160
    printing, 99
    viewing and inserting in Word
        for Windows, 73-74

Word for Windows Equation
Editor, 76
symbols
money, 125
printing in regular fonts, 81
thickness/weight variations, 9
typing outside of margins, 76-77
underlining, breaks between, 81
viewing in test documents, 152
weight, 88, 273
width/height variations, 9-10
chart objects, 84
viewing, 75
clip art, 105, 264
libraries, storing on
CD-ROM, 105
codes, 264
error, CorelDRAW!, 112
hashed, 98
hidden, 141-142
printer control, embedding in
documents, 153-154
color printers
ink-jet, 23
laser, 22
columns in spreadsheets, displaying
more, 158-159
COM ports, 264
CompuServse Information Services,
70, 250
finding printer drivers, 57
Computer Support Corporation, 250
Arts & Letters, 102, 105-108
computers
acting strangely when using
TrueType fonts, 48
connecting printers to, 175-177
locking up
using TrueType fonts, 47-48
when printing, 56

ports
configuring for printers,
178-179
connecting to printer drivers,
182-183
condensed (narrow) fonts, 9-10,
264, 269
configuring
computer ports for printers,
178-179
printers, 177-178
Control Panel (Windows), 47-50,
63-64, 69, 75-76, 81, 180-182, 264
control points, 265
converted fonts, 12
converters, saving files with, 213
converting
characters between word-
processing files, 214-215
font formats, 234-235
fonts to TrueType fonts, 48-49
text to freeform graphics, 107-108
copyrights of fonts, 240-243
Corel Corporation, 251
CorelDRAW! (Corel
Corporation), 251
custom fonts, 111-112
error codes, 112
PostScript Type 1 fonts, display
speed, 111
using fonts, 108-126
cost
color ink-jet printers, 23
color laser printers, 22
dot-matrix printers, 24
ink-jet printers, 23
laser printers, 21
Courier font, 76-77
CRYSTAL fonts, 46
curving text, 232

D

daisywheel, 265
 printers, printing speed, 153
DataProducts ink-jet printers, 23
DDE (Dynamic Data
 Exchange), 265
DECOMP decompression utility
 (Lotus Development Corporation),
 71-72
decompressing Ami Pro style sheets,
 71-72
decorative fonts, 7, 265
default printers, 180
deleting fonts, 47
Designer Plus OLE (Micrografx,
 Inc.), 112-114, 254
DeskJet printers (Hewlett-Packard
 Company), 23
 500 printers, 253
 550C printers, 194, 253
  fonts, 197-198
 printing TrueType fonts, 59
desktop publishers
 FrameMaker for Windows, 87-91
 PageMaker for Windows, 93-97
 Publisher, 91-93
 Ventura Publisher, 97-99
Desktop Solutions (Monotype
 Typography Inc.), 256
Desktop Styles (Agfa Division, Miles
 Inc.), 247
dialog boxes
 Ami Pro font selection, 68
 Control Panel Printer Font
  Installer, 188-189
 Control Panel Printer Setup, 188
 Control Panel Printers for
  PostScript printers, 217
 Control Panel Printers
  selection, 194

CorelDRAW! text and character
 spacing, 109-110
CorelDRAW! text attributes, 109
CorelDRAW! Text Roll-Up,
 109-110
Designer font selection, 114
Designer Text Spacing, 114-115
Excel Font selection, 83-84
font
 fonts appearing in, 49, 57
 only TrueType fonts appearing
  in, 50
 unknown fonts appearing
  in, 51
Fontographer Font Attributes, 239
Harvard Graphics Text, 122
Harvard Graphics Text Anchor
 Point, 123-124
Harvard Graphics Text Attributes,
 122-123
Hewlett-Packard Font
 Installer, 208
PageMaker Type specification, 95
PostScript printer Advanced
 Options, 209-210
PostScript printer Substitution,
 209-211
PowerPoint Replace Fonts, 117
reading in Excel, 85
Windows Add Printers, 181
Windows Control Panel Printers,
 180-181
Windows Font, 64
Windows Font control, 64
Windows Install Printer
 Fonts, 197
Windows Printer Connect,
 182-183
Windows Printers Connect to file,
 217-218
Word Character, 145-146

Word Font selection, 146-147
Word for Windows Convert
File, 212
Word for Windows Open, 211
Word for Windows Save As, 213
WordPerfect for Windows
Font, 78
WordPerfect Typesetting
options, 79
Digital Typeface Corporation
(DTC), 251
Discovery TrueType Pack (Agfa
Division, Miles Inc.), 247
diskettes
buying fonts on, versus font
cartridges, 192-193
printing large documents to,
218-219
display fonts, 7, 265
distorting character shapes, 232
dithering, dot-matrix printers, 199
DLLs (Dynamically Linked
Libraries), 265
DOC file extension, 265
documents
embedding printer control codes,
153-154
exchanging between computers
both using Word for Windows,
204-209
sending to service bureaus,
215-222
with different printers, 209-211
with different word processors,
printing, 211-215
printing
large, to diskettes, 218-219
one at a time, 57
service bureaus duplicating,
216-218

test, for viewing font
characters, 152
viewing
in Word for DOS, 147-150
in WordPerfect for DOS,
136-137
DOS (Disk Operating System), 265
configuring computer ports for
printers, 178-179
exchanging documents with
Windows, 211-213
fonts, 129-131
graphics mode, 130
printers working in, 54-55
sending files to service bureaus
using Macintosh, 215-216
testing printing from, 173-174
DOT file extension, 210
dot-matrix printers, 23-24, 265
fonts, 199-201
internal (built-in), 27-29
installing, 198-199
printing pages, 26
setting controls, 199
downloaded, 265
scalable outline fonts, 30-31
soft fonts, 29-30
dpi (dots per inch), 265
draft quality printing mode, 58, 153
Draw Plus OLE (Micrografx, Inc.),
112, 254
drivers, 31-32, 265
installing, 48
printer, 180
Hewlett-Packard DeskJet, 59
TrueType-compatibility, 76
updating, 57, 80-81
WordPerfect support, 79
video, reinstalling, 86
drop-down font list, scrolling in
PageMaker for Windows, 97

dropped capitals, 266
DRV file extension, 206
DTC Type Library, 251
Dynamic Data Exchange
  (DDE), 265
Dynamically Linked Libraries
  (DLLs), 265

E

Eastern European Library (Casady &
  Greene), 250
editing
  Bézier curves, 233
  character outlines, 111
  characters as graphic elements,
    119-120
  fonts, 235-239
  text converted to graphics, 108
EGA (Extended Graphics
  Adapter), 266
elite, 266
embedding, 101-102, 266
  fonts, 242-243
  printer control codes in
    documents, 153-154
environments, 35
EPS file extension, 218
Equation Editor special
  characters, 76
Error 21 message, 58
error
  codes, CorelDRAW!, 112
  messages, laser printers, 191-192
ethical aspects of fonts, 240-243
Excel (Microsoft Corporation), 255
  formatting individual
    characters, 85
  overlapping characters in narrow
    spreadsheet rows, 87
  page orientation, 86-87

reading dialog boxes and icon
    labels, 85
  screen fonts
    affected by applications, 86
    improving readabilty, 85
  spreadsheet columns as print
    titles, 87
  using fonts, 82-99
exchanging documents between
  computers
  both using Word for Windows,
    204-209
  sending to service bureaus,
    215-222
  with different
    printers, 209-211
    word processors, printing,
      211-215
EXE file extension, 266
expanded fonts, 10, 266
extended
  characters, 169
  sets, 266
extensions, *see* files

F

FaceLift (Bitstream Inc.), 14, 40,
  42-43
  for Windows, 249
  for WordPerfect, 249
families, 8
FENCES files, 76
file conversion utility programs,
  213-214
files
  Adobe Font Metrics (AFM), 151
  AMIFONT.DLL, 70-71
  CDCONFIG.SYS, 112
  extensions, 266
    BMP, 237, 264
    DOC, 265

DOT, 210
DRV, 206
EPS, 218
EXE, 266
FON, 266
FOT, 64, 229, 266
PRD, 180
TTF, 64, 207, 229, 273
TXT, 174
FENCES, 76
font, viewing, 65
header, 219
HPPCL.DRV, 76
HPPCL5A.DRV, 76
MTEXTRA, 76
PostScript, printing to, 217-218
WIN.INI, 208-209
finding slides, 119
fixed fonts, 133
fixed space characters, 10-11
flickering text, 53
Fluent Laser Fonts (Casady &
Greene), 250
FON file extension, 266
FoneFonts (Monotype Typography
Inc.), 256
Font Assistant (Microsoft
Corporation)
displaying and printing fonts, 229
font information, 230
grouping fonts, 226-227
font cartridges, 13-18, 29, 266
buying fonts on, versus buying
diskettes, 192-193
fonts appearing in font dialog
boxes, 59-60
with laser printers, 188-189
font dialog boxes
fonts appearing in, 49
after installing font cartridges,
59-60
after switching printers, 54, 57

only TrueType fonts appearing
in, 50
unknown fonts appearing in, 51
font files, viewing, 65
font libraries, 166
font list, dropping down as mouse
pointer slides by, 118
font managers, 12, 14, 31-32,
38-44, 266
Adobe Type Manager (ATM),
65-66
printers as, 45-46
font metrics tables (VFMs), 99
font sets, 162
adding fonts, 163
changing fonts, 163-164
saving to font libraries, 165-166
FontBank Inc., 251
FontHaus Inc., 251
FontHaus Type Library, 251
FontHopper (Ares Software
Corporation), 234, 248
FontMinder (Ares Software
Corporation), 248
font information, 231
grouping fonts, 228
printing lists of available
fonts, 229
FontMonger (Ares Software
Corporation), 248
converting font formats, 234-235
editing characters, 236
mixing-and-matching characters
from multiple fonts, 236
Fontographer for Windows (Altsys
Corporation), 237-239, 248
fonts, 266
aliases, 90
angles, 88
Arial, 40
attributes, *see* attributes
base, 133

bitmapped, 17-18, 27
black, 264
bold, 264
broken, 264
buying, 12-14
    cartridges versus diskettes,
        192-193
condensed (narrow), 9-10,
    264, 269
consisting of handwriting,
    237-238
converted, 12
converting
    formats, 234-235
    to TrueType fonts, 48-49
Courier, 76-77
creating, 5-6, 235-239
custom
    sources for shapes, 111
    using, 111-112
deciding which to buy, 14-15
decorative, 7, 265
deleting, 47
display, 7, 265
displaying and printing samples,
    228-229
editing, 235-239
embedding, 242-243
expanded, 10, 266
families, 8
fixed, 133
formats, 11-12
generating with video boards, 46
graphics, with laser printers, 191
grouping, 225-228
hashed codes, 98
heavy, 267
illuminated, 267
importance, 4
in 1-2-3 for DOS, 160-170
in Ami Pro, 67-72

in Arts & Letters, 102, 105-108
in CorelDRAW!, 108-112
in Designer Plus OLE, 112-114
in Excel, 82-87
in FrameMaker for Windows,
    87-91
in Harvard Graphics for
    Windows, 120-126
in PageMaker for Windows, 93-97
in PowerPoint, 115-120
in Publisher, 91-93
in Quattro Pro, 154-160
in Ventura Publisher, 97-99
in Windows
    controlling in all applications,
        63-66
    displaying, 52-54
    installing and accessing, 47-49
    printing, 54-60
    selecting and using, 49-52
in Word for DOS, 143-154
in Word for Windows, 72-77
in WordPerfect for DOS, 131-143
in WordPerfect for Windows,
    77-82
information about, 229-231
internal (built-in), 15-18, 27-29,
    187-191, 267
italic, 267
legal and ethical aspects, 240-243
light, 268
medium, 268
metrics, 31-32, 65
monospace (fixed space), 10-11
MS Sans Serif, 85
Nimbus-Q format, 269
oblique, 269
outline, 17-18, 65, 192, 269
permanent, 189, 270
PostScript Type 1, *see* PostScript
    Type 1 fonts

printer, *see* printer fonts
proportional, 10-11, 270
rasterizing, 25-26, 38, 65
regular, 271
rendering, 36-38
roman, 271
sans serif, 8, 271
scalable, 133, 271
scalable outline, 17-18, 28
    downloaded, 30-31
screen, *see* screen fonts
script, 272
serif, 8, 272
sizes, 10-11
    affecting line length on-screen,
      135, 151
    setting percentages, 139-141
soft, 15-18, 29-30, 272
    installing for WordPerfect for
      DOS, 139
    with laser printers, 188-189
sources for laser printers, 187
special effects, 231-234
Speedo (Bitstream), 12, 113, 121,
    159, 272
storing, 64-65
    on CD-ROM, 105
styles, 272
symbol, 7, 51-52, 272
    printing in regular fonts, 81
temporary, 189, 272
text types, 7
TrueType, *see* TrueType fonts
Type 3, 273
variations, 88
vector, 38, 273
vendors, 11-12, 245-261
versus typefaces, 3-4
viewing characters in test
  documents, 152
weight, 88, 273

with dot-matrix printers, 199-201
with inkjet printers, 197-198
WYSIWYG, 31-32
Fonts icon, 47-50
foreign language characters,
  50-51, 125
    inserting in Quattro Pro
      spreadsheets, 159-160
formats
    character, 89
    converting, 234-235
    fonts, 11-12
    master, 5
formatting
    individual characters in Excel, 85
    losing in WordPerfect for DOS,
      141-142
FOT file extension, 64, 229, 266
Frame Technology Corporation, 252
FrameMaker for Windows (Frame
  Technology Corporation), 252
    PostScript fonts
      accessing, 91
      displaying, 90
      starting with, 90
    rotating type, 91
    using fonts, 87-99
frames, 122, 266
freeform, 104
    converting text to, 107-108
Freehand for Windows (Aldus
  Corporation), 247

G

Genigraphics, 252
Glasnost Cyrillic Library (Casady &
  Greene), 250
glossaries, 267
graphical user interfaces (GUIs), 35

graphics
  accelerators, 46
  characters
    custom, sources for shapes, 111
    editing, 119-120
    editing outlines, 111
    oblique, 110
    special effects, 107
  fonts
    editing for special effects, 234
    sources for laser printers, 187
    using with laser printers, 191
  in 1-2-3 for DOS, 161-162
  objects, 101
    inserting, 119-120
  printers, 25, 267
    connecting to computers, 177
    see also inkjet printers, laser printers
  printing, 80
  storing on CD-ROM, 104-105
  viewing, 75
graphics mode, 267
  DOS, 130
  Word for DOS, 144-145
    speeding up, 150
Graphics UltraPro (ATI Technologies, Inc.), 245
Greek characters, 125
  inserting in Quattro Pro spreadsheets, 159-160
grouping fonts, 225-228
GUIs (Graphical User Interfaces), 267

H

handles, 102
handwriting, creating fonts consisting of, 237-238
hard drives, using after WordPerfect for Windows printer changes, 82

Harvard Graphics for DOS (Software Publishing Corporation), 257
Harvard Graphics for Windows (Software Publishing Corporation), 257
  centering text in slides, 125
  changing fonts, 124
  displaying ruler, 124
  selecting text, 124
  TrueType fonts, rotating text, 125-126
  using fonts, 120-126
hashed codes, 98
header files, 219
headlines
  creating in Word for Windows, 74
  special effects, 231
  zooming in to view fit, 96
heads, 267
  dot-matrix printers, 23
heavy characters/fonts, 267
Hendon, Rufus, 239
Hewlett-Packard Company, 252
  DeskJet printers, *see* DeskJet printers
  HP-GL (Hewlett-Packard Graphics Language), 186
  inkjet printers, 22-23
  Intellifont font format, 12
    font manager, 41
  laser printers, 21
  LaserJet printers, *see* LaserJet printers
  PCL (Printer Control Language), 185
Hewlett-Packard Font Pack (Microsoft Corporation), 255
hidden codes, 141-142
high-quality printing mode, 153
hinting, 5, 267

HP-GL (Hewlett-Packard Graphics
 Language), 186
HPPCL.DRV file, 76
HPPCL5A.DRV file, 76

I

icons
 Fonts, 47-50
 Ports, 55
 Printers, 55, 57, 59, 69, 75-76,
  81, 180-182
 reading labels in Excel, 85
IDs (fonts), Ventura Publisher, 98
illuminated characters/fonts, 267
inkjet printers, 22-23, 193-194
 cartridges, 195-196
 fonts, 197-198
 installing, 194-195
 internal (built-in) fonts, 27-29
 paper, 196-197
 printing pages, 26
installing
 drivers, 48
  printer, 180-182
  video, 86
 fonts
  in Windows, 47-49
  soft, for WordPerfect for
   DOS, 139
 inkjet printer cartridges, 195
 printers
  dot-matrix, 198-199
  inkjet, 194-195
  laser, 186
 Ventura Publisher, 98
Intellifont font format (Agfa/
 Hewlett-Packard), 12, 267
 font manager, 41
intensity control, dot-matrix
 printers, 199

internal (built-in) fonts, 15-18,
 27-29, 267
 bitmapped fonts
  sources for laser printers, 187
  using with laser printers,
   187-188
 scalable fonts
  sources for laser printers, 187
  using with laser printers,
   189-191
italic characters/fonts, 267
 oblique, 6

J-K

jagged edges to characters, 52

kerning, 6, 267
 pair, 89, 268
 track, 94, 272
 TrueType fonts in Ami Pro, 69
kilobytes (Kb), 267, 268
KX-P1124 printers (Panasonic), 198
 fonts, 199-200

L

landscape orientation, 27, 268
 in Excel, 86-87
laser printers, 21-22, 268
 connecting to computers, 177
 error messages, 191-192
 font cartridges, 29, 188-189
 fonts
  buying, cartridges versus
   diskettes, 192-193
  graphics, 191
  internal (built-in), 27-29
  internal bitmapped, 187-188
  internal scalable, 189-191
  PostScript Type 1, 193
  soft, 188-189
  sources, 187

installing, 186
locking up, 191-192
PostScript-compatible versus
    PCL, 193
printer drivers, TrueType-
    compatibility, 76
printing pages, 26-27
reverse characters, 75-76
types, 185-186
LaserJet printers (Hewlett-Packard
Company)
    as font managers, 45
    Error 21 message, 58
    LaserJet II, III printers, 252
    LaserJet IIp, IIIp printers, 252
    LaserJet 4 printers, 252
        fonts, 30-31
        internal scalable fonts, 189-191
        new features, 186
        soft fonts or font cartridges,
            188-189
        TrueType fonts, 192
        versions, 186
    resetting during print jobs, 59
LaserTools, 253
    PrimeType for WordPerfect, 142
layout view, Word for DOS,
    148-149
leading, 95, 268
legal aspects of fonts, 240-243
Lexmark laser printers, 21
libraries
    clip art, storing on
        CD-ROM, 105
    font, 166
licenses for fonts, 241-242
light characters/fonts, 268
L'il Bits (Bitstream Inc.), 249
lines
    breaks, matching on-screen and
        printed, 56

expanded, 266
spacing, 95, 268
linking, 268
Linotronic fonts, substituting for
    TrueType fonts, 220
loading paper into printers, 174-175
locking up
    computers
        using TrueType fonts, 47-48
        when printing, 56
    laser printers, 191-192
Logitech, Inc., 253
logos as symbols in fonts, 238-239
Lotus Development
    Corporation, 253
    1-2-3 for DOS, 160-170
    Ami Pro, 67-72
    DECOMP decompression utility,
        71-72
LPT ports, 268

M

Macintosh
    character spacing in Ventura
        Publisher, 99
    System 7, 272
    used by service bureaus, sending
        DOS files for review, 215-216
MakeUp (Bitstream Inc.), 232, 249
managers, *see* font managers
margins, typing text outside of, 53,
    76-77
master formats, 5
media, 268
medium characters/fonts, 268
megabytes (Mb), 104, 268
memory
    RAM (Random-Access
        Memory), 271
    requirements
        laser printrs, 191-192

printers, 58
   TrueType fonts, 48
ROM (Read-Only Memory), 28, 271
menus, font list dropping down as mouse pointer slides by, 118
messages, Error 21, 58
metrics, 31-32, 65, 268
   VFMs (font metrics tables), 99
Micrografx, Inc., 254
   Designer Plus OLE, 112-114
   Draw Plus OLE, 112
MicroLogic Software, 254
   MoreFonts, 143, 151
   TrueType for DOS, 143, 152
Microsoft Corporation, 254
   Excel, 82-87
   Font Assistant, 226-227, 229-230
   PowerPoint, 115-120
   Publisher, 91-93
   TrueType font format, 11-12
   Windows, *see* Windows
   Windows Printing System (WPS), 273
   Word for DOS, 143-154, 180, 215-216
   Word for Windows, 51, 72-77, 204-209, 215-216
   WordArt, 231
modes
   1-2-3 display, 163
   draft, 58, 153
   graphics, 267
      DOS, 130
      Word for DOS, 144-145, 150
   high-quality printing, 153
   preview, 270
   Text, 272
      1-2-3 for DOS, 167
      Word for DOS, 144-145, 150-151

WYSIWYG, Quattro Pro, 155, 158
money symbols, 125
monitors, WYSIWYG text, 31-32
monospace fonts, 10-11, 269
Monotype Type Library (Monotype Typography Inc.), 256
Monotype Typography Inc., 256
MoreFonts for DOS (MicroLogic Software), 143, 151, 254
MS Sans Serif font, 85
MS-DOS (Microsoft Corporation), 255, 269
MTEXTRA files, 76

N

narrow (condensed) fonts, 9-10, 264, 269
NEC laser printers, 21
Nimbus-Q font format, 269
NISCA Inc., 256
NISCAN Spectra (NISCA Inc.), 256
nodes, 102
Notepad (Windows)
   [AmiPro] section, 69
   [Microsoft Word 2.0] section, 75-76

O

objects, 84
   graphics, 101
      inserting, 119-120
   viewing, 75
oblique characters/fonts, 6, 110, 269
OEMs (manufacturers), 48
OLE (Object Linking and Embedding), 101-102, 269
orientation, 27, 269
   in Excel, 86-87
   landscape, 268
   portrait, 270

outline fonts, 17-18, 192, 269
outlines, 65
    curving and shaping text
        around, 232
overhead transparencies, 25
    PowerPoint presentations as,
        221-222
overlapping characters
    in narrow spreadsheet rows, 87
    on-screen, 70-71

P

Page Descriptor Language
    (PDL), 269
PageMaker for Windows (Aldus
    Corporation), 247
    headlines, zooming in to view
        fit, 96
    scrolling drop-down font list, 97
    text, greeked after zooming out,
        96-97
    using fonts, 93-99
pages
    layout
        headlines, zooming in to view
            fit, 96
        text, greeked after zooming out,
            96-97
    printing
        comparing printers, 26-27
        partially, 58
paintjet printers, 22-23, 193-194
    see also inkjet printers
pair kerning, 89, 268
Panasonic
    KX-P1124 printers, 198-200
    laser printers, 21
paper
    for inkjet printers, 196-197
    loading and feeding into printers,
        174-175

parallel, 269
    printer ports, configuring, 177
    printers, connecting to computers,
        175-177
parity, 269
pasteboard, 269
PCL (Printer Control Language),
    185, 269
    printers, versus PostScript-
        compatible printers, 193
PDL (Page Descriptor
    Language), 269
permanent fonts, 189, 270
Persuasion for Windows (Aldus
    Corporation), 247
picas, 270
pictures
    inserting, 119-120
    viewing, 75
pins, dot-matrix printers, 23
pixels, 270
plotters, 25, 270
Plus Pack (Adobe Systems Inc.), 246
points (pt), 10, 270
portrait orientation, 27, 270
    in Excel, 86-87
ports, 270
    COM, 264
    computer
        configuring for printers,
            178-179
        connecting to printer drivers,
            182-183
    LPT, 268
    printer, 54-56, 175
    RS-232, 271
Ports icon, 55
PostScript, 270
    cartridges (Adobe Systems Inc.),
        246, 270
    files (EPS), printing to, 217-218

Type 1 fonts (Adobe Systems
Inc.), 12, 273
  accessing, 91
  displaying, 90
  in Ami Pro style sheets, 71-72
  in CorelDRAW!, 109, 111
  in Word for DOS, 151
  in WordPerfect for DOS, 138,
    142-143
  starting FrameMaker for
    Windows with, 90
  with laser printers, 193
PostScript-compatible printers, 16,
  28-29, 185-186
  as font managers, 46
  downloaded scalable outline fonts,
    30-31
  font managers, 32
  versus PCL printers, 193
power sources, printers, 174
PowerPoint (Microsoft
  Corporation), 255
  affecting Excel screen fonts, 86
  editing characters as graphic
    elements, 119-120
  enlarging text multiple sizes, 119
  finding slides, 119
  font list dropping down as mouse
    pointer slides by, 118
  presentations as slides or overhead
    transparencies, 221-222
  using fonts, 115-126
PRD file extension, 180
presentation applications, 115
preview mode, 270
PrimeType for WordPerfect
  (LaserTools), 142, 253
Print Manager (Windows), printing
  multiple documents, 57
Print Preview, Word for DOS,
  149-150

print sharing devices, 56
printer control codes, embedding in
  documents, 153-154
Printer Control Language (PCL),
  185, 269
printer drivers, 180
  connecting computer ports to,
    182-183
  installing, 180-182
  selecting for printing documents
    exchanged between computers,
    205-206
  TrueType-compatibility, 76
  updating, 57
    Windows, 81
    WordPerfect for Windows, 80
  WordPerfect support, 79
printer fonts, 15-18, 270
  DOS, 130-131
  downloaded scalable outline,
    30-31
  font cartridges, 29
  internal (built-in), 27-29
  screen fonts not matching, 51, 56
  soft, 29-30
  versus screen fonts, 37
printers
  as font managers, 45-46
  bitmaps, 27
  changng setup, 82
  configuring, 177-178
    computer ports for, 178-179
  connecting to computers, 175-177
  daisywheel, printing speed, 153
  default, 180
  DeskJet, *see* DeskJet printers
  dot-matrix, 23-24, 198-201, 265
  emulating listed models, 181
  exchanging documents between,
    209-211

fonts not appearing in font dialog
  boxes after switching, 54
graphics, 25, 267
inkjet, *see* inkjet printers
laser, *see* laser printers
LaserJet, *see* LaserJet printers
loading and feeding paper,
  174-175
memory requirements, 58
not printing, 54-56
overhead transparencies, 25
paintjet, *see* inkjet printers
plotters, 25, 270
PostScript-compatible, *see*
  PostScript-compatible printers
power sources, 174
printing pages, 26-27
    partially, 58
rasterizing, 25-26
selecting, 58-59, 183-184
    for displaying documents
      exchanged between
      computers, 205
slides, 25
testing, 173-174
viewing printable characters, 152
with Word for DOS, 146-147
with WordPerfect for DOS,
  137-138
WYSIWYG text, 31-32
Printers icon, 55, 57, 59, 69, 75-76,
  81, 180-182
printing
  bidirectional, 263
  documents exchanged between
    computers, 205-215
  draft quality, 58
  font samples, 228-229
  fonts in Windows, 54-60
  graphics, 80
  large documents to diskettes,
    218-219

reverse characters, 69, 75-76
special characters in Ventura
  Publisher, 99
spreadsheet columns as print
  titles, 87
symbol characters in regular
  fonts, 81
test documents, 152
to PostScript (EPS) files, 217-218
programs, *see* applications
proportional
  sizing, 117
  fonts, 10-11, 270
pt (points), 10, 270
Publisher (Microsoft
  Corporation), 255

Q

Quattro Pro (Borland)
  bullets, 159
  displaying more columns in
    spreadsheets, 158-159
  special characters, 159-160
  Speedo fonts (Bitstream), 159
  using fonts, 154-158
  WYSIWYG mode, 158

R

RAM (Random-Access
  Memory), 271
ranges, 3-D, 160
rasterizing, 25-26, 38, 65, 271
regular characters/fonts, 271
RenameTT freeware, 239
rendering fonts, 36-38
resolution, 271
RET (Resolution Enhancement
  Technology), 271
reverse characters, printing, 69,
  75-76
ribbon, 150-151

ROM (Read-Only Memory),
    28, 271
roman characters/fonts, 271
rotating text, 91
    in Harvard Graphics for
        Windows, 125-126
rows, adding to 1-2-3 spreadsheet
    displays, 169-170
RS-232 ports, 271
rulers
    changing measurement scale, 77
    displaying in Harvard Graphics
        for Windows, 124

S

Samna Corp. of Atlanta, 67
sans serif fonts, 8, 271
saving font sets to font libraries,
    165-166
scalable fonts, 133, 271
    internal, using with laser printers,
        189-191
    outline, 17-18, 28
        downloaded, 30-31
    sources for laser printers, 187
ScanMan 256 (Logitech Inc.), 253
screen fonts, 31, 271
    changing sizes, 66
    display speed in
        CorelDRAW!, 111
    DOS, 129-131
    Excel, affected by applications, 86
    flickering text, 53
    improving readabilty, 85
    in Windows, 35-36
    jagged edges to characters, 52
    not matching printer fonts, 51, 56
    overlapping characters, 70-71
    TrueType, for laser printers, 190
    typing text outside of margins, 53,
        76-77
    versus printer fonts, 37

screens
    Aldus PageMaker 4.0, 94
    Ami Pro 3.0, 67
    ARES FontMinder, 228
    Arts & Letters, 106
    Character Map, 50
    FrameMaker for Windows 3.0, 88
    Harvard Graphics for Windows,
        120-121
    Microsoft Excel 4.0, 83
    Microsoft Font Assistant, 226-227
    PowerPoint, 115-116
    Word for DOS, affecting line
        length with font sizes, 151
    Word for Windows 2.0, 73
    WordPerfect for DOS, affecting
        line length with font sizes, 135
    WordPerfect for Windows 5.2, 78
script characters/fonts, 272
scrolling drop-down font list in
    PageMaker for Windows, 97
serial, 272
    printer ports, configuring,
        177-178
    printers, connecting to computers,
        175-177
serif fonts, 8, 272
service bureaus, 203
    duplicating documents printed on
        laser printers, 216-218
    PowerPoint presentations as slides
        or overhead transparencies,
        221-222
    sending large documents, 218-219
    substituting Linotronic fonts for
        TrueType fonts, 220
    using Macintosh, sending DOS
        files for review, 215-216
Setup (Windows), 48
    installing video drivers, 86
shaping text, 232
shareware, 272

buying fonts as, 13
for changing font attributes, 239
Sharp laser printers, 21
site licenses for fonts, 242
sizes
  fonts
    affecting line length on-screen,
     135, 151
    changing, 133-135
    setting percentages, 139-141
  text, enlarging multiple, 119
slide shows
  Harvard Graphics for Windows,
    120-126
  PowerPoint, 115-120
slides, 25
  centering text, 125
  enlarging multiple sizes of
    text, 119
  finding, 119
  PowerPoint presentations as,
    221-222
small capitals (small caps) in Ami
  Pro, 68
soft fonts, 15-18, 29-30, 272
  installing for WordPerfect for
    DOS, 139
  sources for laser printers, 187
  using with laser printers, 188-189
Software Bridge (Systems Compatibility Corporation), 213, 257
Software Publishers Association,
  240, 256
Software Publishing
  Corporation, 257
  Harvard Graphics for Windows,
    120-126
spacing
  advanced properties, 89
  characters in Macintosh docu-
    ments in Ventura Publisher, 99

expanded, 266
kerning, 267
  pairs, 89, 268
  track, 94, 272
leading, 95, 268
metrics, 65, 268
spread, 89
TrueType fonts in Ami Pro, 69
special characters, 50-52
  1-2-3 for DOS, 169
  bullets, 264
  disappearing, 53
  entering in text, 138-139, 153
  extended, 169
  inserting in Quattro Pro
    spreadsheets, 159-160
  printing in Ventura Publisher, 99
  viewing and inserting in Word
    for Windows, 73-74
  Word for Windows Equation
    Editor, 76
special effects, 231
  distorting text, 232
  graphics editing, 234
  headlines, 231
speed
  1-2-3 for DOS without
    Wysiwyg, 167
  baud rate, 177-178
  daisywheel printers, 153
  Word for DOS graphics
    mode, 150
  WYSIWYG mode, Quattro
    Pro, 158
Speedo fonts (Bitstream Inc.),
  12, 272
  included with
    Designer Plus OLE, 113
    Harvard Graphics for
     Windows, 121
    Quattro Pro, 159

spread, 89
spreadsheet applications
    1-2-3 for DOS, 160-170
    Excel, 82-87
    Quattro Pro, 154-160
spreadsheets
    3-D, 263
    adding fonts, 163
    adding rows to display, 169-170
    changing fonts, 163-164
    columns as print titles, 87
    displaying more columns,
      158-159
    inserting bullets, 159
    inserting special characters,
      159-160
    overlapping characters in narrow
      rows, 87
    zooming, 166-167
starting FrameMaker for Windows
  with correct fonts, 90
storing
    graphics on CD-ROM, 104-105
    Windows fonts, 64-65
style sheets, specifying PostScript
  fonts, 71-72
styles, 8, 272
Super ATM (Adobe Systems
  Inc.), 246
SuperPrint (Zenographics), 14, 41,
  43-44, 258
sweep effect, 122
SWFTE International, Ltd., 257
symbol
    characters
      logos as, 238-239
      printing in regular fonts, 81
    fonts, 7, 51-52, 272
System 7 (Macintosh), 272
Systems Compatibility
  Corporation, 257
    Software Bridge, 213

T

tables, VFMs (font metrics
  tables), 99
templates, 272
    files, for documents exchanged
      between computers, 210
temporary fonts, 189, 272
test documents, viewing font
  characters, 152
testing printing, 173-174
text
    artistic, 109
    attributes, *see* attributes
    centering, 125
    changing fonts, 124
    converted to graphics, editing, 108
    converting to freeform, 107-108
    curving and shaping, 232
    distorting, 232
    entering special characters,
      138-139, 153
    flickering, 53
    greeked after zooming out, 96-97
    on-screen
      changing sizes, 66
      overlapping, 70-71
    printing
      garbled, 56
      reverse characters, 69, 75-76
      with TrueType fonts, 57
    rotating, 91
      in Harvard Graphics for
        Windows, 125-126
    sizes
      changing, 133-135
      enlarging multiple, 119
      proportional, 117
    typing outside of margins, 53,
     76-77
    underlining, breaks between
     characters, 81

viewing
in Word for DOS, 147-150
in WordPerfect for DOS,
136-137
see also characters
text faces, 7
Text mode, 272
1-2-3 for DOS, 167
Word for DOS, 144-145
viewing character attributes,
150-151
track kerning, 6, 94, 272
troubleshooting
1-2-3 for DOS, 162-170
Ami Pro, 69-72
Arts & Letters, 107-108
CorelDRAW!, 111-112
Excel, 85-87
exchanging documents between
computers, 204-222
FrameMaker for Windows, 90-91
Harvard Graphics for Windows,
124-126
organizing fonts, 225-228
PageMaker for Windows, 96-97
PowerPoint, 118-120
printers not printing, 173-184
Quattro Pro, 158-160
Windows fonts, 47-60
Word for DOS, 150-154
Word for Windows, 75-77
WordPerfect for DOS, 138-143
WordPerfect for Windows, 80
TrueType Font Pack (Microsoft
Corporation), 255
TrueType Font Pack 2 (Microsoft
Corporation), 255
TrueType fonts, 11-12, 38-40, 273
appearing in font dialog boxes,
49-50, 57
compatibility of printer drivers, 76

computers acting strangely when
using, 48
converting fonts to, 48-49
displaying, 53
font managers, 32
in CorelDRAW!, 109
in PowerPoint, 115
in Word for DOS, 151-152
in WordPerfect for DOS,
138, 143
information about, 229-231
installing, 47
kerning in Ami Pro, 69
locking up computers, 47-48
memory requirements, 48
printing, 57, 59
rotating text in Harvard Graphics
for Windows, 125-126
screen, for laser printers, 190
storing, 64-65
substituting Linotronic fonts
for, 220
text outside of margins, 76-77
turning off, 48
using same for printing documents
exchanged between computers,
206-207
with Hewlett-Packard LaserJet 4,
192
TrueType for DOS (MicroLogic
Software), 143, 152, 254
TrueType Value Pack (Monotype
Typography Inc.), 256
TTF file extension, 64, 207,
229, 273
TXT file extension, 174
Type 1 fonts, *see* PostScript Type 1
fonts
Type 3 fonts, 273
Type Companion (FontBank
Inc.), 251

Type On Call (Adobe Systems Inc.), 246
Type Set Value Pack (Adobe Systems Inc.), 246
Type Sets packages (Adobe Systems Inc.), 246
TypeAlign (Adobe Systems Inc.), 232, 246
TypeCase I and II (SWFTE International, Ltd.), 257
TypeCase TrueType Font Variety (SWFTE International, Ltd.), 257
typefaces, 273
  design category, 8-10
  importance, 4
  origin of designs, 4-5
  use category, 7
  versus fonts, 3-4
  see also fonts

U-V

Ultra Graphics Pro (ATI Technologies), CRYSTAL fonts, 46
underlining, breaks between characters, 81
undoing deleted hidden codes, 141-142
updating printer drivers, 57
  Windows, 81
  WordPerfect for Windows, 80

variations, 88
vector fonts, 38, 273
vendors, 11-12, 245-261
Ventura Publisher (Ventura Software Company), 258
  character spacing in Macintosh documents, 99
  font IDs, 98
  installing time, 98
  special characters, printing, 99
  using fonts, 97-99

Ventura Software Company, 257
VFMs (font metrics tables), 99
VGA (Video Graphics Adapter), 273
video
  boards, generating Windows fonts, 46
  display cards, displaying spreadsheet columns, 159
  drivers, reinstalling, 86

W

weight, 88, 273
WIN.INI file, [FontSubstitutes] section, 208-209
Windows (Microsoft Corporation), 35-36, 255
  applets
    Character Map, 50-51, 65
    Control Panel, 47-50, 63-64, 69, 75-76, 81, 180-182, 264
    Notepad, 69, 75-76
    Print Manager, 57
    Setup, 48, 86
  applications, 63
  documents
    exchanging with DOS word processors, 211-213
    printing one at a time, 57
  font dialog boxes
    fonts appearing in, 49, 54, 59-60
    only TrueType fonts appearing in, 50
    unknown fonts appearing in, 51
  font managers, 38-44
  fonts
    Adobe, installing, 47
    controlling in all applications, 63-66
    generating with video boards, 46

grouping, 225-228
rendering, 36-38
screen, not matching printer
    fonts, 51, 56
installing printer drivers, 180-182
jagged edges to characters, 52
printer drivers, updating, 81
printers
    configuring computer ports
        for, 179
    not printing, 54-56
    resetting during print jobs, 59
    selecting, 58-59
printing
    locking up computers when, 56
    partial pages, 58
    testing, 174
special characters, 50-52
    disappearing, 53
text
    flickering, 53
    garbled when printed, 56
    typing outside of margins, 53
TrueType fonts, *see* TrueType
    fonts
Windows Printing System (WPS)
(Microsoft Corporation), 255, 273
Word for DOS (Microsoft
Corporation), 143-144, 255
    embedding printer control codes
        in documents, 153-154
    fonts
        attributes, changing, 145-146
        PostScript, 151
        sizes, affecting line length
            on-screen, 151
        TrueType, 151-152
    graphics mode, 144-145
        speeding up, 150
    installing printer drivers, 180
    printers, 146-147
        daisywheel, printing speed, 153

sending Word for Windows files
    to, 215-216
special characters, entering in
    text, 153
text mode, 144-145, 150-151
viewing
    character attributes, 150-151
    documents, 147-150
    font characters in test
        documents, 152
Word for Windows (Microsoft
Corporation), 255
    exchanging documents between
        computers, 204-209
    printer drivers, TrueType-
        compatibility, 76
    printing reverse characters, 75-76
    rulers, changing measurement
        scale, 77
    sending files to Word for DOS,
        215-216
    special characters, 51
        in Equation Editor, 76
    typing text outside of margins,
        76-77
    using fonts, 72-75
    viewing graphics, 75
word processors
    Ami Pro, 67-72
    exchanging documents between
        computers
        using different, 211-215
        using same, 204-209
    FrameMaker for Windows, 87-91
    PowerPoint, 115-120
    Word for DOS, 143-154
    Word for Windows, 72-77
    WordPerfect for DOS, 131-143
    WordPerfect for Windows, 77-82
WordArt (Microsoft Corporation),
    74, 93, 231
WordPerfect Corporation, 258

WordPerfect for DOS (WordPerfect
Corporation), 77-80, 131, 258
  font sizes
    affecting line length
      on-screen, 135
    changing, 133-135
    setting percentages, 139-141
  fonts, 131-132
    attributes, changing, 132-133
    PostScript Type 1, 138
    soft, installing, 139
    TrueType, 138, 143
    using characters from, 139
    using PostScript Type 1
      without PostScript printers,
      142-143
  losing formatting, 141-142
  printers, 137-138
  special characters, entering in text,
    138-139
  viewing documents, 136-137
WordPerfect for Windows
  (WordPerfect Corporation), 258
  printers, changng setup, 82
  printing graphics, 80
  text, adding bold attributes, 82
  underlining, breaks between
    characters, 81
  using fonts, 77-80
WPS (Windows Printing System)
  (Microsoft Corporation), 45,
  255, 273
Wysiwyg (What You See Is What
  You Get), 31-32, 273
  in 1-2-3 for DOS (Lotus),
    161-162
    display modes, 163
    requirements for running,
      162-163
WYSIWYG mode, Quattro Pro,
  155, 158

X-Z

Z-Script (Zenographics), 258
Zenographics, 258
  SuperPrint, 14, 41, 43-44
zooming
  1-2-3 spreadsheets, 166-167
  greeked text after, 96-97
  headlines to view fit, 96